FIFTH EDITION

Methods in Behavioral Research

FIFTH EDITION

Methods in Behavioral Research

Paul C. Cozby
California State University, Fullerton

 Mayfield Publishing Company
Mountain View, California
London • Toronto

Library of Congress Cataloging-in-Publication Data

Cozby, Paul C.
  Methods in behavioral research / Paul C. Cozby.--5th ed.
    p.   cm.
  Includes index.
  ISBN 1-55934-098-3
    1. Psychology--Research--Methodology.   2. Social sciences-
-Research--Methodology.   I. Title.
BF76.5.C67   1992
150'.72--dc20   92-10768
                                                      CIP

Manufactured in the United States of America

10   9   8   7   6   5   4   3   2   1

Mayfield Publishing Company
1240 Villa Street
Mountain View, California 94041

Sponsoring editor, Franklin C. Graham; production editor, Lynn Rabin
Bauer; manufacturing manager, Martha Branch; manuscript editor, Rene
Lynch; cover designer, Richard Kharibian. The text was set in 10/12 Zapf
International Light by Maryland Composition and printed on 50# Finch
Opaque by Malloy Lithographing.

Contents

CHAPTER 8
Conducting Research   117

CHAPTER 9
Understanding Research Results   138

CHAPTER 10
Correlation Coefficients   163

Preface

This fifth edition of *Methods in Behavioral Research* builds upon the previous editions. Communicating to the student reader remains my highest priority. I have tried to present material clearly, use interesting examples, and mention the same concepts at numerous points throughout the text. An outline precedes each chapter, and study questions containing key terms and issues appear at the end of each chapter along with activities to increase student involvement. There is also a glossary, and glossary terms appear in bold type to help students recognize important terms. My hope is that both instructors and students will find the book useful for teaching and learning about research methods. An instructor's manual is also available, which includes a number of activities and sources of ideas for activities. And for the first time a set of transparency masters is available to instructors.

The organization generally follows the sequence of planning and conducting a research investigation. However, the chapters are relatively independent to afford the instructor flexibility in changing the order of chapters assigned or omitting chapters according to the needs of a particular class. Chapter 1 provides an overview of the scientific method and distinguishes between basic, applied, and program evaluation research. Chapter 2 discusses sources of ideas for research and library research. Chapter 3 discusses scientific variables, issues of reliability and validity, relationships among variables, and the distinction between experimental and correlational research. Chapter 4 contains a discussion of descriptive methods, including field observation, systematic observation, case histories, survey research, and archival research. Chapters 5 through 7 describe experimental and quasi-experimental research designs. Many practical aspects of conducting research are described in Chapter 8—obtaining subjects and controlling for extraneous variables, for example. The logic and basic procedures of statistical inference are covered in Chapters 9 and 10. Issues of generalization and ethics are presented in Chapters 11 and 12. Appendices on writing research reports, analyzing data, and constructing Latin Squares are included as well.

I would be grateful to receive comments and suggestions from readers. My postal mail address is the Department of Psychology, California State University, Fullerton, CA 92634. My computer mail address is COZBY@FULLERTON.EDU.

NOTES FOR USERS OF THE FOURTH EDITION

Instructors who used the fourth edition will recognize some significant changes in the ordering of material and the addition of new material. Most of these changes were prompted by comments from both instructors and students who used the previous edition. Issues of sampling have been consolidated in Chapter 4 along with the material on survey research. Longitudinal versus cross-sectional designs in developmental research are now presented in Chapter 4 along with time-based survey designs. New material on library research has been added to Chapter 2, and there is expanded coverage of techniques to control for order effects. I have also used the commonly accepted "mixed design" terminology to describe experimental designs that include both independent groups and repeated measures variables. Finally, a number of new examples have been added to the text.

ACKNOWLEDGEMENTS

Many individuals helped to produce this and the previous editions of the book. I would particularly like to thank Josh Cozby, Jeanne King, Don Schweitzer, Elaine Hutchison, Sharon Hagar, Marcy Boswell, and Bunny Casas. These friends and colleagues motivated me and gave me time to work on the book. A special note of thanks is due to Claire Palmerino for her efforts in revising and expanding the instructor's manual and test bank.

Most important, I thank Frank Graham at Mayfield Publishing Company, the individuals who reviewed the book, and those who took the trouble to send me their comments and suggestions: Bernardo J. Carducci, Indiana University Southeast; Margaret Thomas, University of Central Florida; Hong C. Chen, Grand Valley State University; Daniel Leger, University of Nebraska; Theodore Steiner, San Francisco State University; Helen Crawford, Virginia Polytechnic University; Art Graesser, Memphis State University; Steve McNeil, Bethel College; David Perkins, California State University, Fullerton; Felice Gordis, California State University, Fullerton; and Lewis Edgel, University of Tennessee, Knoxville.

1

The Scientific Method

W hat are the causes of aggression and violence? How do we remember things, what causes us to forget, and how can memories be improved? What are the effects of stressful environments on health and social interactions? How do early childhood experiences affect later development? Curiosity about questions such as these is probably the most important reason why many students decide to take courses in the behavioral sciences. Scientific research provides us with a means of addressing such questions and providing answers. In this book, we will examine the methods of scientific research in the behavioral sciences. This introductory chapter discusses ways in which a knowledge of research methods can be useful to people in understanding the world around them. Further, it describes the characteristics of a scientific approach to the study of behavior and the general types of research questions that concern behavioral scientists.

USES OF RESEARCH METHODS

A knowledge of research methods is increasingly needed by informed citizens in our society. Your daily newspaper, general-interest magazines, and other media are continually reporting research results: "Type A personalities more likely to suffer from heart attacks" or "Smoking linked to poor grades." Articles and books make claims about the beneficial or harmful effects of particular diets or vitamins on sex life, personality, or health. Survey results are frequently reported that draw conclusions about how we feel about a variety of topics. How do you evaluate such reports? Do you simply accept the findings because they are supposed to be scientific? A background in research methods will help you to read these reports critically, evaluate the methodology employed, and decide if the results are valid.

Many occupations require the use of research findings. Mental health professionals must make decisions about treatment methods, assignment of patients to different types of facilities, medications, and testing procedures. Such decisions are made on the basis of research; to make good decisions, the mental health professional must be able to read the research conducted by others and judge its adequacy and relevance for the particular setting in which he or she works. Similarly, people who work in business environments frequently need to rely on research to make decisions about marketing strategies, ways of improving employee productivity and morale, and methods of selecting and training new employees. Educators must keep up with research on topics such as the effectiveness of different teaching strategies or programs to deal with special student problems. Knowledge of research methods and the ability to evaluate research reports are useful in many fields.

It is also important to recognize that scientific research has become increasingly important in decisions of public policy. Legislators and political leaders at all levels of government frequently take political positions and propose legislation based on research findings. Research may also influence judicial decisions: A major example of this is the *Social Science Brief* that was prepared by psychologists and accepted as evidence in the U.S. Supreme Court case of *Brown v. Board of Education* in 1954. This case banned school desegregation in the United States. One of the studies cited in the brief was conducted by Clark and Clark (1947). The study found that when allowed to choose between light-skin and dark-skin dolls, both black and white children preferred to play with the light-skin dolls (see Stephan, 1983, for a further discussion of the implications of this study). More recently, legislation and public opinion regarding the availability of pornographic materials have been informed by behavioral research investigations of this topic (see, for example, Koop, 1987; Linz, Donnerstein, & Penrod, 1987), and psychological research on sex stereotyping greatly influenced the outcome of a Supreme Court decision on sex discrimination by employers (Fiske, Bersoff, Borgida, Deaux, & Heilman, 1991). Research is also important when pilot programs are funded to develop and assess the effectiveness of programs designed to achieve certain goals—increase retention of students in school or influence people to engage in behaviors that reduce their risk of AIDS, for example. If successful, such programs may be implemented on a large scale. The fact that so many policy decisions and political positions are based on research makes knowledge of research methods particularly important for all of us who, as informed citizens, must ultimately evaluate the policies at the voting booth.

THE SCIENTIFIC APPROACH

We opened this chapter with several questions about human behavior and suggested that scientific research is a valuable means of answering them. What makes the scientific approach different from other ways of learning about behavior? People have always observed the world around them and sought explanations for what they see and experience. However, instead of using a scientific approach, many people rely on authority and intuition as ways of knowing.

Authority and intuition

The philosopher Aristotle was concerned with the factors that determine persuasion or attitude change. In his *Rhetoric*, Aristotle describes credibility: "Persuasion is achieved by the speaker's personal character when the speech is so spoken as to make us think him credible. We believe good men more fully and readily than others." Thus, Aristotle would argue that we are more likely to be persuaded by a speaker who seems prestigious, trustworthy, and respectable than by one who lacks such qualities.

Many of us might accept Aristotle's arguments simply because he is considered a prestigious "authority" and his writings continue to be important. Similarly, many people are all too ready to accept anything they learn from the news media, a book, government officials, or a religious figure. They

3

believe that the statements of such authorities must be true. As we shall see, the scientific approach rejects the notion that one can accept on faith the statements of any authority.

Intuition as a way of knowing is in many ways the opposite of authority. When you believe in an authority, you accept unquestioningly what someone else tells you about the world. In contrast, when you rely on intuition, you accept unquestioningly what your own personal judgment tells you about the world. The intuitive approach takes many forms. Often it involves finding an explanation for our own behaviors or the behaviors of others. For example, you might develop an explanation for why you keep having conflicts with a co-worker such as "that other person wants my job" or "having to share a telephone puts us in a conflict situation." A problem with this approach is that numerous biases affect our perceptions, and we often cannot accurately identify the true causes of our behavior (cf. Fiske & Taylor, 1984; Nisbett & Wilson, 1977; Nisbett & Ross, 1980). On a more general level, you might use intuition to decide that "women are more romantic than men" or "studying all night is the best way to prepare for an exam." Perhaps your personal experience is consistent with these generalizations about human behavior; however, they are intuitive nevertheless because your own experience is limited.

Skepticism and science

The scientific approach recognizes that both authority and intuition are sources of ideas about behavior. However, the scientist does not accept on faith the pronouncements of anyone, regardless of that person's prestige or authority. Nor does a scientist unquestioningly accept his or her own intuitions—scientists recognize that their ideas are just as likely to be wrong as are anyone else's. Scientists are skeptical. They insist that scientific methods be used to evaluate assertions about the nature of behavior and refuse to trust either authority or intuition.

The essence of the scientific method is the insistence that all propositions be subjected to an empirical test. The scientific method embodies a number of rules for testing ideas through research, and these will be explored throughout the book. The important point here is that empirical tests of ideas allow the scientist to investigate an idea under conditions in which the idea may be either supported or refuted. Further, the research is done in a way that can be observed, evaluated, and replicated by others. Thus, the scientific method, in contrast to authority or intuition, does not rely on accepting assertions generated by someone else or on one's own personal perceptions of the world.

Conclusion

The advantage of the scientific approach over other ways of knowing about the world is that it provides an objective set of rules for gathering, evaluating, and reporting information. It is important to qualify this point, however. There is nothing wrong with accepting the assertions of authority as long as we don't accept them as scientific evidence. Often scientific evidence isn't obtainable, as, for example, when religions ask us to accept certain beliefs on faith. Some beliefs, such as whether God exists, cannot be tested and thus are beyond the realm of science. Scientific ideas must be testable—there must be some way of verifying them. In general, there is nothing wrong with having opinions or beliefs as long as they are presented simply as opinions or beliefs. However, it is good to ask whether the opinion can be tested scientifically or whether scientific evidence exists that relates to the opinion. For example, opinions on whether exposure to violence on television is harmful are only opinions until scientific evidence on the question is gathered.

As you learn more about scientific methods, you will become increasingly skeptical of the assertions of scientists. You should be aware that scientists often become authorities when they express their ideas. When someone claims to be a scientist, should we be more willing to accept what he or she has to say? The answer depends on whether the scientist has scientific data that support the assertions he or she is making: If there is no such evidence, the scientist is no different from any other authority; if scientific evidence is presented, you will want to evaluate the methods used to gather it. Also, there are many "pseudoscientists," who use scientific terms to substantiate their claims (astrologers or new age channelers, for example). A general rule is to be highly skeptical whenever someone who is labeled as a scientist makes assertions that are supported by only vague or improbable evidence.

GOALS OF SCIENCE

Scientific research has four general goals: (1) to describe behavior, (2) to predict behavior, (3) to determine the causes of behavior, and (4) to understand or explain behavior.

Description of behavior

The scientist begins with careful observation, because the first goal of the scientist is to describe events. In a classic experiment conducted in the late 19th century, Ebbinghaus carefully observed his own rate of forgetting material after it had been learned. He studied the amount of retention of material (actually, nonsense syllables like TAV) at periods ranging from 20 minutes to 31 days after the original learning. His results produced the "forgetting curve" shown in Figure 1-1 (see Schwartz, 1986). Many questions that interest researchers concern describing the ways in which events are systematically related to one another. Does greater speaker credibility lead to greater attitude

**Figure 1-1
Ebbinghaus
forgetting curve**

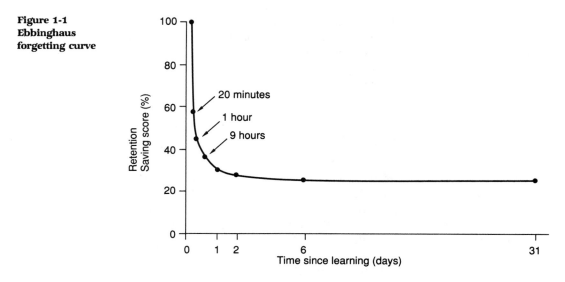

change? In what ways do intellectual abilities change throughout the life cycle? Does noise affect performance on cognitive tasks?

Prediction of behavior

Another goal of science is to predict behavior. Once it has been observed with some regularity that two events are systematically related to one another (e.g., greater credibility is associated with greater attitude change), it becomes possible to make predictions. One implication of this is that we can anticipate events. If we know that one candidate in an election is considered more credible than the other, we may be able to predict the outcome of the election. Further, the ability to predict often helps us make better decisions. For example, if research data show that aptitude test scores and high school grades are related to success in college, college admissions officers can predict which applicants are most likely to succeed and can use this information to decide whom to admit to the school.

Determining the causes of behavior

A third goal is to determine the causes of behavior. Although we might accurately predict the occurrence of a behavior, we might not have correctly identified its cause. For example, college grades are not caused by aptitude test scores. The aptitude test is an indicator of other factors that are the actual causes; research may be undertaken to study these factors. Similarly, research has shown that a child's aggressive behavior may be predicted by knowing how much violence the child views on television. Unfortunately, unless we know that viewing violence is a *cause* of behavior, we cannot assert that aggressive behavior can be reduced by limiting scenes of violence on television. Thus, to know how to *change* behavior, we need to know the *causes* of behavior.

Explanation of behavior

A final goal is to explain the events that have been described. The scientist seeks to understand *why* the behavior occurs. Thus, for example, it is important to ask why the forgetting curve appears as it does in Figure 1-1. It is clear that forgetting increases over time, but time is not sufficient to explain the psychological processes that might be responsible for the forgetting. To explain the finding, you might ask whether there is a decay in the memory trace, or whether other events increasingly interfere with the ability to remember what was learned. Or consider the relationship between television violence and aggression; even if we know that TV violence is a cause of aggressiveness, we need to explain this relationship. Is it due to imitation or "modeling" of the violence seen on TV? Is it the result of psychological desensitization to violence and its effects? Or does watching TV violence lead to a belief that aggression is a normal response to frustration and conflict?

Further research is necessary to shed light on possible explanations of what has been observed. Usually, additional research like this is carried out by testing theories that are developed to explain a particular observed behavior.

Description, prediction, determination of cause, and explanation are all closely intertwined. The problems of finding a cause of a behavior and an explanation of the behavior are particularly close. This is because it is difficult to ever know the true cause or all the causes of any behavior. An explanation that appears satisfactory may turn out to be inadequate when other causes are identified in subsequent research. For example, when early research showed that speaker credibility is related to attitude change, the researchers explained the finding by stating that people are more willing to believe what is said by a person with high credibility than by one with low credibility. This explanation has given way to a more complex theory of attitude change that takes into account many other factors that are related to persuasion (Petty & Cocioppo, 1986). There is a certain amount of ambiguity in the enterprise of scientific inquiry. New research findings almost always pose new questions that must be addressed by further research; explanations of behavior often must be discarded or revised as new evidence is gathered. Such ambiguity is part of the excitement and fun of science.

BASIC AND APPLIED RESEARCH

Behavioral research falls into two general categories: basic research and applied research. A special type of applied research, called program evaluation, will be described in a subsequent section.

Basic research

Basic research tries to answer fundamental questions about the nature of behavior. Studies are often designed to address theoretical issues concerning phenomena such as cognition, emotion, motivation, psychobiology, or social behavior. Here are citations of a few journal articles that illustrate some basic research questions:

> Kyllonen, P. C., Tirre, W. C., & Christal, R. E. (1991). Knowledge and processing speed as determinants of associative learning. *Journal of Experimental Psychology: General, 120,* 57–79.

> Pashler, H. (1990). Do response modality effects support multiprocessor models of divided attention? *Journal of Experimental Psychology: Human Perception and Performance, 16,* 826–842.

> Preston, R. A., & Fantino, E. (1991). Conditioned reinforcement value and choice. *Journal of the Experimental Analysis of Behavior, 55,* 155–175.

> Breckler, S. J., & Wiggins, E. C. (1991). Cognitive responses in persuasion: Affective and evaluative determinants. *Journal of Experimental Social Psychology, 27,* 180–200.

Applied research

The research articles listed above were not concerned with any immediate practical application or the solution of a particular problem. To address issues like these and to find solutions to problems, applied research is conducted. To illustrate, here are a few journal article titles:

> Grant, J. M., & Bateman, T. S. (1990). An experimental test of the impact of drug-testing programs on potential job applicants' attitudes and intentions. *Journal of Applied Psychology, 75,* 127–131.

> Harris, S. L., Handleman, J. S., & Alessandri, M. (1990). Teaching youths with autism to offer assistance. *Journal of Applied Behavior Analysis, 23,* 297–305.

> O'Neill, M. J. (1991). Effects of signage and floor plan configuration on wayfinding accuracy. *Environment and Behavior, 23,* 553–574.

> Burn, S. M. (1991). Social psychology and the stimulation of recycling behaviors: The block leader approach. *Journal of Applied Social Psychology, 21,* 611–629.

Much applied research is conducted in settings such as large business firms, marketing research companies, and public polling organizations and is not published but rather is used within the company or by clients of the company. Whether or not such results are published, however, they are used to help people make better decisions concerning problems that require immediate action.

Comparing basic and applied research

Both basic and applied research are important, and neither can be considered superior to the other. In recent years, many in our society, including legislators who control the budgets of research-granting agencies of the government, have demanded that research be directly relevant to specific social issues. Certainly research that has immediate practical applications is attractive, but basic, theory-oriented research is important, too. In fact, much applied research is guided by the theories and findings of basic research investigations. Most important, insistence that research have obvious applications could result in the neglect of potentially important areas of research. Psychologist B. F. Skinner, for example, conducted basic research in the 1930s on operant conditioning, which carefully described the effects of reinforcement on such behaviors as bar pressing by rats. This research led, years later, to many practical applications in therapy, education, and industrial psychology. Research with no apparent practical value can ultimately be very useful. The fact that no one can predict the eventual impact of basic research leads to the conclusion that support of basic research is necessary both to advance science and benefit society.

PROGRAM EVALUATION

Program evaluation research evaluates the social reforms and innovations that occur in government, education, the criminal justice system, industry, health care, and mental health institutions. Here are a few journal article titles that illustrate program evaluation research:

> Neenan, P. A., & Bowen, G. L. (1991). Multimethod assessment of a child-care demonstration project for AFDC recipient families: The genesis of an evaluation. *Evaluation Review, 15*, 219–232.
>
> Land, K. C., McCall, P. L., & Williams, J. R. (1991). Something that works in juvenile justice: An evaluation of the North Carolina court counselors' intensive protective supervision randomized experimental project. *Evaluation Review, 14*, 574–606.
>
> Blomberg, T. G., Waldo, G. P., & Bullock, C. A. (1989). An assessment of victim service needs. *Evaluation Review, 13*, 598–627.
>
> Levin, H. M., Glass, G. V., & Meister, G. R. (1987). Cost-effectiveness of computer-assisted instruction. *Evaluation Review, 11*, 50–72.

In an influential paper on "reforms as experiments," Donald Campbell (1969) noted that social programs are really experiments designed to achieve certain outcomes. He argued persuasively that social scientists should evaluate each program to determine whether it is having its intended effect. If it is not, alternative programs should be tried. This is an important point that people in all organizations too often fail to remember when new ideas are implemented; the scientific approach dictates that new programs should be evaluated.

9

Figure 1-2
Four phases of program evaluation

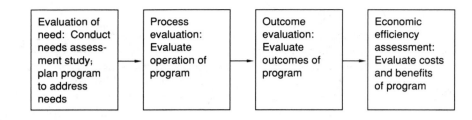

The initial focus of evaluation research was "outcome evaluation." Did the program result in the positive outcome for which it was designed (e.g., higher grades, lower absenteeism, or lower recidivism)? However, as the field of program evaluation has progressed since Campbell's 1969 paper, it has become clear that evaluation research is concerned with much more than outcome evaluation (Posavac & Carey, 1989; Rossi & Freeman, 1989). In fact, evaluation research itself has become an important applied discipline in the behavioral sciences, composed of researchers in psychology, sociology, political science, and education, among others.

There are four general types of evaluations, depicted in Figure 1-2 as the four phases of the evaluation process. The first is the evaluation of need. Needs assessment studies ask whether there are in fact problems that need to be addressed in a target population. Is illiteracy a problem in the community; what services do the elderly need; what is the pattern of high school drop-out rate among various ethnic groups; why do they drop out? Once a need has been established, programs can be planned to address the need.

The second type of program evaluation question is process evaluation or program monitoring. When the program is under way, the evaluation researcher monitors it to determine whether the program is reaching the target population being served, whether it is attracting enough clients, and whether the staff is providing the services planned by the program. In sum, the researcher wants assurance that the program is providing the resources or services it is supposed to provide. This research is extremely important because we would not want to conclude that a program is ineffective if, in fact, it is the implementation of the program that is not working.

The third question concerns outcome evaluation: Are the intended outcomes of the program being realized? Is the goal—to increase literacy, decrease the drop-out rate from high school, or provide job skills—being achieved? To determine this, the research evaluator must devise a way of measuring the outcome and then study the impact of the program on the outcome measure.

The final program evaluation question addresses economic efficiency. Once it is shown that a program does have its intended effect, researchers must determine whether the program is "worth it." The cost of the program must be weighed against its benefits. Also, the researchers must answer the question of whether there might be some better use of the resources that were used to implement the program.

You can see that evaluation research differs greatly from basic research. The evaluation researcher takes immediate action on the basis of the results. He or she must determine clearly whether a program is successful and valuable enough to be continued. Basic researchers can afford to be tentative and conduct more research before they draw strong conclusions about their results.

Behavioral research is important in many fields and has important applications to public policy. This chapter has introduced you to the major goals and general types of research. All researchers, whether they are interested in basic, applied, or program evaluation questions, use scientific methods. The themes and concepts in this chapter will be expanded in the remainder of the book. They will be the basis on which you evaluate the research of others and plan your own research projects as well.

STUDY QUESTIONS

1. Why is it important for anyone in our society to have a knowledge of research methods?
2. Why is scientific skepticism useful in furthering our knowledge of behavior? How does the scientific approach differ from other ways of gaining knowledge about behavior?
3. Distinguish between description, prediction, determination of cause, and explanation as goals of scientific research.
4. Distinguish between basic and applied research.
5. Describe what a program evaluation researcher's goals would be when addressing each of the four types of evaluation research questions.

ACTIVITY QUESTION

Suppose you have been appointed to a task force on the issue of homelessness in your community. Your role is to advise the task force on program evaluation. Design a complete evaluation plan using the four phases of program evaluation.

CHAPTER

2

Where to Start

W here do you get ideas about problems to study? And how do you find out about other people's ideas and research on a problem? In this chapter, we will explore some sources of scientific ideas. We will also consider the nature of research reports published in professional journals.

HYPOTHESES AND PREDICTIONS

Most research studies are attempts to test a **hypothesis** formulated by the researcher. A hypothesis is really a type of idea or question; it makes a statement about something that may be true. A hypothesis is only a tentative idea or question that is waiting for evidence to support or refute it. Sometimes hypotheses are very general and informal questions. For example, Geller, Russ, and Altomari (1986) had general questions about beer drinking among college students. How much beer is consumed in an average sitting in a college bar; how long do people stay; do males and females differ in their drinking? With such questions in mind, the researchers developed a procedure for collecting data to answer the questions. Research problems formulated in this way are informal hypotheses or simply questions about behavior.

Hypotheses are often stated in more specific and formal terms. Usually such formal hypotheses state that two or more variables are related to one another. Thus, a researcher might develop the hypothesis that "crowding results in lowered performance on mental tasks," or another researcher might formulate the hypothesis that "attending to more features of something to be learned will result in greater memory." Such hypotheses are formulated on the basis of past research findings and theoretical considerations. The researcher will then design a study to test the hypothesis. In the crowding example, the researcher might place one group of subjects in a crowded room and another group in an uncrowded room to work on a series of tasks, and their performance will be observed.

At this point, the researcher would make a specific **prediction** concerning the outcome of this experiment. Here the prediction might be that "subjects in the uncrowded condition will perform better on the tasks than will subjects in the crowded condition." If this prediction is confirmed by the results of the study, the hypothesis is supported. If the prediction is not confirmed, the researcher will either reject the hypothesis (and believe that crowding does not lead to poor performance) or conduct further research using different methods to study the hypothesis. It is important to note that when the results of a study confirm a prediction, the hypothesis is only *supported*, not *proven*. Researchers study the same hypothesis using a variety of methods, and each time a hypothesis is supported by a research study, our confidence that the hypothesis is correct increases.

13

SOURCES OF IDEAS

It is not easy to say where good ideas come from. Many people are capable of coming up with worthwhile ideas, but verbalizing the process by which they are generated is difficult. Cartoonists know this—they show a brilliant idea as a light bulb flashing on over the person's head. But where does the electricity come from? Let's consider five sources of ideas: common sense, observation of the world around us, theories, past research, and practical problems.

Common sense

One source of ideas that can be tested is the body of knowledge called common sense—the things we all believe to be true. Do "opposites attract" or do "birds of a feather flock together"? If you "spare the rod," do you "spoil the child"? Is a "picture worth a thousand words"? Asking questions such as these can lead to research programs studying attraction, the effects of punishment, and the role of visual images in learning and memory.

Testing a commonsense idea can be valuable because such notions don't always turn out to be correct, or research may show that the real world is much more complicated than our commonsense ideas would have it. For example, pictures can aid memory under certain circumstances, but sometimes pictures detract from learning (see Levin, 1983). Actually conducting research to test commonsense ideas often forces us to go beyond a commonsense theory of behavior.

Observation of the world around us

Observations of personal and social events can provide many hypotheses that merit testing. The curiosity that is aroused in you by your observations can lead you to research asking about all sorts of phenomena.

Have you ever had the experience of storing something away in a "special place" where you were sure you could find it later (and perhaps where no one else would possibly look for it) and then later discovering that you couldn't recall where you had stored it? Such an experience could lead to systematic research on whether it is a good idea to put things in special places. In fact, Winograd and Soloway (1986) conducted a series of experiments on this very topic. Their research demonstrated that people are likely to forget where something is placed when two conditions are present: (1) The location where it is placed is judged to be highly memorable and (2) the location is considered a very unlikely place for the object. Thus, while it seems to be a good idea at the time, storing something in an unusual place is generally not a good idea.

Events you read about can also lead to research ideas. In 1961, Eliot Aronson read a Gallup Poll that showed that President Kennedy's popularity actually increased following a failed attempt to invade Cuba at the Bay of

Pigs. The invasion attempt was widely viewed as a tremendous blunder by the United States, so Aronson wondered why Kennedy's popularity would increase rather than drop. Aronson then developed the idea that the rise in popularity resulted from the fact that Kennedy was almost "too perfect," with his good looks, charm, athletic ability, and intelligence. Perhaps the blunder of the invasion made him more "human" in the eyes of the public, thus causing the increase in popularity. This was an intriguing idea, but it had not been proven; there was no necessary connection between the blunder and the rise in popularity because many other events were occurring simultaneously that could have caused Kennedy's increased popularity.

To rule out the possibility of these other events, Aronson conducted an experiment to test the hypothesis that a blunder committed by a perfect person will result in increased liking for that person (see Aronson, 1984). In the experiment, subjects listened to a tape recording of a person who was a candidate for the "College Quiz Bowl." Some subjects heard a person who was nearly perfect, with high scores on the quiz answers and an impressive series of accomplishments in his background; other subjects listened to an average person. Some of the subjects listening to each candidate then heard that person commit a blunder: He spilled coffee all over himself. Thus, four conditions were created: a perfect person who did or did not commit the blunder and an average person who did or did not commit the blunder. Subjects then indicated how much they liked the person they listened to. The results showed that subjects most liked the perfect person who had committed the blunder; they least liked the average person who had spilled coffee. Thus, the research supported Aronson's idea that a blunder by a perfect person can increase liking for that person.

A more recent example demonstrates the diversity of ideas that can be generated by curiosity about things that happen around you. During the past few years, there has been a great deal of controversy about the effects of rock music on teenagers—a fear that rock music leads to sexual promiscuity, drug use, and violence. Some groups, such as the Parents' Music Resource Center (PMRC), would like to censor music lyrics or put warning labels on records. There have even been congressional hearings on this topic. Some researchers noted this controversy and decided to conduct research to examine the issue. In one study, Prinsky and Rosenbaum (1987) asked teenagers to name their favorite songs and explain what the songs were about. Most of their subjects could explain the songs in only vague terms, such as "the beat is good" or "it's about love." The researchers concluded that teenagers do not pay a great deal of attention to the lyrics of songs.

The world around us is a rich source of material for scientific investigation. After the Three Mile Island nuclear power plant accident, researchers studied the impact of this disaster on people (see, for example, Baum, Gachtel, & Schaeffer, 1983; Richardson, Sorenson, & Soderstrom, 1987). When the Cable News Network (CNN) presented a live national broadcast of a trial involving a woman who was gang-raped in a bar in Massachusetts in 1983, researchers studied attitudes toward such televised trials and women's perceptions of whether televised rape trials would influence their likelihood of reporting a rape (Swim & Borgida, 1987). When psychologist Robert Levine was teaching in Brazil several years ago, he noticed that Brazilian students were much more casual both in getting to class on time and leaving afterwards than were their counterparts in the United States. That observation led him to begin studying the pace of life in a variety of countries and numerous cities in the United States (Levine, 1990). Investigations such as these illustrate a point made in Chapter 1: Personal opinions and personal experiences provide insights about behavior, but scientific thinking requires us to test ideas through research.

Theories

Much research in the behavioral sciences tests theories of behavior. Theories serve two important functions in increasing our understanding of behavior. First, theories *organize and explain* a variety of specific facts. Specific facts or descriptions of behavior are not very meaningful by themselves, and so theories are needed to impose a framework on them. This framework makes the world more comprehensible by providing a few abstract concepts around which we can organize and explain a variety of behaviors. As an example, consider how Darwin's theory of evolution organized and explained a variety of facts concerning the characteristics of animal species. Similarly, in psychology one theory of memory asserts that there are separate systems of short-term memory and long-term memory. This theory accounts for a number of specific observations about learning and memory, including such phenomena as the different types of memory deficits that result from a blow to the head versus damage to the hippocampus area of the brain, and the rate at which a person forgets material he or she has just read.

Second, theories *generate new knowledge* by focusing our thinking so that we notice new aspects of behavior: Theories guide our observations of the world. The theory generates hypotheses about behavior, and the researcher conducts studies to see if these are correct. If the studies confirm the hypotheses, the theory is supported. A theory is never proven, though; research can only provide support for it. However, research also can reveal weaknesses in a theory and force researchers to modify the theory or develop a new, more comprehensive one.

The necessity of modifying theories is illustrated by the theory of short-term versus long-term memory discussed above. The original conception of the long-term memory system described long-term memory as a storehouse of permanent, fixed memories. However, research by cognitive psychologists, including Loftus (1979), has shown that memories are easily reconstructed and reinterpreted. In one study, subjects saw a film of an automobile accident, and later they were asked to tell what they saw in the film. Loftus found that subjects' memories were influenced by the way they were questioned. For example, subjects who were asked whether they saw "the" broken headlights were more likely to answer yes than were subjects who were asked whether they saw "a" broken headlight. Results such as these have required a more complex theory of how long-term memory operates.

Past research

A fourth source of ideas is past research. Becoming familiar with a body of research on a topic is perhaps the best way to generate ideas for new research. Virtually every study raises questions that can be addressed in subsequent research. The research may lead to an attempt to apply the findings in a different setting, to study the topic with a different age group, or to use a different methodology to replicate the results. The Geller et al. (1986) study on beer drinking reported that people who buy pitchers drink more beer than people who purchase bottles, that males drink more than females, that people in groups drink more than people alone, and that females stay longer in the bar than males. Knowledge of this study and its results might lead, for example, to research on ways of reducing excess drinking by college students.

In addition, as you become increasingly familiar with the research literature on a topic, you may see inconsistencies in research results that need to be investigated, or you may want to study alternative explanations for the results. Also, often what you know about one research area can be successfully applied to another research area. The main point here is that research ideas do not exist in a vacuum; knowledge of past research leads to new research ideas.

Practical problems

Research is also stimulated by practical problems that require immediate solutions. Groups of city planners and citizens might survey bicycle riders to determine the most desirable route for a city bike path, for example. On a larger scale, researchers have guided public policy by conducting research on the effects of exposure to pornographic materials, as well as other social and health issues. Much research in the behavioral sciences is aimed at addressing practical problems such as these.

LIBRARY RESEARCH

Before an investigator can conduct any research project, he or she must have a thorough knowledge of earlier research findings. Even if the basic idea has been formulated, a review of past studies will help the researcher clarify the idea and design the study. Thus, it is important to know how to search the literature on a topic and how to read research reports in professional journals. In this section we will discuss only the fundamentals of conducting library research; for further information, you may refer to the excellent guides to library research in psychology and to preparing papers that review research by Reed and Baxter (1991) and Rosnow and Rosnow (1992), respectively.

17

The nature of journals

If you've walked through the periodicals section of your library, you've noticed the enormous number of professional journals. It is in these journals that researchers publish the results of their investigations. After a research project has been completed, the study is written as a report, many of which are then submitted to the editor of an appropriate journal. The editor solicits reviews from other scientists in the same field and then decides whether the report is to be accepted for publication. Because each journal has a limited amount of space and receives many more papers than it has room to publish, most papers are rejected. Those that are accepted are published about a year later.

Most psychology journals specialize in one or two areas of human or animal behavior. Even so, the number of journals in many areas is so large that it is almost impossible for anyone to read them all. Table 2-1 lists some of the major journals in several areas of psychology. You can see how difficult it would be to read all of them, even in a single research area in psychology such as learning and memory. If you were seeking research on a single specific topic, it would be impractical to look at every issue of every journal in which relevant research might be published. Fortunately, you don't have to.

**Table 2-1
Some major
journals in
psychology**

General
*Contemporary Psychology** (book reviews)   *Current Directions in Psychological Science*   *Psychological Bulletin** (literature reviews; methodology)   *Psychological Review** (theoretical articles)   *Psychological Science*   *American Psychologist** (general articles on a variety of topics)
Experimental areas of psychology
*Journal of Experimental Psychology: General**   *Journal of Experimental Psychology: Human Learning and Memory**   *Journal of Experimental Psychology: Perception and Performance**   *Journal of Experimental Psychology: Animal Behavior Processes**   *Journal of Comparative Psychology**   *Behavioral Neuroscience**   *Journal of Verbal Learning and Verbal Behavior*   *Bulletin of the Psychonomic Society*   *Learning and Motivation*   *Memory and Cognition*   *Cognitive Psychology*   *Cognition*   *Cognitive Science*   *Discourse Processes*   *Journal of Mathematical Psychology*   *Journal of the Experimental Analysis of Behavior*   *Animal Learning and Behavior*   *Physiological Psychology*   *Biological Psychology*

Table 2-1
(*continued*)

Psychophysiology
Behavior Genetics
Behavior Research Methods, Instruments, and Computers

Clinical and counseling psychology

---

*Journal of Abnormal Psychology**
*Journal of Consulting and Clinical Psychology**
*Journal of Counseling Psychology**
Behaviour Research and Therapy
Journal of Clinical Psychology
Behavior Therapy
Biofeedback and Self-Regulation
Journal of Autism and Developmental Disorders
Journal of Abnormal Child Psychology
Psychosomatic Medicine
Addictive Behaviors
Journal of Social and Clinical Psychology

Developmental psychology

---

*Developmental Psychology**
*Psychology and Aging**
Child Development
Journal of Experimental Child Psychology
Journal of Applied Developmental Psychology
Infant Behavior and Development
Developmental Review
Journal of Abnormal Child Psychology
Infant Behavior and Development
Merrill-Palmer Quarterly
Human Development
Experimental Aging Research
Developmental Psychobiology

Personality and social psychology

---

*Journal of Personality and Social Psychology**
Personality and Social Psychology Bulletin
Journal of Experimental Social Psychology
Journal of Research in Personality
Journal of Personality
Journal of Social Issues
Social Psychology Quarterly
Journal of Applied Social Psychology
Basic and Applied Social Psychology
Journal of Social and Personal Relationships

Applied areas of psychology

---

*Journal of Applied Psychology**
*Journal of Educational Psychology**
Journal of Applied Behavior Analysis
Journal of Applied Behavioral Science
Journal of Conflict Resolution

19

Table 2-1
(continued)

Health Psychology
Journal of Human Stress
Educational and Psychological Measurement
American Educational Research Journal
Evaluation Review
Evaluation and Program Planning
Evaluation and Change
Environment and Behavior
Journal of Environmental Psychology
Journal of Consumer Research
Journal of Marketing Research
Organizational Behavior and Human Performance
Academy of Management Journal
Personnel Psychology
Journal of Vocational Psychology
Occupational Psychology
Law and Human Behavior
Forensic Psychology
Intelligence
Public Opinion Quarterly

Family studies and sexual behavior

Journal of Marriage and the Family
Family Coordinator
Journal of Marital and Family Therapy
Journal of Sex Research
Journal of Sexual Behavior
Journal of Homosexuality

Gender, ethnic, and cross-cultural issues

Hispanic Journal of Behavioral Sciences
Journal of Black Psychology
Sex Roles
Psychology of Women Quarterly
Journal of Cross-Cultural Psychology

Some Canadian and British Journals

Canadian Journal of Psychology
Canadian Journal of Behavioral Science
British Journal of Psychology
British Journal of Social and Clinical Psychology

* Published by the
American Psychological
Association

Psychological Abstracts

Psychological Abstracts, or "*Psych Abstracts*," publishes "nonevaluative summaries of the world's literature in psychology and related disciplines." It is published monthly by the American Psychological Association, and each volume contains about 40,000 abstracts of published articles. To find articles on a specific topic in which you are interested, you would use the index at the end of each volume. The summaries of the articles are brief descriptions of the research findings. On the basis of the abstract, you can determine the relevance of a particular article for your purposes. (The reference section of the library has similar abstracts of literature in many disciplines. For example, sociology journal articles are abstracted in *Sociological Abstracts*.)

The following example will illustrate how to use *Psychological Abstracts*. First, locate the index that accompanies each volume. The index is organized by subject category; some categories, such as "cognitive development" or "mental retardation," are quite large, while others, such as "clothing fashions" or "startle reflex," are narrower and contain relatively few references. The more general the category, the greater the number of references. As a general rule, you can search most efficiently when you have narrowed the category as much as possible—that is, when it is as specific as you can get it.

Suppose you are interested in finding out about research on stress management. You locate the index for a recent volume, say volume 77 for 1990. There you find categories labeled "stress," "stress management," and "stress reactions." If you want to know more about the categories used in the abstracts, you can consult the separate thesaurus of terms. Under stress management, 51 articles are listed; here are five of them:

> group stress management training with relaxation & cognitive restructuring & assertiveness skills, symptomatic 19–56 yr olds, 10441
>
> relaxation vs biofeedback vs stress management training, perceived pain & medication consumption, patients with chronic headache & excessive self-medication, 2274
>
> stress management techniques, reduction of Type A behavior & serum cholesterol & hypertension, adults at risk for coronary heart disease, literature review, 17519
>
> stress reduction techniques in sexual & marital therapy, sexual dysfunction & marital discord, husbands vs wives, 20461
>
> use of self-hypnosis & meditation after stress management training, 38–45 yr old executives, 6 mo followup, 8260

Usually only some of the articles will be of interest. You can locate those that do appear relevant in the appropriate volume of abstracts (in this case, volume 77). The abstracts are listed in numerical order. If you looked up article 2274, you would find the following information:

2274. **Michultka, Denise M.; Blanchard, Edward B.; Appelbaum, Kenneth A.; Jaccard, James et al.** (State U New York, Ctr for Stress & Anxiety Disorders, Albany) **The refractory headache patient: II. High medication consumption (analgesic rebound) headache.** *Behaviour Research & Therapy*, 1989, Vol 27(4), 411–420. —Conducted 3 studies on the identification, prognosis, and prediction of analgesic rebound headache. 231 individuals with chronic headache pain were selected on the basis of self-reported medication consumption over a 4-wk baseline period. 60 headache sufferers taking excessive amounts of primarily analgesic medication and still experiencing high levels of headache pain (high medicators [HMs]) had less relative success with a behavioral treatment of headache pain, although they reduced their medication consumption more than 171 low medicators. A relationship between medication reduction and success in treatment unique to the HMs was revealed.

After copying the information about this article, you could then go on to look up any other abstracts that seem relevant. To continue the search, you could then go to prior volumes.

After you complete the abstract search, your final step is to find the most useful original articles in the journals. If your library has the journal, you can read it in the library or make a photocopy. If the journal is not in your library, find out how your library can obtain a copy through an interlibrary loan service.

In addition to *Psychological Abstracts* and *Sociological Abstracts*, you might find several other abstracting services useful. These include:

ERIC, *Resources in Education*
Child Development Abstracts and Bibliography
Animal Behavior Abstracts
Biological Abstracts
Business Periodicals Index
Personnel Literature
Psychopharmacology Abstracts
Family Studies Abstracts
Criminal Justice Abstracts
Index Medicus

Social Science Citation Index

A different and often useful method of searching for articles is offered by the *Social Science Citation Index* (SSCI), which uses the "key article" method. To use this method, you need to first identify a "key article" on your topic, usually an article published sometime in the past that is particularly relevant to your interests. The SSCI then allows you to search for articles that have been published since then that cited the key article. This will give you a bibliography of articles that will be relevant to your topic. As you become familiar with this list, one or more of the articles might become new "key articles" and you can make further searches. Eventually you become thoroughly familiar with the research on your topic.

Literature reviews

Articles that summarize the research in a particular area are also useful. The *Psychological Bulletin* publishes reviews of the literature in various topic areas in psychology. The *Annual Review of Psychology* each year publishes articles that summarize recent developments in various areas of psychology. A number of other disciplines have similar annual reviews.

PsycBooks

A great deal of research information in the behavioral sciences is now published in books. These are often edited volumes on specific topics with chapters written by various researchers. These books and chapters may be literature reviews, theoretical developments, or descriptions of research programs. A resource to find books and chapters in psychology is *PsycBooks*, published annually by the American Psychological Association. Each year, *PsycBooks* is organized in five volumes:

Vol. 1	Experimental Psychology: Basic and Applied
Vol. 2	Developmental, Personality, & Social Psychology
Vol. 3	Professional Psychology: Disorders & Treatment
Vol. 4	Educational Psychology & Health Psychology
Vol. 5	Author, Subject, Book Title, & Publisher Indexes

Your search usually begins by examining the subject index in volume 5. If you look up stress management in the 1989 volume, you will find 24 listings. Here are two of them:

The behavioral control of high blood pressure	IV 7700-76
Stress management in work settings	B I 5900-63

The Roman numerals refer to the volume number in which the book or chapter citation may be found. The B in the second listing indicates that the citation is a book rather than a chapter. The numbers, such as 7700-76, refer to a general topic and the number of the citation. For example, 7700 is the code for "health psychology and behavioral medicine" and the article on high blood pressure is number 76 within that category.

Book citations give the table of contents and a brief description based on the preface or book jacket. Chapter citations provide an abstract of the chapter itself.

Computer-assisted searches

There are now a variety of ways of conducting searches using a computer. The contents of *Psychological Abstracts*, as well as other bibliographic information sources, have been stored in data bases on computers, some of which include:

PsychLit—Psychological Abstracts
ERIC—Resources in Education

23

MedLine—Medical/Physiological Abstracts
National Library of Medicine Data Base

When using a computer data base, you specify the search conditions (e.g., research topics), and the computer searches through the data base to find articles that fit your conditions. The computer search procedures you use will depend on the services available in your library.

Sometimes a reference librarian conducts the search for you by accessing a computer over a phone line. Today, however, more libraries are allowing users to do their own searches by providing them with a microcomputer and a data base stored on a compact disk.

Your main concern as a computer-search user is to specify search conditions accurately so that the computer will find what you want. You must specify the terms or "key words" that the computer will look for in the search. If you are interested in anything having to do with stress management, for example, a single search condition will result in a large number of references. Usually, though, your interests are narrower. For example, specifying stress management and exercise would give you only those articles that deal with both of these subjects. You could of course specify a narrower search by requiring that even more key words be included. As a rule, if your search conditions are too general (e.g., the topic of learning), you may get many more articles than you want; if you make the conditions too specific (e.g., learning math from computer games among high school students), you may get fewer articles than you want. It is usually to your advantage to define the search specifications carefully. Reference librarians can often help you plan an efficient search procedure.

ANATOMY OF A RESEARCH ARTICLE

Now that you have selected a research article, what can you expect to find in it? Journal articles usually have five sections: (1) an *abstract*, such as the ones found in *Psychological Abstracts*; (2) an *introduction* that explains the problem under investigation and the specific hypotheses being tested; (3) a *method* section that describes in detail the exact procedures used in the study; (4) a *results* section in which the findings are presented; and (5) a *discussion* section in which the researcher may speculate on the broader implications of the results, propose alternative explanations for the results, discuss reasons why a particular hypothesis may have not been supported by the data, or make suggestions for further research on the problem.

Abstract

The abstract is a summary of the research report and is usually no more than 150 words in length. It includes information about the hypothesis, a brief discussion of the procedure, and the general pattern of results. Usually little information is abstracted from the discussion section of the paper.

Introduction

In the introduction, the researcher describes the problem that has been investigated. Past research and theories relevant to the problem are described in detail. The specific expectations of the researcher are given, often as formal hypotheses. In other words, the investigator introduces the research in a logical format that shows how past research and theory are connected to the current research problem and the expected results.

Method

The method section is divided into subsections; the number of subsections is determined by the author and depends on the complexity of the research design. Sometimes the first subsection presents an overview of the design in order to prepare the reader for the material that follows. The next subsection describes the characteristics of the subjects. Were they male, female, or were both sexes used? What was the average age? How many subjects were there? If the study used human subjects, there would be some mention of how subjects were recruited for the study. The next subsection details the procedure used in the study. As the researcher describes any stimulus materials presented to the subjects, how the behavior of the subjects was recorded, and so on, it is important that no potentially important detail be omitted. Such detail allows the reader to know exactly how the study was conducted and gives information that other researchers need in order to replicate the study. Other subsections may be necessary to describe in detail some piece of equipment or testing materials that were used.

Results

In the results section, the author presents the findings, usually in three ways. First, there is a description in narrative form—for example, "The location of items was most likely to be forgotten when the location was both highly memorable and an unusual place for the item to be stored." Second, the results are described in statistical language. And third, the material is often depicted in tables and graphs.

The statistical terminology of the results section may appear formidable. However, lack of knowledge about the calculations isn't really a deterrent to understanding the article or the logic behind the statistics. Statistics are only a tool the researcher uses in evaluating the outcomes of the study.

Discussion

In the discussion section, the author talks about the research from various perspectives. Do the results support the hypothesis? If they do, the author should give all of the possible explanations for the results and should discuss why one explanation is superior to another. If the hypothesis has not been supported, the author should offer suggestions to explain this. What might have been wrong with the methodology, the hypothesis, or both? The author may also discuss how the results fit in with past research on the topic. This section may also include suggestions for possible practical applications of the research and for future research on the topic.

You should read as many research articles as possible to become familiar with the way information is presented in reports. As you do so, you will develop ways of efficiently processing the information in the articles. It is usually best to read the abstract first, then skim the article to decide whether you can use the information provided. If you can, go back and read the article in detail. Note the hypotheses and theories presented in the introduction, write down anything you find that is unclear or problematic in the method, and read the results in view of the material in the introduction. Be critical when you read the article; students often generate the best criticism. Most important, as you read more research on a topic you will become more familiar with the variables being studied, the methods used to study the variables, important theoretical issues, and problems that need to be addressed by future research. You will find yourself generating your own research ideas and planning your own studies.

STUDY QUESTIONS

1. What is a hypothesis? What is the distinction between a hypothesis and a prediction?
2. Describe the five sources of ideas for research. Do you think any one source is better than the others or that one source is used more frequently? Why?
3. What are the two functions of a theory?
4. Describe the difference between using *Psychological Abstracts*, the *Social Science Citation Index*, and *PsycBooks*.
5. What information does the researcher communicate in each of the sections of a research article?

ACTIVITY QUESTION

Think of ten "commonsense" sayings about behavior (e.g., Spare the rod, spoil the child; Like father, like son; Absence makes the heart grow fonder). For each, develop a hypothesis that is suggested by the saying and a prediction that follows from the hypothesis. Choose one of your hypotheses and develop a strategy for finding research on this topic. (Based on Gardner, 1988).

CHAPTER

3

Studying Behavior

$\mathbf{I}$n this chapter, we will explore some of the basic issues and concepts that are necessary for understanding the scientific study of behavior. We will begin by looking at the nature of variables, including their measurement and the types of relationships among them. We will then examine general methods for studying these relationships.

VARIABLES

A **variable** is a general class or category of objects, events, or situations. Examples of variables a psychologist might study include cognitive task performance, noise level, spatial density, intelligence, gender, reaction time, rate of forgetting, aggression, speaker credibility, stress, and self-esteem. Each of these variables represents a general category; within the category, specific instances will vary. These specific instances are called the levels or values of the variable. For the spatial density variable, there are many possible levels or values, ranging from one square foot per person on up. Task performance values could range from a low of zero percent correct to a high of 100 percent correct.

OPERATIONAL DEFINITIONS

In actual research, the researcher has to decide on a method by which to study the variables of interest. It is important to know that a variable is an abstract concept that must be translated into concrete forms of observation or manipulation. Thus, a variable such as "aggression," "cognitive task performance," "amount of reward," or "self-esteem" must be defined in terms of the specific method used to measure or manipulate it. Scientists refer to the **operational definition** of a variable—a definition of the variable in terms of the operations or techniques the researcher uses to measure or manipulate it.

Variables must be operationally defined so they can be studied empirically. Thus, a variable such as "speaker credibility" might be conceptualized as having two levels and operationally defined as a speaker described to listeners as a "Nobel Prize recipient" or as a "substitute teacher in the Central High School District." The variable of "cognitive task performance" might be defined as the number of errors detected on a proofreading task during a 10-minute period. It is also true that there may be several levels of abstraction when studying a variable. The concept of "stress" is very general, for example; when researchers study stress, they might focus on any of a number of stressors—noise, crowding, major health problems, or job burnout. A researcher interested in stress would probably choose one stressor to study and then develop operational definitions of that specific stressor. He or she would then carry out research investigations that would pertain both to the specific stressor and the more general concept of stress. The general point to remember is that researchers must always translate the variables into specific operations in order to manipulate or measure them.

The task of operationally defining a variable forces the scientist to discuss abstract concepts in concrete terms. The process often results in the realization that the variable is too vague to study. This does not necessarily indicate that the concept is meaningless but rather that systematic research is not possible until the concept can be operationally defined. Sometimes scientific study of a concept depends on the development of a technology that makes operational definition possible. For instance, the scientific study of dreaming was facilitated by development of electrophysiological techniques for studying brain wave patterns during sleep.

Operational definitions also help us communicate our ideas to others. If someone wishes to tell me about aggression, I need to know exactly what is meant by this term because there are many ways of operationally defining it. For example, aggression could be defined as (1) the number and duration of shocks delivered to another person, (2) the number of times a child punches an inflated toy clown, (3) the number of times a child fights with other children during recess, (4) homicide statistics gathered from police records, or (5) a score on a personality measure of aggressiveness. Communication with another person will be easier if we agree on exactly what we mean when we use the term *aggression* in the context of our research.

There is rarely a single, infallible method for operationally defining a variable. A variety of methods may be available, each of which has advantages and disadvantages. Researchers must decide which is best, given the particular problem being studied, the goals of the research, and considerations such as ethics and costs. To illustrate how complex it can be to develop an operational definition of a variable, consider the choices faced by a researcher interested in studying crowding. The researcher could study the effects of crowding on college students in a carefully controlled laboratory experiment. However, the focus of the researcher's interest may be the long-term effects of crowding; if so, it might be a good idea to observe the effects of crowding on laboratory animals such as rats. The researcher could examine the long-term effects of crowding on aggression, eating, sexual behavior, and maternal behavior. But what if the researcher wants to investigate cognitive or social variables such as family interaction or intellectual performance? Here, the researcher might decide to study people who live in crowded housing and compare them to people who live in less crowded circumstances. Because no one method is perfect, it is clear that complete understanding of any variable involves studying the variable using a variety of operational definitions. Several methods will be discussed throughout this book.

MEASUREMENT

Recall from Chapter 1 that describing behavior is one of the primary goals of scientific research. To do this, researchers must measure variables. Sometimes the aim of the research is primarily to describe one or more variables. A social psychologist, for example, might want to develop a taxonomy of ways that people relate to love partners, or a cognitive psychologist might describe the ways that people approach a problem-solving situation. Other research focuses on relationships among variables. Do males and females differ in their love relationships? Which problem-solving strategies are most effective in different situations? Measuring variables is a fundamental part of every research investigation. The researcher begins with an abstract, conceptual variable and then must operationally define it. In this section, three aspects of measurement are discussed: reliability, validity, and the problem of reactivity.

Reliability of measures

A reliable measure is one that is both consistent and, because it gives a stable measure of a variable, precise. **Reliability** then, refers to the consistency or stability of a measure of behavior.

Your everyday definition of reliability is quite close to the scientific definition. For example, you might say that you have a "reliable" watch: Your reliable watch always gives you the precise time, and you rarely find that it is running slow or fast. Similarly, a reliable measure of a psychological variable such as intelligence will yield the same result each time you administer the test to the same person. A measure of intelligence would be unreliable if it measured the same person as average one week, low the next, and bright the following week. Put simply, a reliable measure does not fluctuate. If the measure does fluctuate, there is error in the measurement device.

Any measure can be thought of as made up of two components: (1) a **true score,** which is the real score on the variable, and (2) **measurement error.** An unreliable measure of intelligence contains measurement error and so does not provide an accurate indication of an individual's true intelligence. In contrast, a reliable measure of intelligence—one that contains little measurement error—will yield an identical (or nearly identical) intelligence score each time the same individual is measured.

To illustrate the concept of reliability further, imagine that you know someone whose "true" intelligence score is 100. Now suppose that you administer an unreliable intelligence test to this person each week for a year. After the year, you calculate the person's average score on the test based upon the 52 scores you obtained. Now suppose that you test another friend who also has a true intelligence score of 100; however, this time you administer a highly reliable test. Again, you calculate the average score. What might your data look like? Typical data are shown in Figure 3-1. In each case the average score is 100. However, scores on the unreliable test range from 85 to 115, while scores on the reliable test range from 97 to 103. The error in the unreliable test is revealed in the greater variability shown by the person who took the unreliable test.

When conducting research, you can only measure each person once, you

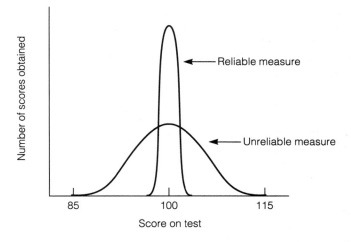

Figure 3-1
Comparing data
of a reliable and
unreliable
measure

can't give the measure 50 or 100 times to discover a true score. Thus, it is very important that you use a reliable measure. Your single administration of the measure should closely reflect the person's true score.

The importance of reliability is obvious. An unreliable measure of length would be useless in building a table; an unreliable measure of a variable such as intelligence is useless in studying that variable. Researchers cannot use unreliable measures to systematically study variables or the relationships among variables. Trying to study behavior using unreliable measures is a waste of time because the results will be unstable and unable to be replicated.

Reliability is an important concept that will be used throughout the book as different research strategies are discussed. In a later chapter, some methods of assessing reliability are described. For now, you should recognize that reliability is achieved when researchers use careful measurement procedures. In some research areas, this might mean carefully training observers to record behavior; in other areas, it might mean paying close attention to the way questions are phrased; or it might mean carefully placing recording electrodes on the body to measure physiological reactions.

Validity

Validity may be defined as the extent to which the operational definition of a variable actually reflects the true theoretical meaning of the variable. Remember that a variable is an abstract concept that can be operationally defined in many ways. Memory, intelligence, attitude, motivation, and self-esteem are all abstract constructs that have theoretical definitions. However, research studying such constructs requires concrete operational definitions. Validity is the extent to which the operational definition does in fact reflect the underlying variable.

In terms of the measurement of behavior, validity is a question of whether the measure that is employed actually measures what it is intended to measure. A measure of scholastic aptitude (such as the Scholastic Aptitude Test, or SAT) is supposed to measure the ability to succeed in school. The validity of such a test is determined by whether it does, in fact, measure this ability. A measure of self-esteem is an operational definition of the self-esteem variable; the validity of this measure is determined by whether it does measure the theoretical self-esteem construct.

A first answer to the question of whether a measure has validity is to examine its **face validity,** which tells whether the measure appears (on the face of it) to measure what it is supposed to measure. Face validity is not very sophisticated; it involves only a judgment of whether, given the theoretical definition of the variable, the measure appears to actually measure the variable. That is, do the procedures used to measure the variable appear to be an accurate operational definition of the theoretical variable? Thus, a measure of a variable such as self-esteem will usually appear to measure self-esteem. The measure might include an item such as "I feel comfortable attending a social function with strangers" but not include items such as "I learned to ride a bicycle at an early age": The first question appears to be more closely related to self-esteem than does the second question. Although it is not very sophisticated, most researchers prefer to use measures that have face validity.

Face validity is not entirely satisfactory, however. Some measures of variables do not have obvious face validity. For example, is it obvious that rapid eye movement during sleep is a measure of dream occurrence? Also, psychological variables are usually discussed in terms of their theoretical meaning. Self-esteem is measured and studied because researchers have developed theories of self-esteem that relate this construct to other variables. People with high self-esteem are hypothesized to differ from people with low self-esteem in a variety of ways; they are expected to behave differently in different situations, for example. Further, certain variables are hypothesized to result in low or high self-esteem. We have now moved to an important question about validity: Does the measure of the variable relate to other variables in meaningful ways?

When a measure does relate to other variables in meaningful ways, the measure is said to have **construct validity.** The construct validity of a measure emerges from research studies in which investigators use the measure to study behavior. The construct validity of rapid eye movement as a measure of dream occurrence is demonstrated when studies find that people who are awakened during rapid eye movement are more likely to report dreaming than are people who are awakened when their eyes are not moving. A measure of self-esteem should be related to variables that are theoretically predicted to be related to self-esteem. Also, the measure should *not* be related to variables with which it should not be related.

The construct validity of a measure is rarely established in a single study but is built up over time as numerous studies investigate the theory of the particular construct being measured. Further, measures of variables usually have a limited life span. As research findings accumulate, researchers discover problems with the measure and develop new measures to correct the problems. This process leads to better measures and more complete understanding of the underlying variable being studied.

The Sensation Seeking Scale developed by Zuckerman (1979) is an excellent example of construct validity issues. Zuckerman's research was stimulated by a psychological theory of optimal levels of physiological arousal. The theory states that people have a need to maintain an optimal level of arousal. When arousal is too low, people will be motivated to do things to increase arousal; if arousal is too high, an attempt to reduce arousal should be observed. The theory helps to explain many behaviors, such as the hallucinations and other disturbances that people experience when they are placed in sensory deprivation environments. Zuckerman decided to study this theory by focusing on individual differences; he asked the question of why some people consistently seem to seek out novel or arousing sensations (e.g., parachute diving, listening to loud music, driving in car races), while other people avoid arousing sensations.

The Sensation Seeking Scale was developed to study such individual differences in personality. The scale itself includes items intended to measure thrill seeking, susceptibility to boredom, and other aspects of sensation seeking. The reliability of the scale was of course assessed. After determining that the scale was reliable, construct validity research could begin. Over a period of many years, research by Zuckerman and others has shown that people who score high on the scale do in fact behave differently from people who score low. High sensation seekers engage in more dangerous activities, drive faster, and prefer less intellectual activities, for example. The measure is also related in expected ways to other personality traits: High sensation seekers are more extraverted. Work on the Sensation Seeking Scale has ultimately led to research on the biological basis for sensation seeking that involves questions of the brain mechanisms responsible for arousal needs, and whether the trait has a genetic basis. Zuckerman's research illustrates a systematic program of research on the validity of a measure of a psychological construct. In other areas of research, the construct validity of measures may be studied less systematically. In all research, though, measures must be useful in studying the variables being investigated.

The problem of reactivity

A potential problem when measuring behavior is **reactivity.** A measure is said to be reactive if awareness of being measured changes the subject's behavior. A reactive measure tells what the person is like when he or she is aware of being observed, but it doesn't tell how the subject would behave under natural circumstances. Simply having various devices such as electrodes and blood pressure cuffs attached to your body may change the physiological responses being recorded. Knowing that a researcher is observing you or recording your behavior on tape might change the way you behave. Measures of behavior vary in terms of their potential reactivity. There are also

33

ways to minimize reactivity, such as allowing time for subjects to become used to the presence of the observer or the recording equipment.

A book by Webb, Campbell, Schwartz, Sechrest, and Grove (1981) has drawn attention to a number of measures that are called nonreactive or unobtrusive. Many such measures involve clever ways of indirectly recording a variable. For example, an unobtrusive measure of preferences for paintings in an art museum is the frequency with which tiles around each painting must be replaced—the most popular paintings are the ones with the most tile wear. Levine's (1990) study on the pace of life in cities, described in Chapter 2, used indirect measures such as the accuracy of bank clocks and the speed of processing standard requests at post offices to measure pace of life. Some of the measures described by Webb et al. (1981) are simply humorous. For instance, in 1872 Sir Francis Galton studied the efficacy of prayer in producing long life. Galton wondered whether British royalty, who were frequently the recipients of prayers by the populace, lived longer than other people. He checked death records and found that members of royal families actually led shorter lives than other people, such as men of literature and science. The book by Webb and his colleagues is a rich source of such nonreactive measures. More important, it draws attention to the problem of reactivity and sensitizes researchers to the need to reduce reactivity whenever possible. We will return to this issue at several points in this book.

RELATIONSHIPS BETWEEN VARIABLES

Recall from Chapter 1 that researchers are often interested in studying the relationship between two variables. The relationship between two variables is the general way in which changes in the values of one variable are associated with changes in the values of the other variable. That is, do the levels of the two variables vary systematically together? As age increases, does the amount of cooperative play increase as well? Does viewing television violence result in greater aggressiveness? Is speaker credibility related to attitude change? The most common relationships found in research are the **positive linear relationship,** the **negative linear relationship,** and the **curvilinear relationship,** and, of course, the situation in which there is no relationship between the variables. These relationships are best illustrated by line graphs that show the way changes in one variable are accompanied by changes in a second variable. The four graphs in Figure 3-2 show these four types of relationships.

Positive linear relationship

In a positive linear relationship, increases in the values of one variable are accompanied by increases in the values of the second variable. Graph A in Figure 3-2 illustrates the relationship between speaker credibility and attitude change, which is a positive linear relationship. In a graph like this, there is

34

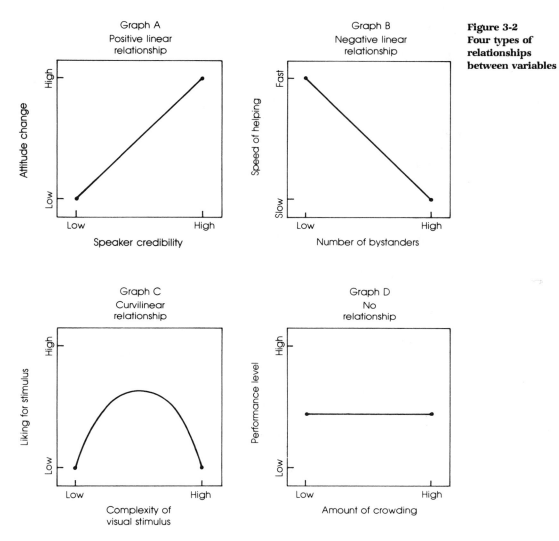

Figure 3-2
Four types of relationships between variables

a horizontal and a vertical axis. Values of the first variable are placed on the horizontal axis, labeled from low to high. Values of the second variable are placed on the vertical axis. Graph A shows that greater amounts of credibility are associated with greater amounts of attitude change.

Negative linear relationship

Variables can also be negatively related. In a negative linear relationship, increases in the values of one variable are accompanied by *decreases* in the values of the other variable. Darley and Latané (1968) were intrigued with a widely publicized incident in which a woman named Kitty Genovese was stabbed outside her apartment building in New York City while 38 of her neighbors looked on. This led to research on the effect of bystanders on helping behavior; the research showed that there is a negative relationship between the number of bystanders present at an emergency and the speed with which the victim receives help. Each subject in the experiment was alone in a cubicle in the laboratory and overheard what he or she thought was another subject having an epileptic seizure (actually each heard a tape record-ing). Some subjects believed that they were the only ones to hear the emer-gency; other subjects thought that there was one other bystander; others believed that there were four other bystanders present. Graph B illustrates the negative relationship between number of bystanders and speed of helping. As the number of bystanders *increased*, the speed of helping *decreased*. The two variables are systematically related, just as in a positive relationship; only the direction of the relationship is reversed.

Curvilinear relationship

In a curvilinear relationship, increases in the values of one variable are accom-panied by both increases and decreases in the values of the other variable. In other words, there is a positive relationship when you look at a portion of the values of one variable and a negative relationship for the other values of the variable. Graph C in Figure 3-2 shows a curvilinear relationship between complexity of visual stimuli and ratings of preferences for the stimuli. This particular relationship is called an inverted-U relationship. Increases in visual complexity are accompanied by increases in liking for the stimulus, but only up to a point. The relationship then becomes negative; further increases in complexity are accompanied by *decreases* in liking for the stimulus (Vitz, 1966).

No relationship

When there is no relationship between the two variables, the graph is simply a flat line. Graph D illustrates the relationship between crowding and task performance found in a study by Freedman, Klevansky, and Ehrlich (1971). Unrelated variables vary independently of one another. Increases in crowding are not associated with any particular changes in performance; thus, a flat line describes a lack of relationship between the two variables.

These graphs illustrate several kinds of shapes; almost any shape can describe the relationship between two variables. Other relationships are de-scribed by more complicated shapes than those in Figure 3-2. Remember that these are general patterns. Even if, in general, there is a positive linear relationship, that does not necessarily mean that everyone who scores high on one variable will also score high on the second variable. There may be individual deviations away from the general pattern. In addition to knowing the general type of relationship between two variables, it is also necessary to know the strength of the relationship. Sometimes two variables are strongly related to one another and there is very little deviation from the general pattern. In other situations, the two variables are not highly correlated. We will return to this issue in a later chapter when statistical analyses are discussed.

CORRELATIONAL VERSUS EXPERIMENTAL METHODS

There are two general approaches to the study of relationships among variables: the correlational method and the experimental method. The **correlational method** is nonmanipulative; the researcher observes or measures the variables of interest (the terms *observation* and *measurement* will be used interchangeably throughout the text). That is, behavior is observed as it occurs naturally. This may be done by asking people to describe their behavior, by directly observing behavior, or even by examining various public records such as census data. The second approach to the study of relationships between variables is called the experimental method. In contrast to the correlational method, the **experimental method** involves manipulation of variables. The researcher directly manipulates one or more variables by establishing the conditions for studying behavior; the behavior is then observed under the different conditions. For example, Loftus (1979) used the experimental method when subjects were asked whether they saw "a" broken headlight or "the" broken headlight. The method of questioning was manipulated and the subjects' answers were then measured.

The correlational method

Suppose a researcher is interested in the relationship between exercise and anxiety. How could this problem be studied? Using the correlational method, the researcher would devise operational definitions to measure both the amount of exercise that people engage in and their level of anxiety. There could be a variety of ways of operationally defining either of these variables; for example, subjects might simply be asked to provide self-reports of their exercise patterns and current anxiety level. The important point to remember here is that both variables are measured when using the correlational method. Now suppose that the researcher collects data on exercise and anxiety from a number of subjects and finds that exercise is negatively related to anxiety. That is, the more people exercise, the lower their level of anxiety.

The correlational method seems like a reasonable approach to studying relationships between variables such as exercise and anxiety. However, two problems arise when interpreting results obtained using the correlational method: (1) direction of cause and effect and (2) the third-variable problem—that is, extraneous variables that may affect the results.

Direction of cause and effect The first problem is that of direction of cause and effect. With the correlational method, it is difficult to determine

37

which variable causes the other. In other words, it can't really be said that exercise causes a reduction in anxiety. Although there are plausible reasons for this particular pattern of cause and effect, there are also reasons why the opposite pattern might occur. Thus, it is possible that anxiety level causes exercise; perhaps the experience of high anxiety interferes with the ability to exercise. This is an important difference. If exercise reduces anxiety, then undertaking an exercise program would be a reasonable way to lower one's anxiety. However, if anxiety causes people to stop exercising, simply forcing someone to exercise would not be likely to reduce the person's anxiety level.

The problem of direction of cause and effect is not the worst problem of the correlational method, however. Scientists have pointed out, for example, that astronomers have been able to make very accurate predictions even though they cannot manipulate variables in an experiment. In addition, the direction of cause and effect is often not crucial because, for some pairs of variables, the causal pattern may operate in both directions. For instance, there seem to be two causal patterns in the relationship between the variables of similarity and liking: Similarity causes people to like each other, and liking causes people to become more similar. In general, the third-variable problem is a much more serious fault of the correlational method.

The third-variable problem   When the correlational method is used, there is the danger that there is no direct causal relationship between the two variables. Exercise may not influence anxiety and anxiety may have no causal effect on exercise. Instead, there may be a relationship between the two variables because some other variable causes both exercise *and* anxiety. This is known as the third-variable problem. Any number of other third variables may be responsible for an observed relationship between two variables. In the exercise and anxiety example, one such third variable could be income level. Perhaps high income gives people more free time to exercise (and the ability to afford a health club membership!), and also high income lowers anxiety. If income is the determining variable, there is no direct cause-and-effect relationship between exercise and anxiety; the relationship was caused by the third variable, income level.

These two problems are serious limitations of the correlational method. Often they are not considered in media reports of research results. For instance, a newspaper may report the results of a correlational study that found a positive relationship between amount of coffee consumed and likelihood of a heart attack. It is easy to see that there is not necessarily a cause-and-effect relationship between the two variables. Numerous third variables (e.g., occupation, personality, or genetic predisposition) could cause both a person's coffee-drinking behavior and the likelihood of heart attack. You can see that the results of such studies are ambiguous.

The experimental method

The experimental method reduces ambiguity such as this in the interpretation of results. With the experimental method, one variable is manipulated and the other is then measured. If a researcher used the experimental method to study whether exercise reduces anxiety, exercise would be manipulated—perhaps by having one group of people exercise each day for a week while another group of people refrains from exercise. Anxiety would then be measured. Suppose it is found that people in the exercise group are lower in anxiety than the people in the group that does not exercise. The researcher can now say something about the direction of cause and effect: In the experiment, exercise came first in the sequence of events. Thus, anxiety level could not influence the amount of exercise that the people engaged in.

Another characteristic of the experimental method is that it attempts to eliminate the influence of all extraneous third variables. This is called control of extraneous variables. Such control is usually achieved by making sure that every feature of the environment except the manipulated variable is held constant. Any variable that cannot be held constant is controlled by making sure that the effects of the variable are random. Through randomization, the influence of any extraneous variables is equal in the experimental conditions. Both procedures are used to make sure that any differences between the groups are due to the manipulated variable.

Experimental control **Experimental control** means that all extraneous variables are kept constant. If a variable is held constant, it cannot be responsible for the results of the experiment. In the experiment on the effect of exercise, the researcher would want to make sure that the only difference between the exercise and no-exercise groups is the exercise. Because people in the exercise group are removed from their daily routine to engage in exercise, the people in the no-exercise group should be removed from their daily routine as well. Otherwise, it is possible that the lower anxiety in the exercise condition resulted from the "rest" from the daily routine rather than the exercise.

Experimental control is accomplished by treating subjects in all groups in the experiment identically; the only difference between groups is the manipulated variable. In the Loftus experiment on memory, both groups will witness the same accident, the experimenter who asks the questions will be the same in both groups, the lighting and all other conditions will be the same, and so on. When there is a difference between the groups in reporting memory, one can be sure that the difference is the result of the method of questioning rather than of some other variable that was not held constant.

Randomization Sometimes it is difficult to keep a variable constant. The most obvious such variable is any characteristic of the subjects. If, in a study using the experimental method, one group of subjects is in the exercise condition and a different group of subjects is in the no-exercise condition, the subjects in the two conditions might be different on some extraneous third variable, such as income. This difference could cause an apparent relationship between exercise and anxiety. How can the researcher eliminate the influence of such extraneous variables in an experiment?

The experimental method eliminates the influence of such variables by **randomization.** Randomization ensures that the extraneous variable is just

39

as likely to affect one experimental group as it is to affect the other group. To eliminate the influence of subject characteristics, the researcher assigns subjects to the two groups in a random fashion. In actual practice, this means that assignment to groups is determined using a list of random numbers. To understand this, think of the subjects in the experiment as forming a line. As each person comes to the front of the line, a random number is given to the subject, much like random numbers are drawn for a lottery. If the number is even, the subject is assigned to one group (e.g., exercise); if the number is odd, the subject is assigned to the other group (e.g., no exercise). By using a random assignment procedure, the researcher is sure that the subject characteristic composition of the two groups will be virtually identical. In this "lottery," for instance, people with low, medium, and high incomes will be distributed equally in the two groups. In fact, randomization ensures that the subject characteristic composition of the two groups will be virtually identical in every way. This ability to randomly assign subjects to groups is an important difference between the experimental and correlational methods.

To make the concept of random assignment more concrete, you might try an exercise such as the one I did with a box full of old baseball cards. The box contained cards of 50 American League players and 50 National League players. The cards were thoroughly mixed up; I then proceeded to select 32 of the cards and assign them to "groups" using the list of random numbers in Appendix C-1. As I selected each card, I used the following decision rule: If the random number is even, the player is assigned to "group 1" and if the number is odd, the player is assigned to "group 2." I then checked to see whether my two groups differed in terms of league representation: Group 1 had nine American League players and seven National League players, while group 2 had an equal number of players from the two leagues. The two groups were virtually identical!

Any other variable that cannot be held constant is also controlled by randomization. For instance, an experiment can be conducted over a period of several days or weeks. Because all subjects in both conditions can't be run simultaneously, researchers use a random order for running subjects. ("Running subjects" is the process of collecting data from individuals who participate in a study. It is perhaps an unfortunate bit of jargon that may have its origins in the process of running rats through mazes.) This procedure prevents a situation in which one group is studied during the first days of the experiment while the other group is studied during later days. Similarly, one group will not be studied only during the morning and the other group only in the afternoon.

Direct control and randomization eliminate the influence of any extraneous variables. Thus, the experimental method allows a relatively unambiguous interpretation of the results. Any difference between groups on the observed variable can be attributed only to the influence of the manipulated variable.

40

INDEPENDENT AND DEPENDENT VARIABLES

When researchers study the relationship between variables, the variables are usually conceptualized as having a cause-and-effect connection. That is, one variable is considered to be the "cause" and the other variable is the "effect." Thus, speaker credibility is considered to be a cause of attitude change; exercise is viewed as having an effect on anxiety. Researchers in both experimental and correlational research view the variables in this fashion, even though, as we have seen, there is less ambiguity about the direction of cause and effect when the experimental method is used. Researchers use the terms **independent variable** and **dependent variable** when referring to the variables being studied. The variable that is considered to be the "cause" is the independent variable, and the variable that is the "effect" is the dependent variable.

In an experiment, the manipulated variable is the independent variable, and the second variable that is measured is the dependent variable. One way to remember the difference is to relate the terms to what happens to a subject in an experiment. The researcher devises a situation to which subjects are exposed, such as watching a violent versus a nonviolent program. This situation is the manipulated variable; it is called the independent variable because the subject has nothing to do with its occurrence. In the next step of the experiment, the researcher measures the subject's response to the manipulated variable. The subject is responding to what happened to him or her; the researcher assumes that what the subject does or says is caused by, or dependent on, the effect of the independent (manipulated) variable. The independent variable, then, is the variable manipulated by the experimenter, and the dependent variable is the measured behavior of the subject that is assumed to be caused by the independent variable.

When the relationship between an independent and a dependent variable is presented in a graph, the independent variable is always placed on the horizontal axis and the dependent variable is always placed on the vertical axis. If you look back to Figure 3-2, you will see that this graphing method was used to present the four relationships. In Graph B, for example, number of bystanders is the independent variable and is placed on the horizontal axis; the dependent variable is speed of helping and is placed on the vertical axis.

It should be noted that some research focuses primarily on the independent variable; the researcher studies the effect of a single independent variable on numerous behaviors. Other researchers may focus on a specific dependent variable and study how various situations affect that one behavior; construct validity research, discussed previously in this chapter, illustrates research that concentrates on a single behavior, such as sensation seeking. To make this distinction more concrete, consider a study of the effect of jury size on the outcome of a trial. One researcher studying this problem might be interested in the effect of group size on a variety of behaviors, including jury decisions or risk taking among business managers. Another researcher could be inter-

41

ested in jury decisions and might study the effects of size of jury or the judge's instructions on the behaviors of jurors. Both emphases lead to important research.

CAUSALITY

Thus far, causality has been discussed only on an intuitive level. When the experimental method is used, causality is inferred on the basis of the fact that, because everything else is held constant, a change in one variable produces a change in another variable. When psychologists speak of "cause," they mean that there is evidence that one variable does affect another. Such evidence is most easily established using the procedures of the experimental method.

Questions of true cause and effect are in fact, however, more difficult than they appear, and they are controversial among both scientists and philosophers. Many argue that a cause-and-effect relationship is proven only if the cause is both necessary *and* sufficient for the effect to occur.

To illustrate, consider the question: "What causes a car to start?" Many people might answer that it is turning the ignition key. Now, it is true that if you have two cars in perfect working order, when you turn the ignition key in one it will start, while the other will not start as long as you do nothing to it. Has causation been proven? The answer is no if we require a cause to be both necessary and sufficient for the effect to occur.

To be necessary, the cause must be present for the event to occur. To prove that turning the ignition key is the cause of the car starting, it must be shown that turning the ignition key must occur for the car to start. To be sufficient, the cause will *always* produce the effect. To prove that turning the key is the cause, it must always result in the car starting.

Is turning the key necessary and sufficient for the car to start? In most cases, turning the key is necessary. However, it is possible to start the car by "hot wiring" the ignition to bypass the ignition key. Thus, "turning the ignition key" is not necessary; rather, turning on an electrical ignition circuit is necessary. Is turning the key sufficient to start the car? Turning the key is not sufficient since it does not always result in the car starting. The car may not start when the key is turned for any number of reasons, including lack of fuel or a dead battery.

The "necessary and sufficient" requirement for establishing cause is rare in psychology. Whenever psychologists assert that there is a necessary and sufficient cause of a behavior, research soon points out that it just isn't true. For example, psychologists once asserted that "frustration causes aggression"; whenever frustration occurs, aggression will result, and whenever aggression occurs, frustration must be the preceding cause. This assertion was shown to be inaccurate. Frustration may lead to aggression, but other responses (such as passive withdrawal or working hard to overcome the frustration) are also possible. Also, aggression may result from frustration, but other events may produce aggression as well, including pain, insult, or direct attack.

42

A typical type of cause-and-effect relationship in psychology is one in which the cause is sufficient but not necessary for the effect to occur. For example, through classical conditioning procedures, the pairing of a painful stimulus with a neutral stimulus will produce a fear of the originally neutral stimulus. However, fears may be acquired in other ways.

Another type of cause and effect is observed when a variable is necessary but not sufficient. The variable by itself cannot produce the effect; other conditions must also be present for the effect to occur. For example, it is necessary to be over 18 years of age to vote, but age is not a sufficient cause. Other conditions, such as motivation to vote, must be present.

Behavioral scientists are not unduly concerned with the issues of ultimate cause and effect. They are concerned with carefully describing behavior, studying how variables affect one another, and understanding the reasons why. The general consensus is that there are few interesting "necessary and sufficient" causes of behavior. Instead, research on numerous variables eventually leads to an understanding of a whole "causal network," in which a number of variables are involved in complex patterns of cause and effect. This book will not focus on these difficult questions but instead will examine the methods used to study behavior.

CHOOSING A METHOD

In this chapter, we have discussed the importance of describing behavior through careful measurement and of studying relationships between variables using the correlational and experimental methods. The advantages of the experimental method have been stressed. However, there *are* disadvantages of experiments and many good reasons for using methods other than experiments. These reasons include the possible artificiality of a laboratory experiment, ethical considerations, the need to study subject variables, and the goals of description and prediction of behavior. When researchers choose a methodology to study a problem, they must weigh the advantages and disadvantages of their options in the context of the overall goals of the research.

Artificiality of experiments

In a laboratory experiment, the independent variable is manipulated within the carefully controlled confines of a laboratory. This procedure permits relatively unambiguous inferences concerning cause and effect and reduces the possibility that extraneous variables could influence the results. It is an extremely valuable way to study many problems. However, the high degree of control and the laboratory setting may sometimes create an artificial atmosphere that limits either the questions that can be addressed or the generality of the results. For this reason, researchers may decide to use correlational methods. Another alternative is to try to conduct an experiment in a field

43

setting. In a **field experiment,** the independent variable is manipulated in a natural setting. As in any experiment, the researcher attempts to control extraneous variables via either randomization or experimental control.

As an example of a field experiment, consider Langer and Rodin's (1976) study on the effects of giving elderly nursing home residents greater control over decisions that affect their lives. One group of residents was given a great deal of responsibility for making choices concerning the operation of the nursing home; a second group was made to feel that the staff would be responsible for their care and needs. The experimenters measured dependent variables such as activity level and happiness of the residents. The results showed that the people in the group that was given responsibility were more active and happy. In a follow-up study, this group even showed greater improvements in physical health (Rodin & Langer, 1977).

The advantage of the field experiment is that the independent variable is investigated in a natural context. The disadvantage is that the researcher loses the ability to directly control many aspects of the situation. The laboratory experiment permits researchers to more easily keep extraneous variables constant, thereby eliminating their influence on the outcome of the experiment. Of course, it is exactly this control that leads to the artificiality of the laboratory investigation.

Ethical considerations

Sometimes the experimental method is not a feasible alternative when choosing a method because experimentation would be unethical or impractical as a way of studying the problem. Child-rearing practices would be impractical to manipulate with the experimental method, for example. Even if it were possible to randomly assign parents to two child-rearing conditions, such as using withdrawal of love versus physical types of punishment, the manipulation would be unethical. Instead of manipulating variables such as child-rearing techniques, researchers usually study them as they occur in natural settings. Many important research areas present similar problems—for example, studies of the effects of alcoholism or divorce and its consequences, or the impact of maternal employment on children. Such problems need to be studied, and generally the only techniques possible are nonexperimental.

Subject variables

Subject variables are characteristics of individuals, such as age, gender, personality, or marital status. These variables are by definition nonexperimental. When subject variables are studied, the variables are measured. For example, to study a personality characteristic such as extraversion, you might have subjects complete a personality test that is designed to measure this variable.

Description of behavior

A major goal of science is to provide an accurate description of events. Thus, the goal of much research is to describe behavior; the issues that experiments address are really not relevant to the primary goals of the research. A classic example of descriptive research in psychology comes from the work of Jean Piaget, who carefully observed the behavior of his own children as they matured and described in detail the changes in their ways of thinking about and responding to their environment (Piaget, 1952). Piaget's descriptions and his interpretations of his observations resulted in an important theory of cognitive development that greatly increased our understanding of this topic. Piaget's theory is still being tested and refined by researchers using a variety of methods (see Flavell, 1985).

Successful predictions of future behavior

In many real-life situations, a major concern is to make a successful prediction about a person's future behavior—for example, success in school, ability to learn a new job, or probable interest in various major fields in college. In such circumstances, there may be no need to be concerned about issues of cause and effect. It is possible to design measures that increase the accuracy of predicting future behavior. School counselors can give tests to decide whether students should be in "enriched" classroom programs, employers can use a test to help determine whether an applicant should be hired, and college students can take tests that can help them decide on a major. These types of measures can lead to better decisions for many people.

When researchers develop measures designed to predict future behavior, they must conduct research to demonstrate that the measure does, in fact, relate to the behavior in question. You may recognize this as a question of validity: If a clerical aptitude test is designed as a measure of the ability to succeed in a clerical training program, does it in fact measure this ability?

The validity of such measures is called **criterion validity.** Research is conducted to examine whether the test, which is called a **predictor variable,** is related to the future behavior, called the **criterion variable.** The criterion validity of a test of clerical aptitude is demonstrated when research shows that people who score high on the test do better in clerical training than people who score low on the test (i.e., there is a positive relationship between the test score and future behavior). When research establishes that the test has criterion validity, the measure can be used to advise people on whether they will be successful in a clerical training program or to select applicants for a program.

At this point, you may be wondering how researchers select a methodology to study a problem. A variety of methods are available, each with advantages and disadvantages. Researchers select the method that best enables them to address the questions that they wish to answer. No method is inherently superior to another. Rather, the choice of method is made after considering the problem that is being investigated and the cost and time constraints that exist. In the remainder of this book, many specific methods will be discussed, all of which are useful under different circumstances. In fact, all

45

are necessary to understand the wide variety of behaviors that are of interest to behavioral scientists. Complete understanding of any problem or issue requires study using a variety of methodological approaches.

STUDY QUESTIONS

1. What is a variable? List at least five different variables and then specify the levels of each variable.
2. Define "operational definition" of a variable. Give at least two operational definitions of the variables you thought of in question 1.
3. What is meant by the reliability of a measure? Distinguish between true score and measurement error.
4. What is meant by validity of a measure? Distinguish between face validity and construct validity.
5. What is a reactive measure?
6. Describe the four general types of relationships between variables. Draw graphs depicting these relationships.
7. What is the difference between the correlational method and the experimental method?
8. What is the difference between an independent variable and a dependent variable?
9. Distinguish between laboratory and field experiments.
10. What is meant by the problem of direction of cause and effect and the third-variable problem?
11. How do direct experimental control and randomization influence the possible effects of extraneous variables?
12. What are some reasons for using the correlational method to study relationships between variables?
13. What is criterion validity?
14. What is meant by a "necessary and sufficient" cause?

ACTIVITY QUESTION

Consider the hypothesis that stress at work causes family conflict at home.

1. What type of relationship is proposed (e.g., positive linear, negative linear)?
2. Graph the proposed relationship.
3. Identify the independent variable and the dependent variable in the statement of the hypothesis.

4. How might you investigate the hypothesis using the experimental and correlational method?

5. Would you use the experimental or correlational method to test the hypothesis? Why? What problems would arise if you use the correlational method?

In Chapter 5, some quasi-experimental designs will be described that might be used to study this problem.

CHAPTER

Descriptive Methods

Description of behavior is important in every research study. This chapter will explore a variety of approaches to describing behavior. These include asking people to describe their behavior, directly observing behavior, or even examining existing records of behavior, such as census data or hospital records.

FIELD OBSERVATION

Observation in natural settings

Field observation is sometimes called "field work" or simply "naturalistic observation" (see Lofland, 1971, 1976; Douglas, 1976). In a **field observation** study, the researcher makes observations in a particular natural setting (the field) over an extended period of time, using a variety of techniques to collect information. The report includes these observations and the researcher's interpretations of the findings.

Gans' (1962) study of "urban villagers" living in Boston's West End is a good example of a field observation study. To examine the impact of living in what was considered a "slum" environment, Gans used a variety of techniques to watch people and listen to conversations in stores, bars, and other public settings. He attended meetings and public gatherings and made friends with people who provided him with information. Gans concluded that, contrary to the beliefs of many city planners and urban renewal advocates, the West End was viewed by its inhabitants as a secure place. The effect of urban renewal (constructing new dwellings to replace the "slum") was to disrupt lives and break strong family and ethnic bonds that existed in the neighborhood.

Field observation is undertaken when a researcher wants to describe and understand how people in a social setting live, work, and experience the setting. If you want to know about bars as a social setting, you will need to visit one or more bars over an extended period of time, talk to people, observe interactions, and become accepted as a "regular" (cf. Cavan, 1966). If you want to know how people persuade or influence others, you can take a job as a car salesperson or take an encyclopedia sales training course (cf. Cialdini, 1988). If you are interested in how people become part of some social group (e.g., marijuana users, prostitutes, a particular religious cult), you can arrange to meet members of such groups to interview them about their experiences (cf. Becker, 1963, on marijuana users). If you want to know what it is really like to be a patient in a mental hospital, you need to get yourself admitted as a patient (cf. Rosenhan, 1973). Of course, you might not want to do any of these things; however, if these questions interest you, the written reports of the researchers will be fascinating.

Field observation demands that a researcher immerse himself or herself in the situation. The field researcher observes everything—the setting itself,

49

the patterns of personal relationships, people's reactions to events that occur, and so on. The goal is to provide a complete and accurate picture, not to test hypotheses formed prior to the study. To achieve this goal, the researcher must keep detailed field notes: On a regular basis (at least once each day), the researcher must write down or dictate everything that has happened. Further, the field researcher uses a variety of techniques to gather information: observing people and events, using key "informants" to provide inside information, talking to people (interviewing them), and examining documents produced in the setting (such as newspapers, newsletters, or memos).

Interpreting the data

The field researcher's first goal is to describe the setting, the events, and the persons observed. The second, equally important goal is to analyze what was observed. The researcher must interpret what occurred, essentially generating hypotheses that help explain the data and make them understandable. Such an analysis is done by building a coherent structure to describe the observations. The final report, while sensitive to the chronological order of events, is usually organized around the structure developed by the researcher. Specific examples of events that occurred during observation are used to support the researcher's interpretations.

A good field observation report will support the analysis by using multiple confirmations. For example, similar events may occur several times, similar information may be reported by two or more people, and several different events may occur that all support the same conclusion.

The data in field observation studies are primarily "qualitative" in nature; that is, they are the descriptions of the observations themselves rather than "quantitative" statistical summaries. However, there is no reason why quantitative data cannot be gathered in a field observation study. If circumstances allow it, data can be gathered on income, family size, education levels, and other easily quantifiable variables. Such data can be reported and interpreted along with qualitative data gathered from interviews and direct observations.

Issues in field observation

Participation and concealment   Two related issues facing the field observation researcher are whether to be a participant or a nonparticipant in the social setting and whether to conceal one's purposes from the other people in the setting. Do you become an active participant in the group or do you observe from the outside? Do you conceal your purposes or even your presence, or do you openly let people know what you are doing?

A nonparticipant observer is an outsider who does not become an active part of the situation. A participant observer, however, is an active participant who observes from the inside. Because participant observation allows the researcher to observe the setting from the inside, he or she experiences events in the same way as natural participants. Friendships and other experiences of the participant observer may yield valuable data. A potential problem in participant observation, however, is that the observer may lose the objectivity necessary in scientific observation. This may be particularly problematic when the researcher already belongs to the group being studied (e.g., a researcher who belongs to Parents Without Partners who undertakes a study of that group). Remember that field observation requires accurate description and objective interpretation with no prior hypotheses: If a researcher has some prior reason to either criticize people in the setting or give a glowing report of a particular group, the research simply should not be done. There are too many reasons in such cases to expect that there will be problems and a lack of objectivity in the results.

Should the researcher be concealed or go ahead and be open about the research purposes? Concealed observation may be preferable because the presence of the observer may influence and alter the behavior of those being observed. Imagine how a nonconcealed observer might alter the behavior of high school students in many situations at a school. Thus, concealed observation is less reactive than nonconcealed observation since people are not aware that their behaviors are being observed and recorded. Still, nonconcealed observation may be preferable from an ethical viewpoint: Consider the invasion of privacy when researchers hid under beds in dormitory rooms to discover what college students talk about (Henle & Hubbell, 1938)! Also, people often quickly become used to the observer and behave naturally in the observer's presence. One widely viewed example of nonconcealed observation was the public television documentary series "An American Family," in which one family's activities were filmed over a period of several months. Many viewers of this series were surprised to see how quickly family members forgot about the cameras and spontaneously showed many private aspects of their family life.

Whether to conceal one's purpose or presence is a decision that must be dependent on the particular group and setting that is being studied. Sometimes a participant observer is nonconcealed to certain members of the group, who give the researcher permission to be part of the group as a concealed observer. Often a concealed observer decides to say nothing directly about his or her purposes but will completely disclose the goals of the research if asked by anyone. Nonparticipant observers are also not concealed when they gain permission to "hang out" in a setting or use interview techniques to gather information (e.g., in Becker's study of marijuana users, some of the subjects who were interviewed first introduced Becker to their network of friends who were also marijuana users). In actuality, then, there are degrees of participation and concealment: A nonparticipant observer may not become a member of the group, for example, but may over a period of time become accepted as a friend or simply part of the ongoing activities of the group. You can see that field observation researchers must carefully determine what their role in the setting will be.

Defining the scope of the observation   A field observation researcher may want to study *everything* about a setting. However, this may not be possible, simply because a setting and the questions one might ask about it are so complex. Thus, it is often necessary for researchers to limit the scope of their observations to behaviors that are relevant to the central issues of the study. For example, we previously mentioned Cialdini's interest in social influence in settings such as car dealerships. In this case, Cialdini might focus only on sales techniques and ignore such things as management practices and relationships among salespersons.

Limits of field observation Field observation obviously cannot be used to study all questions. The approach is most useful when investigating complex social settings; it is less useful for studying well-defined hypotheses under precisely specified conditions.

Field research is also very difficult (cf. Green & Wallaf, 1981). Unlike a typical laboratory experiment, field research data collection cannot always be scheduled at a convenient time and place. In fact, field research can be extremely time-consuming, often placing the researcher in an unfamiliar setting for extended periods. Also, in experimental research, the procedures are well defined and the same for each subject, and the data analysis is planned in advance. In field observation research, there is an ever changing pattern of events—some important and some unimportant; the researcher must record them all and remain flexible in order to adjust to them as the research progresses. The process of analysis that follows the completion of the research is not simple. The researcher must sort through the data again and again, develop hypotheses to explain them, and make sure all the data are consistent with the hypotheses.

If some of the observations are not consistent, the researcher does more analysis. Judd, Smith, and Kidder (1991) emphasize the importance of **negative case analysis.** A negative case is an observation that does not fit the explanatory structure devised by the researcher. When a negative case is found, the researcher revises the hypothesis and again examines all the data to make sure that they are consistent with the new hypothesis. The researcher may even collect additional data in order to examine more closely the circumstances that led to the negative case. The main point here is that field observation research is a difficult and challenging scientific procedure, but when it is done well, knowledge gained from it can be invaluable.

SYSTEMATIC OBSERVATION

Systematic observation refers to the careful observation of one or more specific behaviors in a particular setting. This research approach is much less global than field observation research. The researcher is interested in only a few very specific behaviors, the observations are quantifiable, and frequently the researcher has developed prior hypotheses about the behaviors.

For example, Bakeman and Brownlee (1980; also see Bakeman & Gottman, 1986) were interested in the social behavior of young children. Three-year-olds were videotaped in a room in a "free play" situation. Each child was taped for 100 minutes; observers viewed the videotapes and coded each child's behavior every 15 seconds. The following coding system was used by the observers:

Unoccupied:
Child is not doing anything in particular or is simply watching other children.

Solitary play:
Child plays alone with toys but is not interested in or affected by the activities of other children.

Together:
Child is with other children but is not occupied with any particular activity.

Parallel play:
Child plays beside other children with similar toys but does not play with the others.

Group play:
Child plays with other children, including sharing toys or participating in organized play activities as part of a group of children.

Bakeman and Brownlee were particularly interested in the sequence or order in which the different behaviors were engaged in by the children. They found, for example, that the children rarely went from being unoccupied to engaging in parallel play. However, they frequently went from parallel to group play, indicating that parallel play is a transition state in which children decide whether to go ahead and interact in a group situation.

Coding systems

Numerous behaviors can be studied using systematic observation. The researcher must decide which behaviors are of interest, choose a setting in which these behaviors can be observed, and most important, develop a **coding system** that observers can use to measure the behaviors. Sometimes the researcher develops the coding system to fit the needs of the particular study. Coding systems should be as simple as possible, allowing observers to easily categorize behaviors. This is especially important when observers are coding "live" behaviors rather than viewing videotapes that can be reviewed or even coded on a frame-by-frame basis. An example of a simple coding system comes from a study by Barton, Baltes, and Orzech (1980), in which nursing home residents and the nursing home staff were observed. Only five categories were used: (1) resident independent behavior (e.g., doing something by oneself, such as grooming); (2) resident dependent behavior (asking for help); (3) staff independence-supporting behavior (praise or encouragement for independence); (4) staff dependency-supportive behavior (giving assistance or encouraging taking assistance); and (5) other, unrelated behaviors of both residents and staff. Their results illustrate one of the problems of care facili-

53

ties: Staff perceive themselves as "care providers" and so most frequently engage in dependency-supportive behaviors. Does this lead to greater dependency by the residents and perhaps a loss of feelings of control? If so, the consequences may be serious: Recall the Rodin and Langer (1977) experiment discussed in Chapter 3, in which feelings of control led to greater happiness and general well-being among nursing home residents.

Sometimes researchers can use coding systems that have been developed by others. For example, the Family Interaction Coding System (FICS; see Patterson & Moore, 1979) consists of 29 categories of interaction; these are grouped as aversive (hostility), prosocial (helping), and general activities. Most of the research using the FICS has centered on how children's aversive behaviors are learned and maintained in a family. Another coding system is the Interaction Process Analysis developed by Bales (1970) to code interactions in small groups. In this system, 12 categories are organized into four general types of interactions: (1) positive social-emotional (e.g., expresses agreement); (2) negative social-emotional (shows antagonism); (3) task-related answering (gives opinion); and (4) task-related questioning (asks for information). Interaction process analysis has been used to study such topics as leadership in groups and group satisfaction. A major advantage of using an already developed coding system is that a body of research already exists in which the system has proven useful, and there are usually training materials available.

Methodological issues

Equipment   We should briefly mention several issues in systematic observation. The first concerns equipment. You can directly observe behavior and code it at the same time. For example, without equipment you could directly observe and record the behavior of children in a classroom or couples interacting on campus; however, it is becoming more common to use videotape equipment to make such observations. Videorecorders have become smaller and more inexpensive and have the advantage of providing a permanent record of the behavior observed that can later be coded. Your observations can be coded using paper on a clipboard and a pencil; a stopwatch is sometimes useful for recording the duration of events. Alternatively, you can use a computer recording device that is not much larger than a calculator. Keys on the device are pressed to code the behaviors observed as well as to keep track of their duration. These recorders add to the expense of the research, and initial training of observers may take longer. However, research that requires observing several types of behavior and recording duration of behavior is facilitated by using these computer devices. Also, data analysis may be easier because the data can be automatically transferred from the device to the computer where the analyses will be performed.

Reactivity   A second issue is reactivity—the possibility that the presence of the observer will affect people's behaviors (see Chapter 3). As we noted above, reactivity can be reduced by concealed observation. One-way mirrors, "candid camera" techniques, or hidden microphones may offer ways of concealing the presence of an observer. Alternatively, reactivity can be reduced by allowing enough time for people to become used to the presence of the observer and any recording equipment.

Reliability Recall from Chapter 3 that reliability refers to the degree to which a measure is stable or consistent: A reliable measure is precise. The method used to determine reliability when doing systematic observation is called *inter-rater* or *inter-observer reliability*. This is an index of how closely two observers agree when coding the same observations. Usually, such reliability is expressed as a percentage of the time that two or more observers coded the same behavior in the same way. Very high levels of agreement are reported in virtually all published research using systematic observation (generally 80 percent agreement or higher). For some large-scale research programs in which many observers will be employed over a period of years, observers are first trained using videotapes, and their observations during training are checked for agreement with previous observers (cf. Bakeman & Gottman, 1986).

Sampling Finally, sampling of behaviors should be mentioned. For many research questions, samples of behavior taken over a long period of time will provide more accurate and useful data than single short observations. Consider a study on television viewing in homes (Anderson, Lorch, Field, Collins, & Nathan, 1986). The researchers wanted to know how members of families actually watch TV. They could have studied short periods of TV watching, perhaps during a single evening; however, such data could be distorted by short-term trends—time of day, a particular show, or the variations in family activities that influence TV viewing. A better method to address the question would be to observe TV viewing over a long period of time. This is exactly what the researchers did. Video recorders and cameras were installed in the homes of 99 families; these were set to record in a time-lapse mode whenever the TV was turned on. Using this method, almost 5,000 hours of TV viewing were recorded; coding this much data would be an almost impossible task. To analyze the data, Anderson et al. sampled a segment of TV viewing every 55 minutes. Some of their results included the findings that no one is watching the TV 15 percent of the time and TV viewing increases up to age 10 and then begins to decrease.

CASE STUDIES

A **case study** provides a description of an individual. This individual is usually a person, but it may also be a setting such as a business, school, or neighborhood. Sometimes a field observation study is called a case study, and in fact the field observation and case study approaches sometimes overlap. We have included case studies as a separate category in this chapter because case studies do not necessarily involve field observation. Instead, the case study may be a description of a patient by a clinical psychologist or a historical account of an event such as a model school that failed. A "psychobiography" is a type of case study in which a researcher applies psychological theory to explain the life of an individual—usually an important historical figure (cf. Elms, 1976; Runyan, 1981). Thus, case studies may use such techniques as library research and telephone interviews with persons familiar with the case—there may be no direct observation of the case at all (cf. Yin, 1984).

Depending on the purpose of the investigation, the case study may present the individual's history, symptoms, characteristic behaviors, reactions to situations, or responses to treatment. Typically, a case study is presented when an individual possesses a particularly rare, unusual, or noteworthy condition. One famous case study in clinical psychology was "Sybil," a woman with a rare multiple personality disorder (Schreiber, 1973). During the course of therapy, it was discovered that Sybil had experienced severe beatings and other traumatic experiences during childhood. One explanation of the disorder, then, was that Sybil unconsciously created other personalities who would suffer the pain instead of her. A case study of a man with an amazing ability to recall information was reported by Luria (1968). The man, called "S.," could remember long lists and passages with ease, apparently using mental imagery for his memory abilities. Luria also described some of the drawbacks of S.'s ability. For example, he frequently had difficulty concentrating because mental images would spontaneously appear and interfere with his thinking. A final case study example concerns language development; it was provided by "Genie," a child who was kept isolated in her room, tied to a chair and never spoken to until she was discovered at the age of 14 (Curtiss, 1977). Genie, of course, lacked any language skills. Her case provided psychologists and linguists the opportunity to attempt to teach her language skills and discover which skills could be learned. Apparently Genie was able to acquire some rudimentary language skills, such as forming childlike sentences, but did not develop full language abilities.

Case studies are valuable in informing us of conditions that are rare or unusual and thus not easily studied in any other way. Insights gained through the case study may also lead to the development of hypotheses that can be tested using other methods. Case studies are also very difficult and present unique challenges to the researcher in terms of providing explanations for the events that are described. Runyan (1981), in a discussion of psychobiography research, presents 13 potential explanations for why Vincent Van Gogh cut off his ear. Runyan's analysis emphasized the need to critically examine each explanation in terms of its plausibility and of evidence available.

SURVEY RESEARCH

Surveys use self-report measurement techniques to question people about themselves—their attitudes, behaviors, and demographics (age, income, race, marital status, and so on). Surveys may employ careful sampling tech-

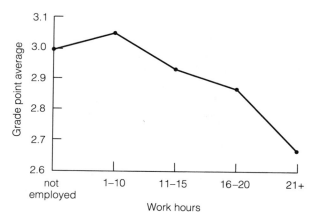

Figure 4-1 Relationship between hours of work and grade point average

Source: Steinberg, L., & Dornbusch, S. M. (1991). Negative correlates of part-time employment during adolescence: Replication and elaboration. *Developmental Psychology, 27,* 303–313. Copyright 1991 by the American Psychological Association. Reprinted by permission.

niques to obtain an accurate description of an entire population; for example, the Gallup Poll conducts surveys to find out what people are thinking about issues such as abortion or nuclear power, or to obtain data on preferences among political candidates. When scientific sampling techniques are used, the survey results can be interpreted as an accurate representation of the entire population. Such accuracy can be achieved by sampling an extremely small percentage of a very large population, such as an entire state or even the nation. Surveys on a much smaller scale are going on all the time. A student may be asked by a school to be part of a survey on student services. Employees of a large corporation might be asked about their opinions of current operations. You might receive a phone call from a marketing research company asking about consumer preferences. Often such surveys are used to help make important policy or marketing decisions.

Most people think of surveys as a way of taking a "snapshot" of current attitudes and behaviors. However, the survey method is also an important way for researchers to study relationships among variables and ways that attitudes and behaviors change over time. Steinberg and Dornbusch (1991) examined the relationship between the number of hours that high school students work and variables such as grade point average, drug and alcohol use, and psychosomatic distress. The sample consisted of 3,989 students in grades 10 through 12 at nine high schools in California and Wisconsin. Results indicated that "long work hours during the school year are associated with lower investment and performance in school, greater psychological and somatic distress, drug and alcohol use, delinquency, and autonomy from parents" (Steinberg & Dornbusch, 1991, p. 304). Figure 4-1 shows a typical finding: There were frequently some positive aspects of working fewer than 10 hours per week (as opposed to not being employed); however, increasingly negative effects are associated with longer work hours.

We will examine two major considerations in survey research: sampling techniques and constructing a survey instrument.

SAMPLING TECHNIQUES

Most research projects involve **sampling** subjects from a population of interest. The **population** is composed of all of the individuals of interest to the researcher. One population of interest to a pollster, for instance, might be all people in the United States who are eligible to vote. This implies that the pollster's population of interest does not include people under the age of 18, people serving prison terms, visitors from other countries, and other people ineligible to vote. With enough time and money, a pollster could, conceivably, contact everyone in the population who is eligible to vote. Fortunately, the pollster can avoid this massive undertaking by selecting a sample from the population of interest. With proper sampling, the pollster can use information obtained from the sample to determine what the population as a whole is like. Sampling is therefore very important in generalization of research results.

There are two basic types of sampling techniques: nonprobability sampling and probability sampling. In **nonprobability sampling,** we don't know the probability of any particular member of the population being chosen. In **probability sampling,** each member of the population has a specifiable probability of being chosen. Probability sampling is very important when you want to make exact statements about a population on the basis of the results of your survey. That is, probability sampling is necessary to accurately generalize results from a sample to a population.

Nonprobability sampling

Nonprobability sampling techniques are quite arbitrary. A population may be defined but little effort is expended to make sure that the sample accurately represents the population. However, nonprobability samples are cheap and convenient, and there are reasons why they are used. Two types of nonprobability sampling are haphazard sampling and quota sampling.

Haphazard sampling   One form of nonprobability sampling is called **haphazard sampling** or "accidental" sampling. Haphazard sampling could be called a "take them where you find them" method of obtaining subjects (or *respondents*—the term that is typically used to describe subjects in survey research). For example, a television reporter might poll people who happen to walk past a particular street corner at a particular time of day and are willing to say a few words to the camera. The population of interest might be "people who live in this city," but the results of this poll could not really be generalized to this population. It would not be possible to specify the probability of a city resident being chosen as a participant in this poll. The probability would be high for some people (those who live or work near the street corner) and low for others. The haphazard sampling technique would exclude everyone who, for any reason, wasn't present at that location at that particular time. Thus, any generalization of the results to the entire city would probably be inaccurate.

Quota sampling Another form of nonprobability sampling is called **quota sampling.** A researcher who uses this technique chooses a sample that reflects the numerical composition of various subgroups in the population. For instance, suppose your city has the following composition: 60 percent white, 20 percent African-American, 10 percent Latino/Hispanic, 8 percent Asian, and 2 percent Native American. A quota sampling technique that uses nationality and ethnic subgroups would produce a sample that numerically reflects these percentages. Thus, a sample of 100 people from your city would have 60 whites, 20 African-Americans, 10 Hispanics, 8 Asians, and 2 Native Americans. Similarly, subgroups might be based on age, gender, socioeconomic class, the number of people in each major at a school, and so on. Quota sampling is a bit more elegant than haphazard sampling. However, there are still problems because no restrictions are placed on how individuals in the various subgroups are chosen. Although the sample reflects the numerical composition of the whole population of interest, subjects within each subgroup are selected in a haphazard manner; thus, quota sampling has the same problems of generalization as haphazard sampling.

Much of the research in psychology and the behavioral sciences uses nonprobability sampling techniques. The advantage of these techniques is that the investigator can obtain subjects without spending a great deal of money or time on selecting a specific sample group. It is, for example, common practice to select subjects from students in introductory psychology classes. Often these students are required to participate in studies being conducted by faculty and students; the introductory psychology students can then choose which experiments they wish to participate in. With this kind of sampling technique, it is difficult to even define the population of interest. Usually, we want to generalize to "people in general" or at least to "adults who live in the United States." Obviously, generalizing to these populations is risky when the haphazard sample is composed of students at a particular college who have decided to take introductory psychology and have volunteered for a particular study.

If generalization is such a problem, why do researchers use these techniques? Most important, many researchers are mainly interested in finding relationships between variables rather than accurately describing a population. The purpose of the research is to test a hypothesis that certain variables are related to one another. Nonprobability samples are inexpensive and convenient, and so researchers may prefer to spend their limited resources on their experiments rather than on obtaining representative samples using probability sampling techniques. Also, it may be difficult to find a sample of the general population willing to come into the lab for an experiment. If a relationship between the variables being studied is found, one can ask whether the same relationship between variables would be observed in some other population of subjects. Usually there isn't a compelling reason to believe or suspect that the relationship would not be found among other groups. When there is a reason to hypothesize that other groups (e.g., children, the elderly, or various ethnic groups) would behave differently, researchers usu-

59

ally conduct research to test their hypotheses. These issues are discussed further in Chapter 11.

Thus, generalization to a specific population is usually not the first priority in scientific studies designed to test ideas about relationships between variables. However, when the research goal is to accurately describe some particular aspect of a specific population, probability sampling techniques must be used. For example, research that is aimed at determining how many people will vote for a particular political candidate, or how many people use the parks in a city, must use a truly representative sample. Let's examine three general types of probability sampling: simple random sampling, stratified random sampling, and cluster sampling.

Probability sampling

Simple random sampling   With **simple random sampling,** every member of the population has an equal probability of being selected for the sample. If the population has 1,000 members, each has one chance out of a thousand of being selected. Suppose you want to sample students who attend your school. A list of all students would be needed; from that list, students would be chosen at random to form the sample. This procedure doesn't introduce any biases about who gets chosen. A haphazard procedure in which you sampled from students walking by a certain location at 9 A.M. would involve all sorts of biases. For example, that procedure eliminates students who don't frequent this location, and it may also eliminate afternoon and evening students.

When conducting telephone interviews, it is common to have a computer randomly generate a list of telephone numbers with the dialing prefixes used in the city or area being studied. This will produce a random sample of the population because most people today have telephones. There are even companies that will provide researchers with a list of telephone numbers for a survey in which the phone numbers of businesses and numbers that phone companies do not use have been removed.

Stratified random sampling   A somewhat more complicated procedure is called **stratified random sampling.** This is analogous to quota sampling in that the population is divided into subgroups (or strata). Random sampling techniques are then used to select sample members from each stratum. A number of dimensions could be used to divide the population. The dimension (or dimensions) used should be relevant to the problem under study. For instance, a survey of sexual attitudes might stratify on the basis of age, gender, and amount of education, because these factors are related to sexual attitudes. Stratification on the basis of height or hair color would be ridiculous. Stratified random sampling has the advantage of a built-in assurance that the sample will accurately reflect the numerical composition of the various subgroups. This kind of accuracy is particularly important when some subgroups comprise very small percentages of the population. For instance, if African-Americans comprise 5 percent of a city of 100,000 population, a simple random sample of 100 people might not include any African-Americans. But a stratified random sample would include five African-Americans chosen randomly from the population. In practice, when it is very important to represent a small group within a population, researchers will "oversample" that group to make sure that a representative sample of the group is surveyed. Thus, if you need to compare attitudes of African-Americans and whites on your campus, you might need to sample a large percentage of the African-American students and only a small percentage of the white students in order to obtain a reasonable number of respondents from each group.

Cluster sampling It might have occurred to you that obtaining a list of all members of a very large or unusual population (for instance, people who work in county health care agencies throughout the nation) might be difficult. In such situations, a technique called **cluster sampling** can be used. Rather than randomly sampling from a list of individuals, the researcher can identify "clusters" of individuals. The researcher can then sample from these clusters. After the clusters have been sampled, all individuals in the cluster will be included in the sample. Most often, use of cluster analysis requires a series of sampling from larger to smaller clusters—a "multistage" approach. For example, a researcher interested in studying county health care agencies might first randomly determine a number of states to sample and then randomly sample counties from each state chosen. The researcher would then go to the health care agencies in each of these counties and study the people who work in them. The main advantage here is that the researcher does not have to sample from lists of individuals.

All attempts to form a representative sample of the population can be fouled up in the data collection phase. Biases are still possible if some people in the sample are not contacted. For example, if the researcher were to bypass dilapidated houses, low-income individuals would be systematically excluded from the sample. A similar bias would develop if an interviewer didn't follow up on people who weren't home but only did this in the slum areas of town. Survey researchers must also be prepared to ask questions in languages other than English if a truly random sample of a population is needed. A random sample can quickly become nonrandom unless care is taken to collect data from the entire sample.

Critically evaluating survey samples

Surveys are frequently used to collect information about questions that intrigue behavioral researchers. In actual practice, few researchers who conduct surveys have the resources to conduct a true probability sample unless the population is limited in scope, or considerable resources are available to conduct the survey. Professional polling organizations, including survey research centers at many universities, conduct surveys using probability samples of a city, county, state, or even the entire nation. However, most researchers do not have the resources to conduct a true probability sample.

A concept in survey research is the sample frame: the actual set of people who might be included in the sample after the population is defined. If you define your population as "residents in my city," the actual sampling frame may be residents who can be contacted by telephone. The sampling frame excludes persons who do not have telephones or whose schedule prevents them from being at home when you are making calls. If you are using your printed telephone directory to obtain numbers, you will exclude persons who have unlisted numbers. When evaluating the results of the survey, you need to consider how well the sample frame matches the population of interest. In the study of high school students cited above (Steinberg & Dornbusch, 1991), the population of interest was teenagers in the United States; however, the sample frame included only high school students in California and Wisconsin. Although this sample obviously excludes many potential subjects in other areas of the United States, it is superior to those used in previous studies of teenage employment. Again, it should be emphasized that research conducted to study relationships among variables is less concerned about generalization. In the Steinberg and Dornbusch study, for example, the researchers were not interested in accurately describing the number of hours that teenagers in the United States work; they were more interested in whether the number of hours that teenagers work is related to variables such as grade point average and alcohol use.

When research is intended to tell us very precisely what a population is like (e.g., state or national opinion polls), careful sampling procedures must be used. This requires defining the population and sampling people from the population in some random fashion so no biases will be introduced into the sample. Thus, in order to learn what elderly people think about the social services available to them, a careful sample of the elderly population is needed. Obtaining the sample by going only to nursing homes would bias the results because these individuals are not representative of all elderly people in the population.

When evaluating survey data, it is important to examine how the responses were obtained and what population was investigated. Major polling organizations typically take great care to obtain representative samples of adults in our society. However, many other surveys, such as surveys on marital satisfaction or sexual practices that are published in a magazine, have limited generalizability because the results are based on people who read the particular magazine and are sufficiently motivated to complete and mail in the questionnaire. When Dear Abby asks readers to write in to tell her whether they have ever "cheated" on their spouse, the results may be interesting but would not give a very accurate estimate of the true extent of extramarital activity in our society.

CONSTRUCTING SURVEYS

Questionnaires vs. Interviews

Survey research may use either questionnaires or interviews to ask people questions about themselves. In questionnaires, the questions are presented in written format and the respondents write their answers. Interviews involve a one-on-one verbal interaction between an interviewer and respondent, either face to face or over a telephone. The questionnaire approach is generally cheaper than interviews. Questionnaires can be administered in groups, or they can be mailed to people. Questionnaires thus allow anonymity of the respondents; however, questionnaires require that the respondents can read and understand the questions. In addition, many people find it dull to sit by themselves to read questions and then write down answers; thus, there may be a problem of motivation.

With interviews, there is a greater chance that the interviewer and respondent can establish a rapport, that the respondent will find it interesting to talk to the interviewer, and that all questions are understood. Telephone interviews are less expensive than face-to-face interviews, and new computerized telephone survey techniques lower the cost of telephone surveys by reducing labor and data analysis costs. With a computer-assisted telephone interview (CATI) system, the interviewer's questions are prompted on the computer screen and the data are entered directly into the computer for analysis.

Constructing questions

A great deal of thought must be given to writing questions for a survey. This section describes some of the most important factors that a researcher must consider.

Defining the research questions   When constructing questions for a survey, the first thing the researcher must do is explicitly determine the research questions: What is it that he or she wishes to know? The survey questions must be tied to the research questions. Too often surveys get out of hand when researchers begin to ask any question that comes to mind about a topic without considering exactly what useful information will be gained by doing so.

Using closed- vs. open-ended questions   Questions may be either closed- or open-ended. With closed-ended questions, a limited number of response alternatives are given; with open-ended questions, respondents are free to answer in any way they like. Thus, you could ask a person "Which of the following problems is the greatest one facing this city today?"(a closed-ended question) or simply "What is the greatest problem facing this city today?" (an open-ended question). The closed-ended question would give the person a list to choose from (although an "other" category can be added to allow other possibilities). The open-ended question would allow the person to generate the answer.

Using closed-ended questions is a more structured approach. They are easier to code and the response alternatives are the same for everyone. Open-ended questions require time to categorize and code the responses and are therefore more costly. Sometimes a respondent's response cannot be categorized at all because the response doesn't make sense or the person couldn't

63

think of an answer. Still, an open-ended question can yield valuable insights into what the subjects are thinking. Open-ended questions are most useful when the researcher needs to know what people are thinking and how they naturally understand their world; closed-ended questions are more likely to be used when the dimensions of the variables are well defined. With closed-ended questions, there are a fixed number of response alternatives; these must make sense to people in the context of the question asked. Also, there must be a sufficient number of alternatives to allow people to express themselves—for example, 5- or 7-point scales ranging from "agree to disagree" or "positive to negative" may be preferable to simple "yes vs. no" or "agree vs. disagree" alternatives.

Wording questions Once the questions have been written, it is especially important to edit them and test them out on others. You should look for "double-barreled" questions that ask two things at once; a question such as "Senior citizens should be given more money for recreation centers and food assistance programs" is difficult to answer because it taps two potentially very different attitudes. Researchers must also avoid questions that would "lead" people to answer in a certain way or might be easily misinterpreted. For example, the questions "Do you favor eliminating the wasteful excesses in the public school budget?" and "Do you favor reducing the public school budget?" will likely elicit different answers. It is a good idea to give the questions to a small group of people and have them "talk aloud" while answering them. Ask the people to tell you how they interpret each question and how they respond to the response alternatives. This procedure can provide valuable insights you can use when editing the questions (see Chapter 8 on the importance of pilot studies).

Ordering questions It is always a good idea to carefully consider the sequence in which you will ask your questions. In general, it is best to ask the most interesting and important questions first in order to capture the attention of your respondents. Roberson and Sundstrom (1990) obtained the highest return rates in an employee attitude survey when important questions were presented first and demographic questions (age, gender, and so on) were asked last.

Interviewer bias and response sets

Two major sources of bias can arise when questionnaires and interviews are used. These are called **interviewer bias** and **response sets.**

Interviewer bias Interviewer bias refers to all of the biases that can arise from the fact that the interviewer is a unique human being interacting with another human. Thus, one potential problem is that the interviewer could subtly bias the subject's answers by inadvertently showing approval or disapproval of certain answers. Or, if there are several interviewers, each could possess different characteristics (such as level of physical attractiveness, age, or race) that could influence the way subjects respond. Another problem is that interviewers may have expectations that lead them to "see what they are looking for" in the answers of a subject. Such expectations could bias their interpretations of responses, or might lead them to probe further for an answer from certain subjects but not others—for example, when questioning whites but not people from other groups, or when testing boys but not girls. Careful screening and training of interviewers may help limit some biases, but they remain a possibility in interview research.

Response sets A response set is a tendency to respond to all questions from a particular perspective rather than to provide answers that are directly related to the questions. Thus, response sets can affect the usefulness of data obtained from self-reports.

The most common response set is called social desirability, or "faking good." The social desirability response set leads the individual to answer in the most socially acceptable way—the way that "most people" are perceived to respond, or the way that would reflect most favorably on the person. Social desirability can be a problem in many research areas, but it is probably most acute when the question concerns a sensitive topic such as violent or aggressive behavior, substance abuse, or sexual practices. It should not be assumed, however, that people consistently misrepresent themselves. Jourard (1969) has argued that people are most likely to lie when they don't trust the researcher. If the researcher openly and honestly communicates the purposes and uses of the research, promises that there will be feedback about the results, and assures anonymity, then there is every reason to believe that subjects will provide honest responses.

An interesting approach called the **randomized response technique** has been developed to solve the problem of the social desirability response set for issues that are highly sensitive (cf. Fidler & Kleinknecht, 1977; Soeken & Macready, 1982). The technique is based on the assumption that subjects will respond honestly to questions such as "Have you used cocaine in the last month?" or "Did you cheat on your income tax reporting last year?" only if they feel they have complete anonymity. To achieve complete assurance of anonymity, subjects are shown two questions, one sensitive and the other innocuous—for example:

A. Have you used cocaine in the past month?

B. Were you born in the month of March?

The two questions are followed by a single set of response alternatives: yes and no. The subjects are then told that which question is to be answered depends on the outcome of a random event. For example, subjects could be told to take a dollar bill from their wallets; if the serial number on the bill ends with a 0 through 7, they should answer question A, and if it is an 8 or 9, they should answer question B. Because the researcher cannot possibly know the serial number on the bill, it cannot possibly be determined whether any person had answered question A or B; thereby complete anonymity would be assured. An estimate of the number of people in the survey who actually said yes to question A is determined by applying a statistical formula that takes into account known probabilities, such as the probability that a subject

65

will be asked to answer question A and the probability of being born in March. Using this technique, the researcher in fact cannot identify any individual who may have used cocaine but can obtain a good estimate of the percentage of the whole sample who have used cocaine. Research on obtaining answers using the randomized response technique indicates that estimates of the number of people who say yes to the sensitive question is higher than when more conventional questioning techniques are used.

Another response set is the tendency of some subjects to consistently agree or disagree with questions ("yea-saying" or "nay-saying"). The solution to this is relatively straightforward: Several questions are asked and response alternatives are posed in both positive and negative directions. For example, a study of family communication patterns might ask people how much they agree with the following statements: "The members of my family spend a lot of time together" and "My family members don't usually eat dinner together." Although it is possible that someone could legitimately agree with both items, consistently agreeing or disagreeing with a set of related questions posed in both directions is an indicator that the subject is using a response set.

Sources of self-report measures

If you engage in survey research, you may need to design your own questionnaires or interviews. Good references for advice on constructing such measures are Judd, Smith, and Kidder (1991) and Converse and Presser (1986). You may often find it useful to use questions developed by others, particularly if these have proven useful in other studies and have been shown to have high reliability. A variety of measures of social, political, and occupational attitudes developed by others have been compiled by Robinson and his colleagues (Robinson, Athanasiou, & Head, 1969; Robinson, Rusk, & Head, 1968; Robinson, Shaver, & Wrightsman, 1991).

ARCHIVAL RESEARCH

Archival research involves using already existing information to answer research questions. The researcher doesn't actually collect the original data. Instead, he or she analyzes existing data such as statistics that are part of public records (e.g., number of divorce petitions filed), reports of anthropologists, the content of letters to the editor, or information contained in computer data bases. Judd, Smith, and Kidder (1991) distinguish between three types of archival research data: statistical records, survey archives, and written records.

Statistical records

Statistical records are collected by many public and private organizations. The U.S. Census Bureau maintains the most extensive set of statistical records that are available for analysis by researchers. There are also numerous less obvious ones, such as public health statistics and test score records kept by testing organizations such as the Educational Testing Service.

Researchers Lillian Belmont and Francis Morolla used such statistical records when they examined the intelligence test scores of all 19-year-old men in the Netherlands. They discovered a very interesting pattern in the data: Intelligence was systematically related to both birth order and family size. It is higher in families with fewer children and also higher among early-born than later-born children. Later, Zajonc (1976) developed a mathematical model to explain the data, a model that is based on the amount of intellectual stimulation received by children of differing family size and birth order. Zajonc was also able to replicate the original findings by studying a data base consisting of test scores obtained in the United States.

Various public records can also be used as sources of archival data. For example, Gwaltney-Gibbs (1986) used marriage license applications in one Oregon county in 1970 and 1980 to study changing patterns of premarital cohabitation. She found that only 13 percent of the couples used the same address on the application in 1970 while 53 percent gave the same address in 1980. She was also able to relate cohabitation to other variables such as age and race. The findings were interpreted as support for the notion that premarital cohabitation has become a new step in patterns of courtship leading to marriage. Another example of the use of public records is research by Anderson and Anderson (1984) that demonstrated a relationship between temperature and violent crime statistics in two American cities. Data on both variables are readily available from agencies that keep these statistics.

Survey archives

Survey archives consist of data from surveys that are stored on computers and available to researchers who wish to analyze them. Major polling organizations make many of their surveys available; many universities are part of the Interuniversity Consortium for Political and Social Research (ICPSR), which makes survey archive data available. One very useful data set is the General Social Survey, a series of surveys funded by the National Science Foundation and intended as a resource for social scientists (Russell & Megaard, 1988). Each survey includes over 200 questions covering a range of topics such as attitudes, life satisfaction, health, religion, education, age, gender, and race. This and other survey archives may be available through the computer system on your campus. Some useful descriptions of various surveys available may be found in Clubb, Austin, Geda, and Traugott (1985), Verdonik and Sherrod (1985), and Migdal, Abeles, and Sherrod (1985). These survey archives are extremely important because most researchers do not have the financial resources to conduct large surveys that carefully obtain national samples; the archives allow researchers to access such samples to test their ideas.

Written records

Written records consist of a variety of documents, such as diaries and letters that have been preserved by historical societies; ethnographies of other cultures written by anthropologists; public documents such as speeches by politicians; and mass communications, including books, magazine articles, movies, and newspapers.

Schoeneman and Rubanowitz (1985) studied Dear Abby and Ann Landers letters published in newspapers. They were interested in the causes people gave for problems they wrote about in their letters. Letters were coded according to whether the writers were discussing themselves or other people and whether the causes discussed in the letters were internal (caused by the person's own actions or personality) or external (caused by some situation external to the person). When people discussed themselves, the causes of the problems were primarily external, but when other people were described, more of the problems were seen as internally caused (also see Fischer, Schoeneman, & Rubanowitz, 1987).

Archival data may also be used in cross-cultural research that examines aspects of social structure that differ from society to society. A variable such as the presence versus absence of monogamous marital relationships cannot be studied in a single society. In North America, for example, monogamy is the norm and bigamy is illegal. By looking at a number of cultures, some monogamous and some not, we can increase our understanding of the reasons why one system or the other comes to be preferred. This method was pursued in a study by Rosenblatt and Cozby (1972) on the role of freedom of choice in mate selection. In some societies, there are considerable restrictions on whom one can marry, while other societies give great freedom of choice to young people in deciding upon a spouse. In the study, anthropologists' descriptions (called "ethnographies") of a number of societies were used to rate the societies as being either low or high in terms of freedom of choice of spouse. The ethnographies also provided information on a number of other variables. The results indicated that when there is freedom of choice of spouse, romantic love and sexual attraction are important as a basis for mate selection, and there is also greater antagonism in the interactions among young males and females. The Rosenblatt and Cozby study used the Human Relations Area Files, a resource available in many university libraries, to obtain information from the ethnographies. The Human Relations Area Files consist of anthropologists' descriptions of many cultures, which have been organized according to categories such as courtship and marriage customs, child-rearing practices, and so on. Thus, it is relatively easy to find specific information from many societies by using these files.

Content analysis of documents

Content analysis is the systematic analysis of existing documents such as the ones described above (see Holsti, 1969; Viney, 1983). Like systematic observation, content analysis requires researchers to devise coding systems that raters can use to quantify the information in the documents. Sometimes the coding is quite simple and straightforward; for example, it is easy to code whether the addresses of the bride and groom on marriage license applications are the same or different. More often, the researcher must define categories in order to code the information. In the Rosenblatt and Cozby cross-cultural study, for example, raters had to read the ethnographic information and determine whether each culture was low or high on freedom of choice of spouse. Raters were trained to use the coding system, and reliability coefficients were computed to make sure that there was high agreement among the raters. Similar procedures would be used in studies examining archival documents such as speeches, magazine articles, television shows, or letters.

The use of archival data allows researchers to study interesting questions, some of which could not be studied in any other way. Archival data are a valuable supplement to more traditional data collection methods. There are at least two major problems with the use of archival data, however. First, the desired records may be difficult to obtain: They may be placed in long-forgotten storage places, or they may have been destroyed. Second, we can never be completely sure of the accuracy of information collected by someone else.

PSYCHOLOGICAL TESTS

One major area of psychology is the development of measures to assess individual differences in psychological attributes such as intelligence, self-esteem, or depression. Several such measures are described below. Sources of information about psychological tests that have been developed include the *Mental Measurements Yearbook* (Conoley & Kramer, 1989) and *Test Critiques* (Keyser & Sweetland, 1991). These reference books are published periodically and contain descriptions and evaluations of many psychological tests.

Aptitude and interest measures

Aptitude and interest measures are usually designed for applied purposes. The Strong-Campbell Interest Inventory, for example, is given to many high school and college students to help them decide which vocations they might find personally satisfying. Aptitude tests are frequently given to predict an individual's future performance. Researchers who study tests such as these establish the criterion validity of the tests (recall the discussion of criterion validity in Chapter 3). This research addresses the question of whether the test does in fact relate to the behavior the test is intended to measure.

Personality measures

Many psychologists are involved with research on the assessment of personality characteristics, some of which has direct applications to clinical psychology practice. In clinical psychology, one well-known measure is the MMPI—the Minnesota Multiphasic Personality Inventory. The MMPI (and its revised version, the MMPI-2) consists of over 500 items, such as "I have trouble making new friends." By saying whether each item is descriptive of himself or herself, the respondent provides a thorough self-description. The MMPI is used for both clinical diagnostic purposes and research in clinical psychology. The items are divided into clinical scales such as hypochondriasis, depression, and schizophrenia.

Other personality assessment instruments measure more "normal" personality traits. The NEO Personality Inventory (NEO-PI) (Costa & McCrae, 1985), for example, measures five major dimensions of personality: neuroticism, extraversion, openness to experience, agreeableness, and conscientiousness. Still other tests focus on very specific characteristics of a person, such as "social anxiety" or "loving style." Much basic research in personality is concerned with determining how personality characteristics such as these are related to a person's behavior and interactions with others. For example, you might want to study how Type A (stress-prone) and Type B (more relaxed) personalities perform when placed in stressful and relaxed work situations. We will explore research designs that address such issues in Chapter 7.

STUDYING VARIABLES ACROSS TIME AND AGE

Survey designs to study changes over time

Surveys most frequently study people at one point in time. On numerous occasions, however, researchers wish to make comparisons over time. In the county in which I live, a local newspaper hires a firm to conduct an annual random survey of residents. Because the questions are the same each year, it is possible to track changes over time in such variables as satisfaction with the area, attitudes toward the school system, and perceived major problems facing the county. Similarly, a large number of new freshman students are surveyed each year at colleges throughout the United States to study changes in the composition, attitudes, and aspirations of this group (Astin, 1987). Often researchers will test hypotheses concerning how behavior may change over time. For example, Sebald (1986) compared surveys of teenagers in 1963, 1976, and 1982. The questions focused on the person that teenagers seek advice from on a variety of issues. The primary result was that seeking advice from peers rather than parents increased from 1963 to 1976, but this peer orientation decreased from 1976 to 1982.

Another way to study changes over time is to conduct a **panel study** in which the same people are surveyed at two or more points in time. In a "two-wave" panel study, people are surveyed at two points in time, in a "three-wave" panel study, there are three surveys, and so on. Panel studies allow researchers to study how people change over time, which is particularly important when the research question addresses the relationship between one variable at "time one" and another variable at some later "time two." For example, Hill, Rubin, and Peplau (1976) surveyed dating couples to study variables such as attitude similarity. The same people were surveyed later to determine whether they were still in the dating relationship and, if so, how satisfied they were. This procedure allowed the researchers to decide that attitude similarity is a predictor of how long the dating relationship will last.

Developmental research: Changes across ages

Developmental psychologists are interested in how variables change as a function of age. A researcher might test a theory concerning changes in ability to reason as children grow older, the age self-awareness develops in young children, or the global values people have as they move from adolescence through old age. In all cases, the major variable is age. Studying changes across age is conceptually similar to studying changes over time; some unique issues arise, however, in developmental research. These are discussed below.

Two general methods are used to study the age variable: the **longitudinal method** and the **cross-sectional method.** In the longitudinal method, the same group of people are observed repeatedly as they grow older. This is conceptually similar to the panel survey design described above. In a longitudinal study, a researcher might study the same group of children from age 5 to 13 at one- or two-year intervals.

In the more common cross-sectional design, persons of different ages are studied at only one point in time. A researcher using a cross-sectional design might study five different groups of children grouped by age (e.g., 5, 7, 9, 11, and 13) to compare differences in some behavior as a function of age.

The cross-sectional method is more common than the longitudinal method primarily because it is less expensive and immediately yields useful results. Note that it would take eight years to study the same group of children from age 5 to 13 with a longitudinal design, but with a cross-sectional design, comparisons of different age groups can be obtained relatively quickly.

There are, however, some disadvantages of cross-sectional designs. Most important, the researcher must infer that differences among age groups are due to the developmental variable of age; the developmental change is not observed directly among the same group of people, but rather the comparisons are among different cohorts of individuals. You can think of a **cohort** as a group of people born at about the same time, exposed to the same events in a society, and influenced by the same demographic trends, such as divorce rates and family size. If you think about the hairstyles of people you know who are in their 30s, 40s, 50s, and 60s, you will immediately recognize the importance of cohort effects! More crucial, differences among different cohorts reflect different economic and political conditions in society, different music and arts, different educational systems, and different child-rearing practices. In a cross-sectional study, a difference among groups of different ages may reflect developmental age changes; however, the differences may result from cohort effects (Schaie, 1986). The main point here is that cross-sectional designs confound age and cohort effects (see Chapter 5 for a discussion of confounding and internal validity). Finally, you should note that cohort

71

effects are most likely to be a problem when the researcher is examining age effects across a wide range of ages (e.g., college students through older adults).

The only way to conclusively study changes that occur as people grow older is to use a longitudinal design. Also, longitudinal research is the best way to study how scores on a variable at one age are related to another variable at a later age. For example, if a researcher wants to study how the home environment of children at age 5 is related to school achievement at age 12, a longitudinal study provides the best data. The alternative in this case would be to study 12-year-olds and ask them or their parents about the earlier home environment; this retrospective approach has its own problems when one considers the difficulty of remembering events in the distant past.

Thus, the longitudinal approach, despite being expensive and difficult, has definite advantages. There is one major problem, however: Over the course of a longitudinal study, people may move, die, or become uncooperative about staying in the study. Researchers who conduct longitudinal studies become adept at convincing people to continue, often travel anywhere to collect more data, and compare test scores of people who drop out with those who stay to provide better analyses of their results. In sum, a researcher shouldn't embark upon a longitudinal study without considerable resources and a great deal of patience and energy!

A compromise between the longitudinal and cross-sectional approaches is called a **sequential design.** Here, groups of overlapping ages are tested longitudinally. For example, one group of children could be studied at ages 5, 7, and 9; another group could be studied at ages 9, 11, and 13. This method would take fewer years to complete than a longitudinal study, and also, there are immediate rewards for the researcher because differences in age groups are available even in the first year of the study.

This chapter has provided you with a great deal of information about important methods for describing behavior that can be used to study a variety of questions about behavior. The next three chapters will focus on the experimental method. We will then turn to some practical issues in conducting research, including obtaining subjects, carrying out pilot studies, and making statistical analyses of the results.

STUDY QUESTIONS

1. What is field observation? How does a researcher collect data when conducting field observation research?
2. Why are the data in field observation research primarily "qualitative"?
3. Distinguish between participant and nonparticipant observation; between concealed and nonconcealed observation.

4. What is systematic observation? Why are the data from systematic observation primarily "quantitative"?

5. What is a coding system? What are some important considerations when developing a coding system?

6. What is a case study? When are case studies used? What is a psychobiography?

7. What is a survey? Describe some research questions you might address with a survey.

8. Distinguish between probability and nonprobability sampling techniques. What are the implications of each?

9. Distinguish between haphazard and quota sampling.

10. Distinguish between simple random, stratified random, and cluster sampling.

11. Why don't researchers who want to test hypotheses about the relationships between variables worry about random sampling?

12. What are the advantages and disadvantages of using questionnaires versus interviews in a survey?

13. What are some factors to take into consideration when constructing questions for surveys?

14. Define interviewer bias.

15. Discuss types of response sets and possible solutions to the problem of response sets.

16. What is archival research? What are the major sources of archival data?

17. What is content analysis?

18. Describe some psychological tests.

19. Distinguish between longitudinal, cross-sectional, and sequential designs in developmental research.

20. What is a cohort effect?

ACTIVITY QUESTION

In the Steinberg and Dornbusch (1991) study on teenage employment (see Figure 4-1), longer work hours were associated with lower grade point averages. Can you conclude that working longer hours causes lower grades? Why or why not? How might you expand the scope of this investigation through a panel study?

CHAPTER 5

Experimental Design: Purposes and Pitfalls

In the experimental method all extraneous variables are controlled. Suppose you want to test the hypothesis that crowding impairs cognitive performance. To do this, you might put one group of subjects in a crowded room and another group in an uncrowded room. The subjects in each of the groups would then complete the same cognitive tasks. Now suppose that the subjects in the crowded group do not perform as well on the cognitive tests as those in the uncrowded condition. Can the difference in test scores be attributed to the difference in crowding? Yes, *if* there is no other difference between the groups. But what if the room in which the crowded group was placed had no windows and the room with the uncrowded group did have windows—for example, they were in two different rooms in a high school? In that case it would be impossible to know whether the poor scores of the subjects in the crowded group were due to the crowding or to the lack of windows.

This chapter discusses the fundamental procedures of experimental design. Recall from Chapter 3 that the experimental method has the advantage of allowing a relatively unambiguous interpretation of results. The researcher manipulates the independent variable to create groups that differ in the *levels* of the variable and then compares the groups in terms of their scores on the dependent variable. All other variables are kept constant, either through direct *experimental control* or through *randomization*. If the scores of the groups are different, the researcher can conclude that the independent variable caused the results, because the only difference between the groups is the manipulated variable.

Although the task of designing an experiment seems simple, researchers sometimes make mistakes and use designs that look perfectly acceptable but actually contain serious flaws. A detailed look at the flaws in such designs will lead to a better understanding of good experimental designs. This chapter first considers the concept of internal validity and then examines three poorly designed experiments, with all their flaws. Two true experimental designs are then described. The chapter concludes by briefly considering quasi-experimental designs: experimental designs that have some flaws but are extremely useful in many applied settings.

CONFOUNDING AND INTERNAL VALIDITY

In the hypothetical crowding experiment just described, the variables of crowding and window presence are confounded. **Confounding** occurs when the researcher fails to control some extraneous variable. A variable other than the manipulated variable has been allowed to exert a differential effect in the two conditions. If the window variable had been held constant, the presence or absence of windows might have affected subject performance, but the effect of the windows would be identical in both conditions. Thus, the presence of windows would not be a factor to consider when interpreting the difference between the crowded and uncrowded groups. When the variables of crowding and windows are confounded, the effect of the window variable is *different* in the crowded and the uncrowded conditions.

In the crowding experiment, both rooms should have had windows or both should have been windowless. Because one room had windows and one room did not, any difference in the dependent variable (test scores) cannot be attributed solely to the independent variable (crowding). An alternative explanation can be offered: The difference in test scores may have been caused, at least in part, by the window variable.

Good experimental design involves eliminating possible confounds that result in alternative explanations. A researcher can claim that the independent variable caused the results only when there are no competing explanations. When the results of an experiment can confidently be attributed to the effect of the independent variable, the experiment is said to have **internal validity.** To achieve internal validity, the researcher must design and conduct the experiment so that only the independent variable can be the cause of the results.

When you design an experiment or read about someone else's research, it is important to consider internal validity. Several different experimental designs that have been described by Campbell and Stanley (1966) nicely illustrate the internal validity problem.

POORLY DESIGNED EXPERIMENTS

The missing control group

Suppose you want to see whether sitting close to a stranger will cause the stranger to move away. You might try sitting next to a number of strangers and measure the number of seconds that elapse before they leave. Your design would look like this:

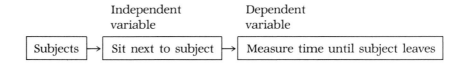

Now suppose that the average amount of time before the subjects leave is 9.6 seconds. Unfortunately, this finding is not interpretable. You don't know whether subjects would have stayed longer if you had not sat down or whether they would have stayed for 9.6 seconds anyway. It is even possible that they would have left sooner if you had not sat down—perhaps they liked you!

This design—formally called a "one-shot case study" by Campbell and Stanley (1966)—lacks a crucial element of an experiment: a control or comparison group. There must be some sort of comparison condition to enable you to interpret your results.[1]

The pitfalls of a one-group pretest-posttest design

One way to obtain a comparison would be to measure subjects before the manipulation (a pretest) and again afterward (a posttest). An index of change from the pretest to the posttest could then be computed. Although this *one-group pretest-posttest design* sounds fine, there are some major problems.

Suppose you wanted to test the hypothesis that a relaxation training program will result in a reduction in cigarette smoking. Using the one-group pretest-posttest design, you would select a group of subjects who smoke, administer a measure of smoking, have the subjects go through relaxation training, and then readminister the smoking measure. Your design would look like this:

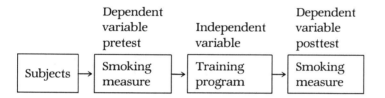

If you did find a reduction in smoking, you would not be able to assume that the result was due to the relaxation training program. This design has failed to take into account several competing alternative explanations, termed **history, maturation, testing, instrument decay,** and **statistical regression.**

History History refers to any event that occurs between the first and second measurements but is not part of the manipulation. For example, the smoking-related death of a famous person might occur during the time between the first and second measures. This event could be responsible for a reduction in smoking rather than the relaxation training. Any such event is a potentially confounding variable that would invalidate the results.

Maturation of subjects People change over time. In a brief period they become bored, fatigued, perhaps wiser, and certainly hungrier; children over

---

1. The one-shot case study with its missing comparison group has serious deficiencies in the context of designing an experiment to precisely measure the effect of an independent variable on a dependent variable. As we noted in Chapter 3, case studies are valuable in other contexts.

a longer period of time become more coordinated and analytical. Any changes that occur systematically over time are called maturation effects. Maturation could be a problem in the smoking reduction example if people generally become more concerned about health as they get older. Such a change might result in a decrease in smoking from the pretest to the posttest that might be mistakenly attributed to the effect of the program rather than maturation.

Testing   Testing becomes a problem if simply taking the pretest changes the subject's behavior. For example, the smoking measure might require subjects to keep a diary in which they note every cigarette smoked during the day. It is possible that simply keeping track of smoking would be sufficient to cause a reduction in the number of cigarettes a person smokes. Thus, the reduction found on the posttest could be the result of taking the pretest rather than of the program itself. In other contexts, taking a pretest may sensitize people to the purpose of the experiment or make them more adept at a skill being tested—again, the experiment would not have internal validity.

Instrument decay   Sometimes the basic characteristics of the measuring instrument change over time. This is particularly true when human observers are used to measure behavior. Over time, an observer may gain skill, become fatigued, or change the standards on which observations are based. In our smoking example, subjects might be highly motivated to record all cigarettes smoked during the pretest when the task is new and interesting, but by the time the posttest is given they may be tired of the task and sometimes forget to record a cigarette. Such instrument decay would lead to an apparent reduction in cigarette smoking.

Statistical regression   Statistical regression is sometimes called *regression toward the mean.* It is likely to occur whenever subjects are selected because they score extremely high or low on some characteristic. When they are retested, their scores tend to change in the direction of the mean. Extremely high scores are likely to become lower, and extremely low scores are likely to become higher.

Statistical regression would be a problem in the smoking experiment if participants were selected because they were initially found to be extremely heavy smokers. By choosing people for the program who scored highest on the pretest, the researcher may have been selecting many subjects who were, for whatever reason, smoking much more than usual at the particular time the measure was administered. The problem is actually rooted in the reliability of the measure. If there is measurement error in the score of a person who scores at the extreme, that score is likely to become less extreme when the measure is re-administered. The overall change from pretest to posttest of a group of very heavy smokers could be due to statistical regression, not the program.

Statistical regression occurs when we try to explain events in the "real world" as well. Sports columnists often refer to the hex that awaits an athlete who appears on the cover of *Sports Illustrated*. The performances of a number of athletes have dropped considerably after they were the subjects of *Sports Illustrated* cover stories. Although it is possible that cover stories cause the lower performance (for example, the notoriety could result in nervousness and low concentration), statistical regression is also a likely explanation. An athlete is selected for the cover of the magazine because he or she is performing at an exceptionally high level, and the principle of statistical regression says that high performance is likely to deteriorate. We would know this for sure if *Sports Illustrated* also covered stories about athletes who were in a slump and this became a good omen for them!

All these problems can be eliminated by the use of an appropriate control group. A group that does not receive the experimental treatment provides an adequate control for the effects of history, statistical regression, and so on. For example, outside historical events would have the same effect on both the experimental and control group. If the experimental group differs from the control group on the dependent measure administered after the manipulation, the difference between the two groups can be attributed to the effect of the experimental manipulation.

In forming a control group, the subjects in the experimental condition and the control condition must be equivalent. If subjects in the two groups are different *before* the manipulation, they will probably be different *after* the manipulation as well. The next design illustrates this problem.

The nonequivalent control group design

The **nonequivalent control group design** employs a separate control group, but the subjects in the two groups—the experimental group and the control group—are not equivalent. The differences become a confounding variable that provides an alternative explanation for the results. This problem, which is called **selection differences,** usually occurs when subjects who form the two groups in the experiment are chosen from existing natural groups. If the relaxation training program is studied with the nonequivalent control group design, the design would look like this:

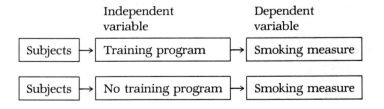

The subjects in the first group are given the smoking frequency measure after completing the relaxation training. The subjects in the second group do not participate in any program. In this design, the researcher does not have any control over which subjects are in each group. It is likely in this case that the subjects in the first group chose to participate in the program, and the subjects in the second group are simply smokers who did not sign up for the training. The problem of selection differences arises because smokers who choose to participate may be different from those who do not. They may already be light smokers, compared to the others, who are more confident that a program can help them. If so, any difference between the groups on the smoking measure would reflect preexisting differences rather than the effect of the relaxation training.

It is important to note that the problem of selection differences arises in this design even when it appears that the researcher has successfully manipulated the independent variable using two similar groups. For example, a researcher might have a group of smokers in the engineering division of a company participate in the relaxation training program while smokers who work in the computer programming division serve as a control group. The problem here, of course, is that the people in the two divisions may have differed in smoking patterns *prior* to the relaxation program.

We could use a pretest to tell us whether the groups were equivalent before the manipulation; such a pretest would improve this design. But it wouldn't completely solve the selection differences problem because the two groups could still differ on other, unmeasured, variables. Such a design will be discussed at the conclusion of this chapter as an example of a quasi-experimental design that can be used when there is no possibility of using a true experimental design.

WELL-DESIGNED EXPERIMENTS

Now that you understand how an experiment is designed and some problems to be avoided, let's look at a well-designed experiment, a "true" experimental design.

The simplest possible experimental design has two variables—the independent variable and the dependent variable—and two groups—an experimental group and a control group. Researchers must make every effort to ensure that the only difference between the two groups is the manipulated variable. Remember, the experimental method involves control over extraneous variables, either through keeping such variables constant (experimental control) or using randomization to make sure that any extraneous variables will affect both groups equally. The simple experimental design can take one of two forms: The first is a posttest-only design; the second is a pretest-posttest design.

Posttest-only design

A researcher who uses the **posttest-only design** must (1) obtain two equivalent groups of subjects, (2) introduce the independent variable, and (3) measure the effect of the independent variable on the dependent variable. The design looks like this:

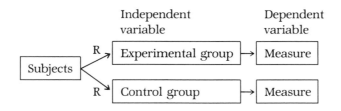

Thus, the first step is to choose the subjects and assign them to the two groups. The procedures used must achieve equivalent groups in order to eliminate the problem of selection differences. Groups can be made equivalent by randomly assigning subjects to the two conditions, or by having the same subjects participate in both conditions. The R in the diagram means that subjects were randomly assigned to the two groups.

Next, the researcher must choose two levels of the independent variable, such as an experimental group that receives a treatment and a control group that does not. Thus, a researcher might study the effect of reward on motivation by offering a reward to one group of children before they play a game while offering no reward to children in the control group. Or a study testing the effect of a method of reducing smoking could compare one group, which receives the treatment, with a control group that does not. Another approach would be to use two different amounts of the independent variable: to use more reward in one group than the other, or to compare the effects of different amounts of relaxation training. Either of these approaches would provide a basis for comparison of the two groups.

Finally, the effect of the independent variable is measured. The same measurement procedure is used for both groups, so that comparison of the two groups is possible. Since the groups were equivalent to begin with, various factors—such as history or maturation—affect both groups equally; thus, any difference between the groups on the dependent variable must be attributed to the effect of the independent variable. The result is an experimental design that has internal validity. In actuality, a statistical significance test would be used to assess the difference between the groups. However, we don't need to be concerned with statistics at this point. An experiment must be well designed, and confounding variables must be eliminated. If not, the results are useless and statistics will be of no help at all.

Pretest-posttest design

The only difference between the posttest-only design and the **pretest-posttest design** is that in the latter a pretest is given before the experimental manipulation is introduced. This design makes it possible to ascertain that the groups

81

were, in fact, equivalent at the beginning of the experiment. However, this precaution is usually not necessary if subjects have been randomly assigned to the two groups. With a sufficiently large sample of subjects, random assignment will produce groups that are virtually identical in all respects. Although there are no clear-cut rules for specifying a "sufficiently large" sample, a minimum of 10 subjects per group is a good rule of thumb. The larger the sample, the less likelihood there is that the groups will differ in any systematic way.

Advantages and disadvantages of the two designs

Each design has advantages and disadvantages that affect the decision as to whether to include or omit a pretest. The first decision factor concerns the equivalence of the groups in the experiment. Although randomization is likely to produce equivalent groups, it is possible that, with small sample sizes, the groups will not be equal. Thus, with a pretest it is possible to assess whether the groups were in fact equivalent to begin with.

Sometimes a pretest is necessary to select a particular type of subject. A researcher might need to give a pretest to find the lowest or highest scorers on a smoking measure, a math anxiety test, or a prejudice measure. Once identified, the subjects would be randomly assigned to the experimental and control groups. Also, the researcher who uses a pretest can measure the extent of change in each subject. If a smoking reduction program appears to be effective for some subjects but not others, attempts can be made to find out why.

A pretest is also necessary whenever there is the possibility that subjects may drop out of the experiment. For example, if a program lasts over a long period of time, some people may drop out of the program. The drop-out factor in experiments is called **mortality.** People may drop out for reasons unrelated to the experimental manipulation, such as illness; but sometimes mortality is related to the experimental manipulation. Even if the groups are equivalent to begin with, different mortality rates can make them nonequivalent. How might mortality affect a program designed to reduce smoking? The heaviest smokers in the experimental group might wind up leaving the program; when the posttest is given, only the light smokers would remain, so that a comparison of the experimental and control groups would show less smoking in the experimental group even if the program had no effect. Use of a pretest makes it possible to assess the effects of mortality; you can look at the pretest scores of the dropouts and know whether mortality affected the final results. Mortality is likely to be a problem when the experimental manipulation extends over a long period of time. In such a situation, a pretest is a very good idea.

Thus, pretests may offer some advantages in the experimental design. One disadvantage of a pretest, however, is that it may be time-consuming and awkward to administer in the context of the particular experimental procedures being used. Perhaps most important, a pretest can sensitize subjects to what you are studying, enabling them to figure out your hypothesis. The subjects may then react differently to the manipulation than they would have without the pretest. When a pretest affects the way subjects react to the manipulation, it is very difficult to generalize the results to people who have not received a pretest. That is, the independent variable may not have an effect in the real world, where pretests are rarely given.

A pretest, then, may be a **demand characteristic.** Any cue, such as that provided by a pretest, which tells subjects what the researcher is trying to find in the experiment is called a demand characteristic. A demand characteristic is any aspect of the experiment that communicates a "demand" for the subject to behave in a particular way. When demand characteristics are present, the researcher's ability to generalize the findings to other situations where the demands aren't present is diminished.

When such a problem seems likely, it is sometimes possible to disguise the pretest. One approach is to measure subjects so they are not aware they are being tested. Concealed observation of behavior is one way to do this (although ethical problems may arise here). Sometimes the pretest can be disguised by conducting it in a completely different situation with a different experimenter. Another approach is to embed the pretest in a set of irrelevant measures so it is not obvious that the researcher is interested in a particular topic. When reading about an experiment in which a pretest-posttest design was used, you should try to determine whether such precautions were taken.

QUASI-EXPERIMENTAL DESIGNS

Sometimes a research problem requires an approach that doesn't allow all the niceties of a true, well-designed experiment. As we noted in the first chapter, researchers frequently confront applied research questions and do evaluation research. This research must often be conducted in settings and under circumstances in which it is impossible to employ a true experimental design. In such situations, an alternative to a true experimental design is a **quasi-experimental design.** Quasi-experimental designs attempt to approximate the control features of true experiments to infer that a given treatment did have its intended effect—that is, there is an attempt to eliminate most alternative explanations for the results by improving upon the three poor designs described previously. Here we will look only at some of the more commonly used quasi-experimental designs. For more detailed discussions, see Campbell (1968, 1969), Cook and Campbell (1979), and Campbell and Stanley (1966).

Nonequivalent control group pretest-posttest design

Earlier in this chapter, we mentioned that the nonequivalent control group design could be improved by including a pretest. When this is done, we have a **nonequivalent control group pretest-posttest design.** The nonequivalent control group pretest-posttest design is one of the most useful quasi-experimental designs; it can be diagrammed as follows:

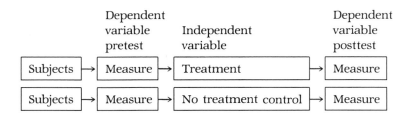

This is not a true experimental design because assignment to groups is not random; it is possible that the two groups are not equivalent. We have the advantage, however, of knowing the pretest scores, thus, we can see whether the groups were the same on the pretest. Even if the groups are not equivalent, we can look at *changes* in scores from the pretest to the posttest. If the independent variable has an effect, the experimental group should show a greater change than the control group (see Kenny, 1979).

Joy, Kimball, and Zabrack (1986) used a nonequivalent control group pretest-posttest design to study the effect of television on children's aggression. A Canadian town that never had television reception until 1974 was the focus of the study (this town was dubbed "Notel" by Joy et al.). Both before and after the introduction of television in Notel, the researchers measured children's physical and verbal aggression. At the same time, they measured aggression in two similar towns: one that received only a single Canadian station ("Unitel") and one that received both Canadian and U.S. networks ("Multitel"). Thus, it was possible to compare the change in aggressiveness in Notel with the aggressiveness change in the control communities of Unitel and Multitel. The results of the study showed that there was a greater increase in aggression in Notel than in either Unitel or Multitel.

Interrupted time series design

Campbell (1969) discusses at length the evaluation of one specific legal reform: the 1955 crackdown on speeding in Connecticut. Although this seems to be an event in the distant past, the example is still a good illustration of an important methodological issue. The crackdown was instituted after a record high number of traffic fatalities occurred in 1955. The easiest way to evaluate this reform is to compare the number of traffic fatalities in 1955 (before the crackdown) with the number of fatalities in 1956 (after the crackdown). Indeed, there was a reduction in the number of traffic deaths, from

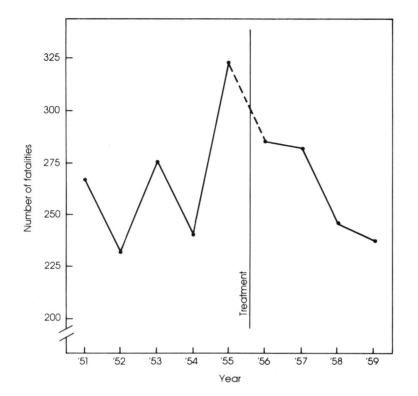

Figure 5-1
Connecticut traffic
fatalities:
1951–1959

Source: Campbell D. T. (1969). Reforms as experiments. *American Psychologist, 24,* 409–429. Copyright 1969 by the American Psychological Association. Reprinted by permission.

324 in 1955 to 284 in 1956. This single comparison is really a one-group pretest-posttest design with all of that design's problems; thus, there are many other reasons why traffic deaths might have declined.

One alternative is to use an **interrupted time series design** that would examine the traffic fatality rates over an extended period of time, both before and after the reform was instituted. Figure 5-1 shows this information for the years 1951 to 1959. Campbell (1969) argues that the drop from 1955 to 1956 does not look particularly impressive, given the great fluctuations in previous years, but there is a steady downward trend in fatalities after the crackdown. Even here, however, Campbell sees a problem in interpretation. The drop could be due to statistical regression: Because 1955 was a record high year, the probability is that there would be a drop anyway. Still, the data for the years extending before and after the crackdown allow for a less ambiguous interpretation than would be possible with only data for 1955 and 1956.

Control series design

One way to improve the interrupted time series design is to find some kind of control group—a **control series design.** In the Connecticut speed crack-

85

Figure 5-2
Control series
design comparing
Connecticut traffic
fatality rate (solid
line on graph)
with the fatality
rate of four
comparable states
(dashed line)

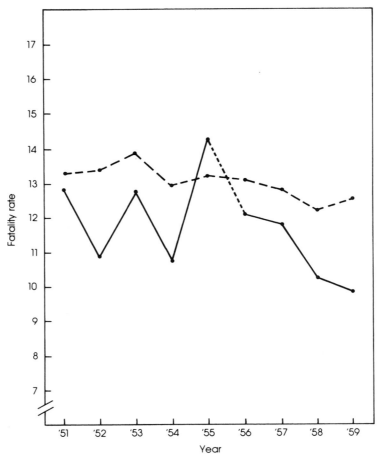

Source: Campbell D. T.
(1969). Reforms as
experiments. *American*
Psychologist, 24,
409–429. Copyright
1969 by the American
Psychological
Association. Reprinted
by permission.

down, this was possible because other states had not instituted the reform.
Figure 5-2 shows the same data on traffic fatalities from Connecticut plus
the fatality figures of four comparable states during the same years. The fact
that the fatality rates in the control states remained relatively constant, while
there was a consistent decline in Connecticut, led Campbell to conclude that
the crackdown did indeed have some effect.

SUMMARY OF DESIGNS

The various designs described in this chapter are shown in Table 5-1 in
summary form. You should familiarize yourself with the designs, the threats
to internal validity, and the reasons why true experimental designs eliminate
these threats.

Design type	Problem(s)
1. One-shot case study	No comparison group
2. One-group pretest-posttest	History
	Maturation
	Testing
	Instrument decay
	Statistical regression
	Mortality
3. Nonequivalent control group	Selection differences
	Mortality
4. Posttest-only true experiment	None; possibly mortality
5. Pretest-posttest true experiment	None; possibly mortality but can assess with pretest information. Sensitizing subjects to the hypothesis is a potential problem.
6. Nonequivalent control group pretest-posttest	A quasi-experimental design used to offset the problems of the nonequivalent control group design when a random assignment to groups is not possible. Groups might not be equivalent, though.
7. Interrupted time series	A quasi-experimental design used to offset the problems of the one-group pretest-posttest design when a true experiment is not possible. There is no independent control group.
8. Control series design	A quasi-experimental design that adds a control group to offset the problems of the interrupted time series design. Groups may not be equivalent.

**Table 5-1
Summary of
designs**

STUDY QUESTIONS

1. What is meant by confounding?

2. What is meant by the internal validity of an experiment?

3. Describe the threats to internal validity discussed in the text: history, maturation, testing, instrument decay, statistical regression, selection differences, and mortality.

4. Consider a program designed to reduce prejudice. Give specific examples of threats to internal validity if a one-group pretest-posttest design is used to evaluate the effectiveness of the program.

5. Why does having a control group eliminate the problems associated with the second poor design—the one-group pretest-posttest design?

6. How do the two true experimental designs eliminate the problem of selection differences?

7. Distinguish between the posttest-only design and the pretest-posttest design. What are the advantages and disadvantages of each?

8. Why might a researcher use a quasi-experimental design rather than a true experimental design?

9. Describe the nonequivalent control group pretest-posttest design. Why is this a quasi-experimental design rather than a true experiment?

10. Describe the interrupted time series and the control series design. What are the strengths of the control series design as compared to the interrupted time series design?

ACTIVITY QUESTION

Dr. Smith learned that one sorority on campus had purchased several Macintosh computers, and another sorority had purchased several IBM computers. Dr. Smith was interested in whether the type of computer affects the quality of students' papers, and so he went to the sorority houses to collect samples of papers from students in the two sororities. Two graduate students in the English Department then rated the quality of the papers. Dr. Smith found that the quality of the papers was higher in one sorority than in the other. What are the independent and dependent variables in this study? Identify the type of design that Dr. Smith used. What variables are confounded with the independent variable? Design a true experiment that would address Dr. Smith's original question.

CHAPTER 6

Types of Experimental Designs

In Chapter 5, the logic of experimental design was presented. The importance of having equivalent groups of subjects in the different experimental conditions was stressed. This chapter will focus on the fundamental procedures of experimental design, primarily the way subjects are assigned to groups in the experiment. Again, only the simplest experiment with two conditions will be used to illustrate the principles of experimental design. However, the topics explored in this chapter will be expanded in Chapter 7, in which more complex experimental methods are considered.

ASSIGNING SUBJECTS TO GROUPS

There are two basic ways of assigning subjects to experimental groups. One way is to randomly assign subjects to the various conditions; each subject participates in only one group. This is called an **independent groups design.** In the second procedure, subjects participate in more than one condition. In the simplest experiment, for example, each subject would be assigned to both levels of the independent variable. This is called a **repeated measures design,** because each subject is measured after receiving each level of the independent variable.

INDEPENDENT GROUPS DESIGNS

As noted above, in an independent groups design, different subjects are assigned to each of the groups. Two assignment procedures may be used: simple random assignment and matched random assignment.

Simple random assignment

The simplest method for assigning subjects to different groups is **simple random assignment.** If there are two groups in the experiment, a possible randomization procedure would be to flip a coin to assign subjects to one or the other group. If there are more than two groups, the researcher would need to use a table of random numbers to assign subjects. A table of random numbers and instructions for using it are shown in Appendix C. The table is made up of a series of the digits 0 through 99 that were arranged randomly by a computer. The researcher can use the arrangement of the numbers in the table to determine which group each subject will be assigned to. Random assignment will prevent any systematic biases, and the groups will be equivalent in terms of subject characteristics, such as social class, intelligence, age, and political attitudes.

Matched random assignment

A somewhat more complicated method of assigning subjects to different groups is called **matched random assignment.** Matching procedures can be used when the researcher wants to make sure that the groups are equivalent on some subject characteristic. Typically, the matching variable will be a subject characteristic that is strongly related to the dependent variable; for example, in a learning experiment, subjects might be matched on the basis of IQ scores. If intelligence is not related to the dependent measure, however, matching on the basis of intelligence would be a waste of time.

When matched random assignment procedures are used, the first step is to obtain a measure of the matching variable from each subject. The subjects are then rank-ordered from highest to lowest on the basis of their scores on the matching variable. Now the researcher can form subject pairs that are approximately equal on the characteristic (the highest two subjects form the first pair, the next two form the second pair, and so on). Finally, the members of each pair are randomly assigned to the conditions in the experiment.

Matched random assignment ensures that the groups are equivalent (on the matching variable) prior to introduction of the independent variable manipulation. This assurance could be particularly important with small sample sizes, because random assignment procedures are more likely to produce equivalent groups as the sample size increases. Matched random assignment, then, is most likely to be used when there are only a few subjects available, or when it is very costly to run large numbers of subjects in the experiment.

The matched random assignment procedure also has an advantage when the results are analyzed for statistical significance. The most obvious reason for this is that, because we know that the groups were exactly equal on the matching variable before the experimental manipulation, it is easier to attribute group differences on the dependent measure to the effect of the experimental manipulation. This is because it is possible to account for individual differences in responses to the independent variable. Suppose you conduct an experiment in which the independent variable is written versus audio presentation of material, and the dependent variable is ability to recall the material. When you examine the results, you may find that the average ability to recall is different in the two groups. You will also find that, within each group, subjects' recall scores vary; subjects do not respond with the same score even though they were in the same group. With simple random assignment, we don't know why this variability exists; it is merely called "error" or unexplained variance in the scores. With matched random assignment to groups, it is possible to account for much of the variability within each group. If IQ is related to the ability to remember material, we can identify the extent to which individual differences in reactions to the independent variable are due to IQ. The ability to explain the variability in scores on the dependent variable reduces the amount of "error," and when error or unexplained variability is reduced, we are more likely to find that the differences in the means are statistically significant.

91

These issues of variability and statistical significance are discussed further in Chapter 9 and Appendix B. The main point here is that matching on a variable makes it more likely that a statistically significant difference between groups will be found in an experiment. However, matching procedures can be costly and time-consuming, requiring that subjects be tested on the matching variable prior to the experiment. Such efforts are worthwhile only when the matching variable is strongly related to the dependent measure and you know that the relationship exists prior to conducting your study. For these reasons, matching is less likely to be used than simple random assignment.

There is a compromise technique that avoids the problems of matching while maintaining some of its statistical advantages. Rather than obtaining data on the subject variable (e.g., intelligence scores) in advance to establish matched pairs, the simple random assignment design is used but time is allotted to collect data on the subject variable. Although these data are collected "after the fact," they can be used in the statistical analysis of the results. You may see research that reports the use of "analysis of covariance" or refers to a variable such as intelligence as a "covariate." A statistical technique called **analysis of covariance** statistically controls for the correlation between the subject variable and the dependent variable in the experiment. This procedure removes the error variance that results from the fact that variability in scores on the dependent variable is due in part to the effect of the subject variable. Analysis of covariance theory and procedures are beyond the scope of this book. After you have familiarized yourself with the simpler statistical methods described in Chapter 9 and Appendix B, however, you will be ready to use techniques such as these.

In both the simple and matched random assignment procedures, each subject participates in only one of the conditions in the experiment. An alternative procedure is to have the *same* subjects participate in all of the groups. This is called a repeated measures experimental design.

REPEATED MEASURES DESIGNS

Consider an experiment conducted to investigate the relationship between the meaningfulness of material and the learning of that material. In an independent groups design, one group of subjects would be given low meaningful material to learn and another group would receive high meaningful material. In a repeated measures design, the same subjects would be used in both conditions. Thus, subjects might first read low meaningful material and take a recall test to measure learning; the same subjects would then read high meaningful material and take the recall test. (You can see why this is called a repeated measures design—subjects are repeatedly measured on the dependent variable after being in each condition of the experiment.)

The problem of order effects

An immediate problem is associated with the repeated measures experiment. Suppose that there is greater recall in the high meaningful condition, a result that could be caused by the manipulation of the meaningfulness variable. However, the result could also simply be an **order effect**—the order of presenting the treatments affects the dependent variable. Thus, greater recall in the high meaningfulness condition could be attributed to the fact that the high meaningful task came second in the order of presentation of the conditions. Performance on the second task might increase simply because of the practice developed on the first task.

There are two general types of order effects. The first is a **practice effect** in which performance improves as a result of repeated practice with the task. The second is a **fatigue effect** in which performance deteriorates as the subject becomes tired, bored, or distracted. Order effects are possible whenever subjects are given a sequence of tasks to perform. For example, suppose you ask a child to play a video game for half-hour periods under different conditions each time (e.g., different rewards for good performance or different amounts of distraction). You might imagine that a child playing the game for the first time might show a practice effect with scores improving over time, but a child familiar with the game might show a fatigue effect with scores deteriorating if there is boredom or fatigue. How do you control for order effects?

Counterbalancing

Complete counterbalancing In a repeated measures design, order effects must be controlled by counterbalancing. With complete **counterbalancing,** all possible orders of presentation are included in the experiment. In the preceding example, half of the subjects would be randomly assigned to the low-high order, and the other half would be assigned to the high-low order. This design is illustrated as follows:

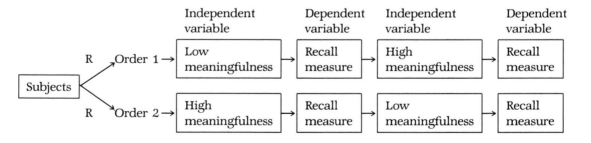

Counterbalancing principles can be extended to experiments with three or more groups; with three groups, there would be six possible orders (3! = 3 × 2 × 1 = 6). With four or more groups, the number of possible orders becomes very large. With four groups, there are 24 possible orders (4! = 4 × 3 × 2 × 1 = 24). You would need a minimum of 24 subjects to represent each order; you would need 48 subjects to have just two subjects per order. Imagine the number of orders possible in an experiment by Shepard and

**Figure 6-1
Three-
dimensional
figures**

Source: Shepard, R. N.,
& Metzler, J. (1971).
Mental rotation of
three-dimensional
objects. *Science, 171,*
701–703. Copyright
1971 by the AAAS.

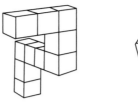
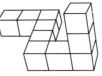

Metzler (1971). In their basic experimental paradigm, each subject is shown a three-dimensional object along with the same figure rotated at one of 10 different angles ranging from 0 degrees to 180 degrees (see the example figures illustrated in Figure 6-1). Each time, the subject presses a button when it is determined whether the two figures are the same or different. The results show that reaction time becomes longer as the angle of rotation increases away from the original. In this experiment with 10 conditions, there are 3,628,800 possible orders! Fortunately, there are alternatives to complete counterbalancing.

Latin Squares   A technique to control for order effects without having all possible orders is to construct a **Latin Square:** a limited set of orders constructed to ensure that (1) each condition appears at each ordinal position and (2) each condition precedes and follows each condition one time. Using a Latin Square to determine order controls for most order effects without having to include all possible orders. Suppose you replicated the Shepard and Metzler (1971) study using only four of the 10 rotations: 0, 60, 120, and 180 degrees. A Latin Square for these four conditions is shown in Figure 6-2. Each row in the square is one of the orders of the conditions (the conditions are labeled A, B, C, and D). The number of orders in a Latin Square is equal to the number of conditions; thus, if there are four conditions, there are four orders. When you conduct your study using the Latin Square to determine order, you need at least one subject per row. Usually, you will have two or more subjects per row; the number of subjects run in each order must be equal. The procedures for constructing Latin Squares with any number of conditions are provided in Appendix D.

Randomized blocks   In many areas of research that use repeated mea-sures designs, the basic experimental procedure is repeated many times. For example, the ten rotations in the Shepard and Metzler study might be re-peated numerous times using different original figures. Each repetition of the basic experiment is called a block of trials. To control for order effects when there are many such blocks of trials, the order of presentation can be randomly determined each time.

We should note that, in an experiment in which subjects are tested over a series of trials, as in many learning studies, "trials" is a repeated measures variable. In this situation, counterbalancing is not an issue—in fact, the order effect of changes in performance over trials is of interest to the researcher.

Order of conditions

	1	2	3	4
Row 1	A (60)	B (0)	D (120)	C (180)
Row 2	B (0)	C (180)	A (60)	D (120)
Row 3	C (180)	D (120)	B (0)	A (60)
Row 4	D (120)	A (60)	C (180)	B (0)

Figure 6-2
A Latin Square with four conditions

Note: The four conditions were randomly given the letter designations. A = 60 degrees, B = 0 degrees, C = 180 degrees, and D = 120 degrees. Each row represents a different order of running the conditions.

ADVANTAGES AND DISADVANTAGES OF REPEATED MEASURES DESIGNS

The repeated measures design has several advantages. An obvious one is that fewer subjects are needed, because each subject participates in all conditions. When subjects are scarce or when it is costly to run subjects, a repeated measures design may be preferred. In much research on perception, for instance, extensive training of subjects is necessary before the actual experiment is begun. Such research often involves only a few subjects who participate in all conditions of the experiment.

An additional advantage of repeated measures designs is that they are extremely sensitive to finding differences between groups. Because subjects in the various groups are identical in every respect (they are the same people), error variability due to subject differences is minimized. As with the matched random assignment procedure described earlier, the error variance or unexplained variability in the scores can be more readily identified, which results in a more sensitive statistical test. The principle is the same as with matching designs, but subjects are not just matched on a single characteristic—they are identical on all characteristics. The result is that we are much more likely to detect an effect of the independent variable if a repeated measures design is used.

Carry-over effects

Despite these advantages, however, repeated measures designs do have limitations. The major drawback is the possibility of **carry-over effects,** which occur when the effects of one treatment are still present when the next treatment is given. Consider an experiment on alcohol and hand–eye coordination. If the alcohol treatment precedes the control (no alcohol) condition, there is the possibility that the effect of the alcohol will carry over and influence how the subject behaves in the control condition. The problem of carry-over effects is present in almost any repeated measures design in which the effect of a drug is being studied; the interval between conditions must be long enough to allow the drug to wear off.

Carry-over effects can also occur in research that does not involve drugs; for example, the effects of heightened anxiety might carry over to the other treatments. In an extreme example, the carry-over effect of a brain lesion would make the use of a repeated measures design impossible, since the brain lesion is irreversible.

Demand characteristics

Another problem in a repeated measures design is that the subjects have knowledge of all the conditions. When subjects participate in all of the groups, they may quickly figure out the true purpose of the experiment, and if this happens, they may behave differently than they would if they were unaware of the hypothesis. It is usually more difficult for subjects to discern the true purpose of the experiment in an independent groups design. The general problem here is one of **demand characteristics:** various aspects of the experiment provide cues that enable the subject to discover the researcher's hypothesis. The general problem of demand characteristics is discussed further in Chapter 8.

Repeated measures designs have both advantages and disadvantages. The advantages are (1) a savings in the number of subjects required to run the experiment and (2) greater control over subject differences and thus greater ability to detect an effect of the independent variable. Obviously, the advantages are worthwhile only if the problems of carry-over effects and demand characteristics seem minimal. The alternative, of course, is to use an independent groups design. Recall that the advantages of the repeated measures design also apply to the matched random assignment procedure described earlier. Researchers must weigh all of these considerations when deciding on the appropriate design for the experiment.

Generalization and repeated measures designs

A final consideration in whether to use a repeated measures design concerns generalization to conditions in the "real world." Greenwald (1976) has pointed out that in actual everyday situations, we sometimes encounter independent variables in an independent groups fashion: We encounter only one condition and no other contrasting condition exists for comparison. However, some independent variables are most frequently encountered in a repeated measures fashion: Both conditions appear and our responses occur in the context of exposure to both levels of the independent variable. Whether or not to use an independent groups or repeated measures design may be partially determined by these generalization issues.

SINGLE-SUBJECT EXPERIMENTS

Single-subject experiments frequently take place within the context of research on reinforcement. This research tradition can be traced to the work of B. F. Skinner (1953) on reinforcement schedules, and it is often seen in applied and clinical settings when behavior modification techniques are used. The techniques and logic of **single-subject experiments** can be readily applied to other research areas, however.

Single-subject designs were developed from a need to determine whether an experimental manipulation had an effect on a single subject. The procedures of single-subject designs share some of the characteristics of the time series designs described in Chapter 5; however, the single-subject procedures are clearly experimental. They also share some characteristics of the repeated measures design. In a single-subject design, the subject's behavior is measured over time during a baseline control period. The manipulation is then introduced during a treatment period, while the subject's behavior continues to be observed. A change in the subject's behavior from baseline to treatment periods is evidence for the effectiveness of the manipulation. There is a problem, however: There could be many reasons for the change other than the experimental treatment. For example, some other event may have coincided with the introduction of the treatment. The single-subject designs described in the following sections address this problem.

Reversal designs

As noted, the basic issue in single-subject experiments is how to determine that the manipulation of the independent variable had an effect. One method is to demonstrate the reversibility of the manipulation. A simple **reversal design** takes the following form:

A (baseline period) − B (treatment period) − A (baseline period)

This design, called an ABA design, requires that behavior be observed during the baseline control (A) period and again during the treatment (B) period, and also during a second (A) baseline period after the experimental treatment has been removed. (Sometimes this is called a "withdrawal design," in recognition of the fact that the treatment is removed or withdrawn.) The effect of a reinforcement procedure on a child's academic performance could be assessed with an ABA design. The number of correct homework problems could be measured each day during the baseline. A reinforcement treatment procedure would then be introduced in which the child receives stars for correct problems that can be accumulated and exchanged for toys or candy. Later, this treatment would be discontinued during the second (A) baseline period. Hypothetical data from such an experiment are shown in Figure 6-3. The fact that behavior changed when the treatment was introduced and reversed when the treatment was withdrawn is evidence for its effectiveness.

The ABA design can be greatly improved by extending it to an ABAB design, in which the experimental treatment is introduced a second time. There are two potential problems with the ABA design. First, a single reversal is not extremely powerful evidence for the effectiveness of the treatment. It could be argued that the observed reversal was due to a random fluctuation in the child's behavior, or perhaps the treatment happened to coincide with

97

**Figure 6-3
Hypothetical data
from ABA reversal
design**

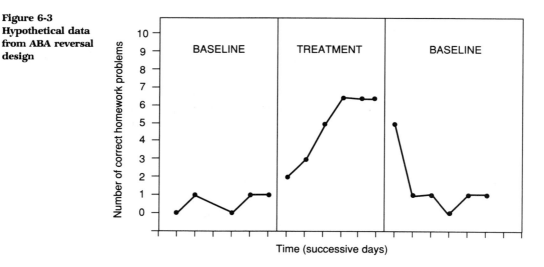

some other event such as the child's upcoming birthday and that was the true cause of the change (and the postbirthday reversal). The second problem is ethical. As Barlow and Hersen (1984) point out, it doesn't seem right to end the design with the withdrawal of a treatment that may be very beneficial for the subject. Using an ABAB design provides the opportunity to observe a second reversal when the treatment is introduced again. Thus, the ethical problem is addressed; also, it is very unlikely that random or coincidental events could be responsible for both reversals. Evidence from an ABAB design is very convincing.

It is also possible to use a control group in a reversal design. For example, one group of researchers used reinforcement to increase ridership on a campus bus system (Everett, Hayward, & Meyers, 1974). Riders were counted on two different buses for 36 days. The experimental manipulation consisted of giving a token to each rider on one of the specially marked buses; the tokens could later be exchanged for goods and services at stores in the community. No tokens were used on the control bus. An ABA design was used. The first 16 days was a baseline period, and during this phase, ridership on each bus was about 250 people per day. The experimental manipulation was introduced on days 17 through 24. During this period ridership on the experimental bus was about 400 per day while there was no change in ridership on the control bus. The token system was discontinued on day 25 and ridership was monitored on both buses through day 36. Ridership on the experimental bus returned to baseline levels during this period and was no longer greater than ridership on the control bus.

Multiple baseline designs

It may have occurred to you that a reversal of some behaviors may be impossible or unethical. For example, it would be unethical to reverse treatment that reduces dangerous or illegal behaviors, such as indecent exposure or alcoholism, even if there is the possibility that a second introduction of the treatment might result in another change. Other treatments might produce a long-lasting change in behavior that is not reversible. In such cases, multiple measures over time can be made before and after the manipulation. If the manipulation is effective, a change in behavior will be immediately observed and the change will continue to be reflected in further measures of the behavior. In a **multiple baseline design,** the effectiveness of the treatment is demonstrated when a behavior changes only when the manipulation is introduced. To demonstrate the effectiveness of the treatment, such a change must be observed under *multiple* circumstances to rule out the possibility that other events were responsible.

There are several variations of the multiple baseline design (Barlow & Hersen, 1984). In the multiple baseline *across subjects*, the behavior of several subjects is measured over time; for each subject, though, the manipulation is introduced at a different point in time. Figure 6-4 shows data from a hypo-

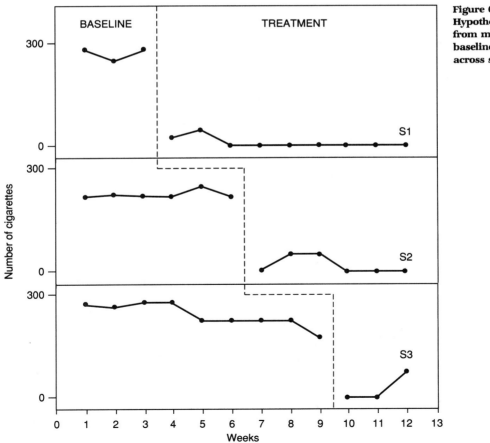

Figure 6-4
Hypothetical data
from multiple
baseline design
across subjects

thetical smoking reduction experiment with three subjects. Note that introduction of the manipulation was followed by a change in behavior for each subject, but because this occurred across individuals and the manipulation was introduced at a different time for each subject, we can rule out explanations based on chance, historical events, and so on.

In a multiple baseline *across behaviors*, several different behaviors of a single subject are measured over time. At different points in time, the same manipulation is applied to each of the behaviors. For example, a reward system could be instituted to increase the socializing, grooming, and reading behaviors of a mental patient, a system that would be applied to each of these behaviors at different points in time. Demonstrating that each behavior increased when the reward system was applied would be evidence for the effectiveness of the manipulation.

The third variation is the multiple baseline *across situations*, in which the same behavior is measured in different settings, such as at home and at work. Again, a manipulation is introduced at a different time in each setting, with the expectation that a change in the behavior in each situation will occur only after the manipulation.

Replications in single-subject designs

The procedures for use with a single subject can, of course, be replicated with other subjects, greatly enhancing the generalizability of the results. Usually reports of research that employs single-subject experimental procedures do present the results from several subjects (and often in several settings). The tradition in single-subject research has been to present the results from each subject individually rather than grouping data and presenting overall means. Sidman (1960), a leading spokesman for this tradition, has pointed out that grouping the data from a number of subjects by using group means can sometimes give a misleading picture of individual responses to the manipulation. For example, the manipulation may be effective in changing the behavior of some subjects but not others. This was true in a study of seat belt use under different seat belt signal conditions (e.g., a second signal that would come on if the subject did not buckle up after an initial signal). Among 13 subjects, six always used their seat belt irrespective of the condition and three never used their seat belt. For the other four subjects, the signal conditions did have an effect. Because the emphasis of the study was on the individual subject, the pattern of results was quickly revealed (Berry and Geller, 1991).

Single-subject designs are useful for studying many research problems. They can be especially valuable for someone who is applying some change technique in a natural environment—for example, a teacher who is trying a new technique in the classroom. In addition, complex statistical analyses are not required for single-subject designs. Despite this tradition of single-subject data presentation, however, there has been an increasing trend to study larger samples using the procedures of single-subject designs and presenting the average scores of groups during baseline and treatment periods (Barlow and

Hersen, 1984). One reason for this trend is the relative lack of generalizability of single-subject research. A more important reason is that not all variables can be studied with the reversal and multiple baseline procedures used in single-subject experiments. Specifically, these procedures are useful only when the behavior is reversible or when one can expect a relatively dramatic shift in behavior after the manipulation.

We have now examined the fundamental aspects of experimental design. In the next chapter, these fundamentals are extended to an understanding of the more complex designs necessary to address more complex questions of behavior.

STUDY QUESTIONS

1. Distinguish between the simple random assignment and matched random assignment designs. When would a researcher decide to use the matched random assignment procedure? What would be the advantage of this design?

2. What is a repeated measures design? Why is counterbalancing necessary in this design?

3. What are the problems of carry-over effects and demand characteristics in a repeated measures design?

4. Why would a researcher use a repeated measures design instead of an independent groups design?

5. What is a reversal design? Why is an ABAB design superior to an ABA design?

6. What is meant by "baseline" in a single-subject design?

7. What is a multiple baseline design? Why is it used? Distinguish between multiple baseline designs across subjects, across behaviors, and across situations.

ACTIVITY QUESTION

A marketing research company conducted a cola taste test. Each subject in the experiment first tasted 2 ounces of Coca-Cola, then 2 ounces of Pepsi, and finally 2 ounces of RC Cola. A rating of the cola's flavor was made after each taste. What are the potential problems with this experimental design and the procedures used? Revise the design and procedures to address these problems. You may wish to consider several alternatives and think about the advantages and disadvantages of each.

CHAPTER 7

Complex Experimental Designs

T hus far we have discussed only the simplest experimental design, containing one independent variable with two levels and one dependent variable. The simple design allows us to examine important aspects of research, such as internal validity and subject assignment procedures, considerations that are common to all research. However, this design has its limitations, and researchers often investigate problems that demand more complicated designs. These complex designs are the subject of this chapter.

INCREASING THE NUMBER OF LEVELS OF AN INDEPENDENT VARIABLE

In the simplest experimental design, there are only two levels of the independent variable. There are several reasons, however, why a researcher would want to design an experiment with more than two levels. First, when the design includes only two levels, the research does not produce a completely accurate description of the relationship between the independent and dependent variables. If there are only two levels of the independent variable, it is possible to show only linear relationships. For example, Figure 7-1 shows the outcome of a hypothetical experiment on the relationship between motivation and performance on a motor task. The solid line describes the results when there are only two levels—no reward for good performance and $4.00 promised for high performance. Because there are only two levels, the relationship can only be described with a straight line. We don't know what the relationship would be if lower or higher amounts were included as levels of the independent variable. The broken line in Figure 7-1 shows the results when $1.00, $2.00, and $3.00 are also included. This result is a more accurate description of the relationship between the amount of reward promised and performance. In the hypothetical experiment, the amount of reward is very effective in increasing performance up to a point, after which only modest increases in performance accompany increases in reward. The experiment with two levels cannot yield such exact information.

An experimental design with only two levels of the independent variable also cannot detect curvilinear relationships between variables. If a researcher predicts a curvilinear relationship, such as the one illustrated in Figure 7-2, at least three levels must be used. Figure 7-2 shows that if only levels 1 and 3 of the independent variable had been used, there would appear to be no relationship between the variables.

Many such curvilinear relationships exist in psychology. The relationship between fear arousal and attitude change is one example. Increasing the amount of fear in a subject increases attitude change up to a moderate level of fear; further increases in fear arousal actually reduce attitude change.

Finally, it is often the case that a researcher is interested in comparing more than two groups. For example, Punnett (1986) tested the hypothesis that setting specific and difficult goals improves performance more than vague goals such as "do your best" or no specific goals at all. The subjects

103

**Figure 7-1
Comparison of
results of a
hypothetical
experiment**

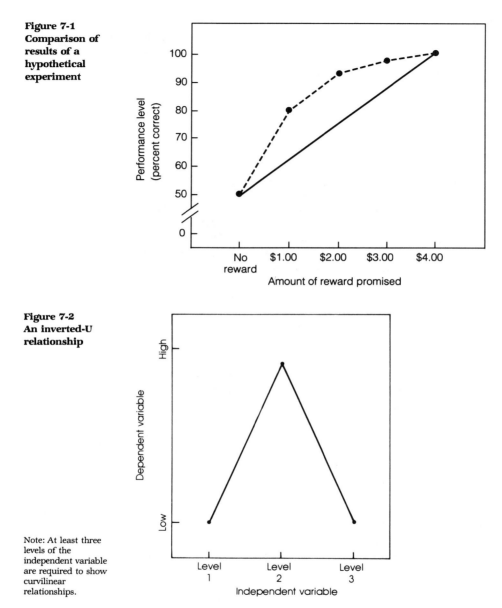

**Figure 7-2
An inverted-U
relationship**

Note: At least three
levels of the
independent variable
are required to show
curvilinear
relationships.

were Caribbean women who work at home sewing childrens' clothes. One group was given the difficult goal of increasing production by 20 percent, another group was instructed to "do your best," and a third group served as a control. Results showed that the subjects in the difficult goal condition earned an average of $1.91 per day, while the subjects in the "do your best" and control conditions earned $1.30 and $.96 per day, respectively.

INCREASING THE NUMBER OF INDEPENDENT VARIABLES: FACTORIAL DESIGNS

Researchers often manipulate more than one independent variable in a single experiment. Typically, two or three independent variables are operating simultaneously. This type of experimental design is a closer approximation of real-world conditions in which independent variables do not exist by themselves. Researchers recognize that in any given situation a number of variables are operating to affect behavior, so they design experiments with more than one independent variable.

Factorial designs are designs with more than one independent variable (or *factor*). In a factorial design, all levels of each independent variable are combined with all levels of the other independent variables. The simplest factorial design has two independent variables, each having two levels.

An experiment by Smith and Ellsworth (1987) illustrates what is called a 2 × 2 (two by two) factorial design; there are two independent variables, each with two levels. Smith and Ellsworth studied the effects of asking misleading questions on the accuracy of eyewitness testimony. Subjects in the experiment first viewed a videotape of a robbery and were then asked questions about what they saw. One independent variable was the type of question—misleading or unbiased. The second independent variable was the questioner's knowledge of the crime: The person asking the questions had either viewed the tape just once (a "naive" questioner) or had seen the tape a number of times previously (a "knowledgeable" questioner).

This 2 × 2 design results in four experimental conditions: (1) knowledgeable questioner-misleading questions, (2) knowledgeable questioner-unbiased questions, (3) naive questioner-misleading questions, and (4) naive questioner-unbiased questions. You may recall from Chapter 2 that Aronson's "blunder" experiment also studied two independent variables in a 2 × 2 design: There was a superior person who did or did not commit a blunder and an average person who did or did not commit a blunder (Aronson, 1984).

Note that a 2 × 2 design always has four groups. The general format for describing factorial designs is:

$$\begin{bmatrix} \text{Number of levels} \\ \text{of first IV} \end{bmatrix} \times \begin{bmatrix} \text{Number of levels} \\ \text{of second IV} \end{bmatrix} \times \begin{bmatrix} \text{Number of levels} \\ \text{of third IV} \end{bmatrix}$$

and so on. A design with two independent variables, one having two levels and the other having three levels, is a 2 × 3 factorial design; there are six conditions in the experiment. A 3 × 3 design has nine groups.

Interpretation of factorial designs

Factorial designs yield two kinds of information. The first is information about the effect of each independent variable taken by itself: the **main effect** of an independent variable. In a design with two independent variables, there

105

**Table 7-1
Results of the
eyewitness
testimony
experiment**

Questioner type (Independent variable B)	Type of question (Independent variable A)		Overall means (main effect of B)
	Unbiased	Misleading	
Knowledgeable	13	41	27.0
Naive	13	18	15.5
Overall means (main effect of A)	13.0	29.5	

are two main effects—one for each independent variable. The second type of information is called an **interaction effect**. If there is an interaction between two independent variables, the effect of one depends on the particular level of the other. In other words, the effect that an independent variable has on the dependent variable depends on the level of the other independent variable. Interactions are a new source of information that cannot be obtained in a simple experimental design in which only one independent variable is manipulated.

To illustrate main effects and interactions, we can look at the results of the Smith and Ellsworth study on accuracy of eyewitness testimony. Table 7-1 illustrates a common method of presenting outcomes for the various groups in a factorial design. The number in each cell represents the mean percent of errors made by subjects in the four conditions.

Main effects   A main effect is the effect each variable has by itself. The main effect of independent variable A, the type of question, is the overall effect of the variable on the dependent measure. Similarly, the main effect of independent variable B, type of questioner, is the effect of the different types of questions on accuracy of recall.

The main effect of each independent variable is the overall relationship between the independent variable and the dependent variable. For independent variable A, is there a relationship between type of question and recall errors? We can find out by looking at the overall means in the unbiased and misleading question conditions. These means are shown in the margins of the table. The overall percent of errors made by subjects in the misleading questions condition is 29.5, while the error percent in the unbiased question condition is 13.0. These overall main effect means are obtained by averaging across all subjects in each group, irrespective of the type of questioner (knowledgeable or naive). Note that the overall mean of 29.5 in the misleading question condition is the average of 41 in the knowledgeable-misleading group and 18 in the naive-misleading group (this calculation assumes equal numbers of subjects in each group). You can see that, overall, subjects make more errors in the misleading questions condition than when the questions are unbiased. Statistical tests would enable us to determine whether this is a significant main effect.

The main effect for variable B (questioner type) is the overall relationship between that independent variable, by itself, and the dependent variable. You can see in Table 7-1 that the overall score of subjects in the knowledgeable questioner condition is 27.0, while the overall score in the naive questioner group is 15.5. Thus, in general there are more errors when the questioner is knowledgeable.

Interaction effects These main effects tell us that overall there are more errors when the questioner is knowledgeable and when the questions are misleading. There is also the possibility that an interaction exists, and if so, the main effects of the independent variables must be qualified. This is because an interaction between independent variables indicates that the effect of one independent variable is different at different levels of the other independent variable. That is, an interaction tells us that the effect of one independent variable depends on the particular level of the other.

We can see an interaction in the results of the Smith and Ellsworth study. The effect of the type of question is different depending upon whether the questioner is knowledgeable or naive. When the questioner is knowledgeable, misleading questions result in more errors (41 percent in the misleading question condition versus 13 percent in the unbiased condition). However, when the questioner is naive, the type of question has little effect (18 percent for misleading questions and 13 percent for unbiased questions). Thus, the relationship between type of question and recall errors is best understood by considering both independent variables: We must consider whether the questions are misleading *and* whether the questioner is knowledgeable or naive.

Interactions can be easily seen when the means for all conditions are presented in a graph. Figure 7-3 is a graph of the results of the eyewitness testimony experiment. Note that all four means have been graphed and that there are two lines to describe the relationship between type of question and errors of recall. One line represents this relationship for the knowledgeable questioner, and the other line shows the relationship for the naive questioner. You can see the relationship that exists when the questioner is knowledgeable; when the questioner is naive, there is no relationship.

The concept of interaction is a relatively simple one that you probably use all the time. When we say "it depends," we are usually indicating that some sort of interaction is operating—it depends on some other variable. For example, a decision to go to a movie tonight may reflect an interaction between two variables: (1) Is an exam coming up? and (2) Who stars in the movie? If there is an exam coming up, you won't go under any circumstance. If you do not have an exam to worry about, your decision will depend on whether you like the person in the movie. That is, you will go only if a favorite star is in the movie.

You might try graphing the movie example in the same way we graphed the eyewitness testimony example in Figure 7-3. The dependent variable (going to the movie) is always placed on the vertical axis. Independent variable A is placed on the horizontal axis. The results for the first level of independent variable B are then placed on the graph and a line is drawn to

107

**Figure 7-3
Interaction
between type of
question and type
of questioner
(Based on data
from Smith &
Ellsworth, 1987)**

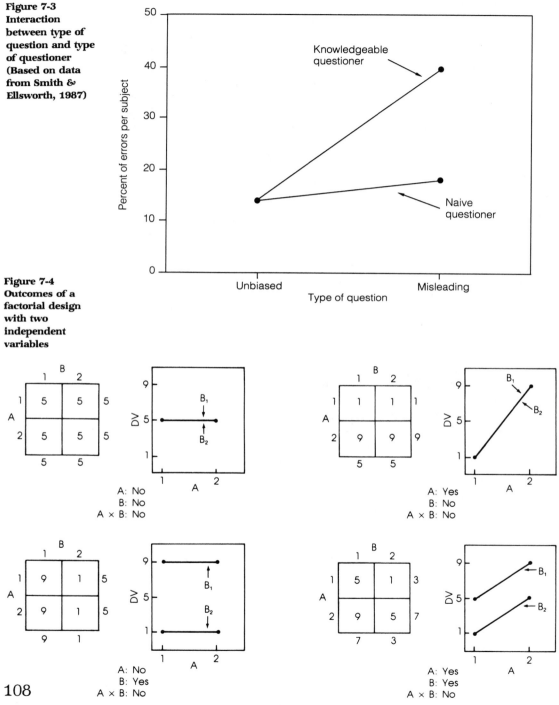

**Figure 7-4
Outcomes of a
factorial design
with two
independent
variables**

108

connect the points. The same is then done for the second level of independent variable B.

Graphing the results in this manner is a useful method of visualizing interactions in a factorial design. In actual research, it is necessary to conduct statistical analyses to determine whether either main effect is statistically significant and whether there is a significant interaction.

Outcomes of a 2 × 2 factorial design

A 2 × 2 factorial design has two independent variables, each with two levels. When analyzing the results, there are several possibilities: (1) There may or may not be a significant main effect for independent variable A; (2) there may or may not be a significant main effect for independent variable B; (3) there may or may not be a significant interaction between the independent variables.

Figure 7-4 illustrates the eight possible outcomes in a 2 × 2 factorial design. For each outcome, the means are given and then graphed. Note on each graph that the dependent variable is placed on the vertical axis, and independent variable A is placed on the horizontal axis. The two means for B_1 are plotted and a line is drawn to represent this level of B. Similarly, the B_1 means are plotted and a second line is drawn to represent this level. In the first two graphs, the lines representing B_1 and B_2 coincide, so only one line is seen.

Figure 7-4
(continued)

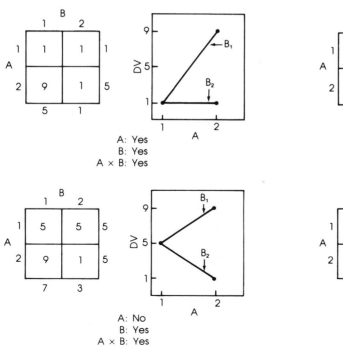

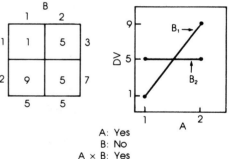

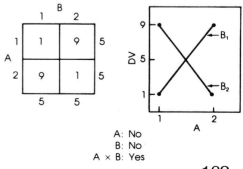

The means that are given in the figure are idealized examples; such perfect outcomes rarely occur in actual research. Nevertheless, you should study the graphs to determine for yourself why, in each case, there is or isn't a main effect for A, a main effect for B, and an A × B interaction.

The first four graphs illustrate outcomes in which there is no A × B interaction effect, and the last four graphs are outcomes in which there is an interaction. When no interaction exists, the lines for B$_1$ and B$_2$ are *parallel*. The parallel lines indicate that the nature of the relationship between independent variable A and the dependent variable is the same at B$_1$ as it is at B$_2$. In the first graph, there is no relationship between A and the dependent variable at either level of B. In each of the first four graphs, the lines are parallel, indicating *no interaction*.

When the lines are *not* parallel, an interaction is present. Such outcomes indicate that the nature of the relationship is different, depending on the particular level of B. In the last four graphs, the two lines are not parallel. In the last graph, a positive relationship exists between A and the dependent variable at B$_1$ but there is a negative relationship for B$_2$. An interesting feature of this last graph is that neither independent variable has an effect *by itself*. However, the interaction shows that A has strong (but opposite) effects, depending on the particular level of B. The interaction indicates that both independent variables must be considered if the relationships involved are to be understood. To make sure that you fully understand these graphs, you might test yourself. Cover the answers or draw a new set of graphs; see if you can say whether or not there are main effects or an interaction.

Factorial designs with manipulated and nonmanipulated variables

One common type of factorial design includes both experimental (manipulated) and correlational (not manipulated) variables. These designs—sometimes called **IV × SV designs** (or independent variable by subject variable)—allow researchers to investigate how different types of subjects respond to the same manipulated variable. The kinds of subject variables studied include gender, age, ethnic group, personality characteristics, and clinical diagnostic category.

An example of this design is a study by Fazio, Cooper, Dayson, and Johnson (1981). These researchers showed that Type A (coronary-prone) and Type B personalities respond differently to the stress that comes when asked to do many things at once. The results of this study are shown in Figure 7-5. The manipulated variable was the number of demands on the subject while working on a proofreading task. Subjects in one condition spent 10 minutes proofreading a manuscript; subjects in the other condition performed the same proofreading task but were also asked to perform other chores, such as tabulate the number of times the word "object" appeared and

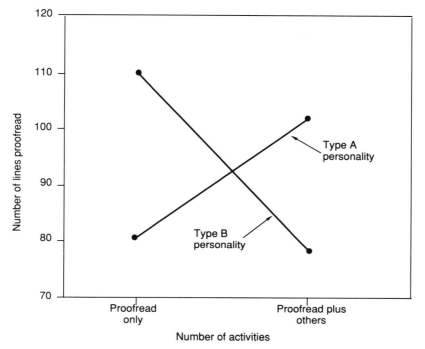

Figure 7-5
An interaction in a mixed design (Based on data from Fazio et al., 1981)

stop to work on a different task whenever the experimenter asked them to do so. The subject variable was the Type A versus Type B personality as measured by a personality test. Type A personalities are said to be "driven" by meeting performance standards and a sense of time urgency. You can see that there was an interaction. People with Type B personalities responded to the multiple demands by decreasing their performance on the proofreading task; the Type A subjects' performance did not decrease but rather actually increased.

Factorial designs with both experimental and correlational variables offer a very appealing method for investigating many problems in the behavioral sciences. Such experiments recognize that full understanding of behavior requires knowledge of both situational variables and the personality and background characteristics of the individuals in the situation.

Subject assignment and factorial designs

The considerations of subject assignment discussed in Chapter 6 can be generalized to factorial designs. There are two basic ways of assigning subjects to groups: In an independent groups design, different subjects are as-

111

Figure 7-6
Number of subjects required to have 10 subjects in each condition

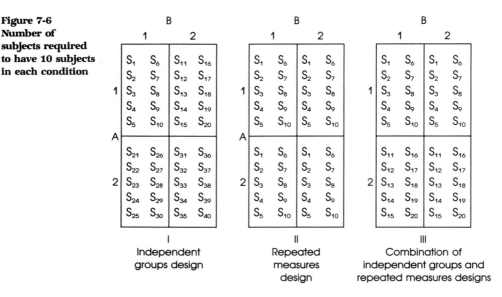

signed to each of the conditions in the study; in a repeated measures design, the same subjects participate in all conditions in the study. These two types of subject assignment procedures have implications for the number of subjects necessary to complete the experiment. We can illustrate these implications by looking at a 2 × 2 factorial design. The design can be completely independent groups, completely repeated measures, or a mixed design that is a combination of the two.

Independent groups In a 2 × 2 factorial design, there are four conditions. If we want a completely independent groups design, a different group of subjects will be assigned to each of the four conditions. If we want to have 10 subjects in each condition, a total of 40 subjects will be needed. You can see this by looking at the first table in Figure 7-6; 40 *different* subjects are shown in the four conditions.

Repeated measures In a completely repeated measures procedure, the same subjects will participate in *all* conditions. The second table in Figure 7-6 shows that we need a total of 10 subjects, because the same 10 subjects participate in each condition. This design offers considerable savings in the number of subjects required. In deciding whether to use a completely repeated measures assignment procedure, however, the researcher would have to consider the disadvantages of repeated measures designs.

Mixed factorial design using combined assignment The third table in Figure 7-6 illustrates the use of both independent groups and repeated measures procedures in a **mixed factorial design.** Independent variable A is an independent groups variable. Ten subjects are assigned to level 1 of this independent variable, and another 10 subjects are assigned to level 2. Independent variable B is a repeated measures variable, however. The 10 subjects assigned to A receive both levels of independent variable B. Similarly, the other 10 subjects assigned to A receive both levels of the B variable. Thus, a total of 20 subjects is required.

Further considerations in factorial designs

The 2 × 2 factorial design is the simplest factorial design. Using this basic design, the researcher can arrange experiments that are more and more complex. One way to increase complexity is to increase the number of levels of one or more of the independent variables. A 2 × 3 design, for example, contains two independent variables: Independent variable A has two levels, and independent variable B has three levels. The 2 × 3 design has six conditions. Table 7-2 shows a 2 × 3 factorial design with the independent variables of task difficulty (easy, hard) and anxiety (low, moderate, high).

The dependent variable is performance on the task. The numbers in each of the six cells of the design indicate the mean performance score of the group. The overall means in the margins show the main effects of each of the independent variables. The results in Table 7-2 indicate a main effect of task difficulty, because the *overall* performance score in the easy-task group is higher than the hard-task mean. However, there is no main effect of anxiety, because the mean performance score is the same in each of the three anxiety groups. Is there an interaction between task difficulty and anxiety? Note that increasing the amount of anxiety has the effect of increasing performance on the easy task but *decreasing* performance on the hard task. The effect of anxiety is different, depending on whether the task is easy or hard, and thus, there is an interaction.

We can also increase the number of variables in the design. A 2 × 2 × 2 factorial design contains three variables, each with two levels. There are eight conditions in this design. A 2 × 2 × 3 design produces 12 conditions, and a 2 × 2 × 2 × 2 design has 16 conditions. The rule for constructing factorial designs remains the same throughout.

Task difficulty	Anxiety			Overall means (main effect)
	Low	Moderate	High	
Easy	4	7	10	7.0
Hard	7	4	1	4.0
Overall means (main effect)	5.5	5.5	5.5	

Table 7-2
2 × 3 factorial design

113

Table 7-3
2 × 2 × 2
factorial design

Instruction method	Class size	
	10	40
	Male	
Lecture		
Discussion		
	Female	
Lecture		
Discussion		

A 2 × 2 × 2 factorial design is constructed in Table 7-3. The variables are (A) instruction method (lecture, discussion), (B) class size (10, 40), and (C) student gender (male, female). Note that gender is a nonmanipulated variable and the other two variables are manipulated variables. The dependent variable is performance on a standard test.

Notice that the 2 × 2 × 2 design can be seen as two 2 × 2 designs, one for the male subjects and another for the female subjects. The design yields main effects for each of the three independent variables. For example, the overall mean for the lecture method is obtained by considering all subjects who experience the lecture method, irrespective of class size or the sex of the subject. Similarly, the discussion method mean is derived from all subjects in this condition. The two means are then compared to see whether there is a significant main effect. Is one method *overall* superior to the other?

The design also allows us to look at interactions. In the 2 × 2 × 2 design, we can look at the interaction between (1) method and class size, (2) method and gender, and (3) class size and gender. We can also look at a three-way interaction that involves all three independent variables, to determine whether the nature of the interaction between two of the variables is different, depending on the particular level of the other variable. Three-way interactions are rather complicated; fortunately, you won't encounter too many of these in your explorations of behavioral science research.

Sometimes students are tempted to include in a study as many independent variables as they can think of. A problem with this procedure is that the design may become needlessly complex and require enormous numbers of subjects. The design above had eight groups; a 2 × 2 × 2 × 2 design has 16 groups; 32 groups would be required by adding another independent variable with two levels. Also, when there are more than three or four independent variables, many of the particular conditions that are produced by the combination of so many variables do not make sense or could not occur under natural circumstances.

STUDY QUESTIONS

1. Why would a researcher have more than two levels of the independent variable in an experiment?
2. What is a factorial design? Why would a researcher use a factorial design?
3. What are main effects and interactions? Identify the main effects and interactions in a factorial design with two independent variables. Graph the results of a factorial design with two independent variables.
4. Describe an IV × SV factorial design in which there are both experimental (manipulated) and correlational (nonmanipulated) variables.
5. Identify the number of subjects required in a factorial design under (a) completely independent groups assignment, (b) completely repeated measures assignment, and (c) a mixed factorial design with both independent groups assignment and repeated measures variables.
6. Identify the number of conditions in a factorial design on the basis of knowing the number of independent variables and the number of levels of each independent variable.

ACTIVITY QUESTION

In a study by Chaiken and Pliner (1987), subjects read an "eating diary" of either a male or female stimulus person. The information in the diary indicated that the person ate either large meals or small meals. After reading this information, subjects rated the person's femininity and masculinity.

1. Identify the design of this experiment.
2. How many conditions are in the experiment?
3. Identify the independent variable(s) and dependent variable(s).
4. Is there a subject variable in this experiment? If so, identify the subject variable. If not, can you suggest a subject variable that might be included?

Chaiken and Pliner reported the following mean femininity ratings (higher numbers indicate greater femininity): male/small meals

(2.02), male/large meals (2.05), female/small meals (3.90), and female/large meals (2.82). Assume there are equal numbers of subjects in each condition.

1. Are there any main effects?
2. Is there an interaction?
3. Graph the means.
4. Describe the results in a short paragraph.

CHAPTER

8

Conducting Research

After you have decided on a topic to study and a specific question to address, you must do a great deal of planning before you actually conduct the study. You must make a number of choices about the design of the study. Should you use the correlational or the experimental method? If you conduct an experiment, should you use an experimental or quasi-experimental design? Should you use an independent groups, repeated measures, or single-subject design? Should you try to use one of the descriptive methods described in Chapter 4?

The previous chapters have laid the foundation for asking these types of questions. In this chapter we will focus on some very practical aspects of conducting research. How do you choose subjects? What should you consider when deciding how to manipulate an independent variable? What should you worry about when you measure a variable? What do you do when the study is completed?

OBTAINING SUBJECTS

Subjects are an integral part of the research process. Whether the subjects are children, college students, schizophrenics, rats, pigeons, rabbits, or primates (even cockroaches and flatworms have been used), they must somehow be selected. The method used to select subjects has implications for generalizing the research results.

Recall from Chapter 4 that most research projects involve sampling subjects from a population of interest. The population is composed of all of the individuals of interest to the researcher. Samples may be drawn from the population using probability sampling or nonprobability sampling techniques. When it is very important to accurately describe the population, you must use probability sampling. Much research, however, is more interested in testing hypotheses about behavior, and in such cases, subjects may be found for experiments or testing in the most convenient way possible. Nonprobability haphazard (or "accidental") sampling is done because such samples are available. You may ask students in introductory psychology classes to be your subjects, you may knock on doors in your dorm to find subjects to fill out a questionnaire, or you may choose a class in which to test children simply because you know the teacher. Nothing is wrong with such methods of obtaining subjects as long as you recognize that they affect the generalizability of your results. The issue of generalizing results is discussed in Chapter 11. Despite the problems of generalizing results based upon convenient haphazard samples, ample evidence supports the view that we can generalize findings to other populations and situations.

MANIPULATING THE INDEPENDENT VARIABLE

To manipulate an independent variable, you have to turn a conceptual variable into a set of specific operations—that is, into a set of specific instructions, events, and stimuli to be presented to subjects. In addition, the independent and dependent variables must be introduced within the context of the total experimental setting. This has been called "setting the stage" (Aronson, Brewer, & Carlsmith, 1985). It is always necessary that your procedures make sense to subjects.

Setting the stage

In setting the stage, you usually have to explain to subjects why the experiment is being conducted. Sometimes the rationale given is completely truthful, although rarely will you want to tell subjects the actual hypothesis. For example, subjects can be told you are conducting an experiment on memory when, in fact, you are studying a specific aspect of memory (that is, your independent variable).

Sometimes the researcher deceives the subjects about the actual purpose of the experiment. Deception is most common in social psychological research, because researchers in this area often find that subjects behave most naturally when they are unaware of the variable that is being manipulated. If subjects know what you are studying, they may try to confirm the hypothesis, or they may try to look good by behaving in the most socially acceptable way.

Deception is not common practice in research, but it may sometimes be necessary if the experiment is to be conducted successfully. You should recognize, though, that deception is ethically questionable and should be used only when necessary. Further, when subjects have been deceived during an experiment, it is very important that the researcher debrief the subjects when the experiment is completed. Of course, subjects may in fact know or suspect that some deception will occur in the experimental procedures, but they generally do not know exactly which aspects of the experiment are part of the crucial experimental manipulation.

There are no clear-cut rules for setting the stage, except that the experimental setting must seem plausible to the subjects. Nor are there any clearcut rules for translating conceptual variables into specific operations. Exactly how the variable is manipulated depends on the variable and the cost, practicality, and ethics of the procedures being considered.

Types of manipulations

Straightforward manipulations　Researchers are usually able to manipulate a variable with relative simplicity by presenting written or verbal material to the subjects. Such a straightforward manipulation is sometimes referred to as an *instructional manipulation* or a *judgment manipulation*.

Straightforward manipulations have been used in many studies of decision making. Tversky and Kahneman (1983), for example, had subjects in one group estimate the probability that the following event would occur in the next year:

119

> A massive flood somewhere in North America, in which more than 1,000 people drown.

Subjects in the second group estimated the probability of a different event:

> An earthquake in California, causing a flood in which more than 1,000 people drown.

The researchers were studying how subjects estimate the probability of joint occurrences (conjunctive events). Subjects in the first group estimated a single event, a flood anywhere in North America, while subjects in the second group estimated a joint occurrence, an earthquake *and* a flood. In theory, the probability of the single event is higher than a conjunctive event; they found, however, that subjects in the second group gave higher probability estimates than did subjects in the first group.

As another example, consider a study by Petty, Cacioppo, and Goldman (1981) on the effect of communicator credibility and personal involvement on attitude change. The subjects were college seniors who read about the reasons why a comprehensive examination should be required for graduation from their university. To manipulate credibility, the arguments were said to be written by a professor of education at Princeton University or a junior at a local school. The manipulation of involvement was accomplished by telling the students that the examination was being considered for implementation the same year (thus affecting the subjects) or 10 years from now. These manipulations, although they involve deception, are relatively straightforward because of the way they are presented to subjects. In the study, it was found that there was an interaction between credibility and involvement: Subjects in the low-involvement condition changed their attitudes more if the communicator was high in credibility, but the credibility of the communicator did not make a difference when the subjects were highly involved.

You will find that most manipulations of independent variables are straightforward. Researchers vary the difficulty of material to be learned, motivation, the way questions are asked, characteristics of people to be judged, and a variety of other factors in a straightforward manner.

We should also note at this point that it is becoming easier and more common for researchers to use computers as a tool for manipulating independent variables. Computers have many advantages in laboratory experimentation. Written material can be presented to be read or visual graphic displays can be presented. The researcher can control the length of time of presentation of the material or record the length of time that each subject studies the material on the screen.

Staged manipulations   Other manipulations are less straightforward —sometimes it is necessary to stage events that occur to subjects in order to manipulate the independent variable successfully. When this occurs, the manipulation is called a *staged* or *event manipulation*.

Staged manipulations are most frequently used for two reasons: First, the researcher may be trying to create some psychological state in subjects, such as frustration or a temporary lowering of self-esteem; second, a staged manipulation may be necessary to simulate some situation that occurs in the real world. For example, in the Fazio et al. (1981) study discussed in Chapter 7, the researchers studied performance under conditions of multiple task demands—subjects were given a proofreading task to perform and were interrupted from time to time and asked to go to another room to perform other tasks.

Staged manipulations frequently employ a confederate: a person who poses as a subject but is actually part of the manipulation. Consider, for example, a typical study on aggression in which the confederate's role is to anger the subject. The confederate and the subject both report to the experiment and are told to wait in a room before the experiment begins. During this waiting period, the confederate insults the subject in an "anger" condition but does not insult the subject in a "no anger" condition. The experimenter then enters and informs the confederate and the subject that learning is being studied and that one of them will be a teacher and the other will be a learner. The assignments to the roles of teacher and learner appear to be random but are actually rigged by the experimenter: The confederate is always the learner and the subject is always the teacher. In the learning task, the subject is permitted to shock the confederate whenever an incorrect answer is given. The amount of shock the subject chooses to give is the measure of aggression; the researcher compares the amount of shock given in the anger and no anger conditions.

Staged manipulations demand a great deal of ingenuity and even some acting ability. They are used to involve subjects in an ongoing social situation, which the subjects perceive not as an experiment but as a real experience. Researchers assume that the result will be natural behavior that truly reflects the feelings and intentions of subjects. However, such procedures allow for a great deal of subtle interpersonal communication that is hard to put into words, which may make it difficult for other researchers to replicate the experiment. Also, a complex manipulation is difficult to interpret. If many things happened to the subject, what *one* thing was responsible for the results? In general, it is easier to interpret results when the manipulation is relatively straightforward, but the nature of the variable you are studying sometimes demands complicated procedures.

Strength of the manipulation

The simplest experimental design has two levels of the independent variable. In planning the experiment, the researcher has to choose these levels. A general principle to follow is to make the manipulation as strong as possible: A strong manipulation maximizes the differences between the two groups and increases the chances that the independent variable will have an effect.

To illustrate, suppose you think that there is a positive linear relationship between attitude similarity and liking ("birds of a feather flock together"). In conducting the experiment, you could arrange for subjects to encounter another person, a confederate. In one group, the confederate and the subject

121

**Figure 8-1
Relationship
between attitude
similarity and
liking**

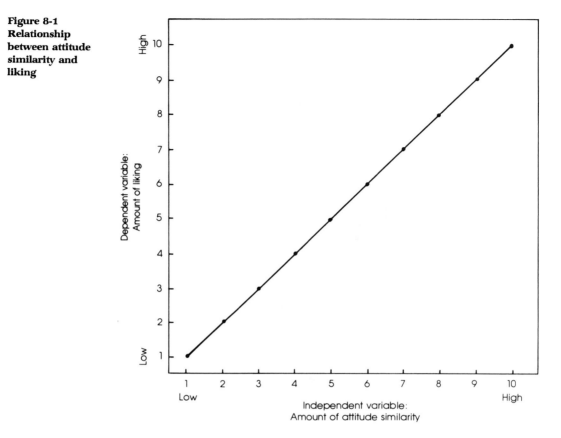

Independent variable:
Amount of attitude similarity

would share similar attitudes; in the other group, the confederate and the subject would be dissimilar. Similarity, then, is the independent variable and liking is the dependent variable, but you have to decide on the amount of similarity. Figure 8-1 shows the hypothesized relationship between attitude similarity and liking at 10 different levels of similarity. Level 1 represents the least amount of similarity and level 10 the greatest. To achieve the strongest manipulation, the subjects in one group would encounter a confederate of level 1 similarity and the subjects in the other group would encounter a confederate of level 10 similarity. This would result in the greatest difference in the liking means. The strong manipulation would result in a 9-point difference in mean liking. A weaker manipulation—using levels 3 and 7, for example—would result in a smaller mean difference.

A strong manipulation is particularly important in the early stages of research, when the researcher is most interested in demonstrating that a relationship does, in fact, exist. If the early experiments are successful in finding a relationship between the variables, later research can systematically manipulate the other levels of the independent variable to provide a more detailed picture of the relationship.

122

The principle of using the strongest manipulation possible should be tempered by at least two considerations. First, the strongest possible manipulation may involve a situation that rarely, if ever, occurs in the real world. For example, an extremely strong crowding manipulation might involve placing so many people in a room that no one could move—a manipulation that might well result in a significant effect on a variety of behaviors. However, we wouldn't know if the results were similar to those occurring in more common situations that are less crowded—as in many classrooms or offices.

A second consideration is ethics: A manipulation should be as strong as possible within the bounds of ethics. A strong manipulation of stress, for example, might not be possible because of the physical and psychological harm that might result.

Cost of the manipulation

Cost is another factor in the decision about how to manipulate the independent variable. When researchers have limited monetary resources, it is difficult to conduct research that calls for expensive equipment or salaries for confederates or subjects in long-term experiments. Also, a manipulation in which subjects must be run individually requires more of the researcher's time than a manipulation that allows running many subjects in a single setting. In this respect, a manipulation that uses straightforward presentation of written or verbal material is less costly than a complex, staged, experimental manipulation. Some government and private agencies offer grants for research, and because much research is costly, continued public support of these agencies is very important.

MEASURING THE DEPENDENT VARIABLE

In previous chapters, we have discussed various aspects of measuring variables. Reliability, validity, and reactivity of measures were described in Chapter 3, and descriptive methods such as systematic observation were presented in Chapter 4. Here we focus on issues that are particularly relevant to experimental research.

Types of measures

The dependent variable in most experiments is one of three general types: self-report, behavioral, and physiological. We consider the distinction among these in the following subsections.

Self-report measures　Self-report measures simply ask people to describe their responses. Usually the self-report is a paper-and-pencil measure in which the experimenter asks questions to which subjects respond using a rating scale. For example, subjects were asked to rate probabilities in the Tversky and Kahneman (1983) study described previously. Self-reports can

123

be used to have subjects indicate attitudes, liking for someone, judgments about the personality characteristics of another person, intended behaviors, emotional states, attributions about why someone performed well or poorly on a task, confidence in one's judgments, and many other aspects of human behavior.

As noted, self-report measures often have subjects use a rating scale with two or more response alternatives for subjects to select. For example, a subject might be asked to respond to the following 5-point scale:

Students at the university should be required to pass a comprehensive examination to graduate.

Strongly agree	Agree	Undecided	Disagree	Strongly disagree

Other rating scales do not label the response alternatives. Thus, a subject could be asked to indicate liking for someone on the following scale, which has seven possible responses:

How much do you like this person?

Dislike very much   Like very much

Self-reports have many uses, and the exact method of obtaining a self-report measure will depend to a large degree on the topic being investigated. Perhaps the best way to gain an understanding of self-report scales is to simply look at a few—some examples are shown in Table 8-1.

Behavioral measures   Behavioral measures are direct observations of subjects' behaviors. Like self-reports, there is an almost endless number of behaviors that can be measured. Sometimes the researcher may record whether or not a given behavior occurs—for example, whether or not a subject helps someone in distress, makes an error on a test, or chooses to engage in one activity rather than another. Often the researcher must decide whether to record the number of times a behavior occurs in a given time period—the *rate* of a behavior; how quickly a response occurs after a stimulus—a *reaction time*; or how long a behavior lasts—a measure of *duration*. The decision of which aspect of behavior to measure depends on which is most theoretically relevant for the study of a particular problem or which measure logically follows from the independent variable manipulation.

Sometimes the nature of the variable being studied requires either self-report or behavioral measurement. A measure of helping behavior is almost by definition a behavioral measure, while a measure of perception of the personality characteristics of someone will employ a self-report measure. For many variables, however, both self-reports and behavioral measures could be appropriate. Thus, liking could be measured on a rating scale, or with a behavioral measure of the distance two people place between themselves or the amount of time they spend looking into each other's eyes. When both options are possible, a series of studies may be conducted to study the effects of an independent variable on both types of measures.

Physiological measures Physiological measures are recordings of the physiological responses of the body. Many such responses are available: Examples include the galvanic skin response (GSR), electromyogram (EMG), and electroencephalogram (EEG). The GSR is a measure of general emotional arousal and anxiety; it measures the electrical conductance of the skin, which changes when sweating occurs. The EMG measures muscle tension and is frequently used as a measure of tension or stress. The EEG is a measure of electrical activity of brain cells. It can be used to record general brain arousal as a response to different situations, activity in different parts of the brain as learning occurs, or brain activity during different stages of sleep.

The GSR, EMG, and EEG have long been used as physiological indicators of important psychological variables. Many other physiological measures are available, including temperature, heart rate, and information that can be gathered from blood or urine analysis. Often such measures offer valuable alternatives to self-report and behavioral measures (also see Cacioppo & Tassinary, 1990).

Sensitivity of measures

The dependent variable should also be sensitive enough to detect differences between groups. A measure of liking that asks "Do you like this person?" (yes or no) is less sensitive than one that asks "How much do you like this person?" on a 5- or 7-point scale. The first measure allows only for a yes or no response; it is possible that most subjects will be nice and say yes even if they have some negative feelings about the person. The second measure allows for a gradation of liking. Such a scale would make it easier to detect differences in the amount of liking.

The issue of sensitivity is particularly important when measuring human performance. Memory can be measured using recall, recognition, or reaction time; cognitive task performance might be measured by examining speed or number of errors during a proofreading task; physical performance can be measured through various motor tasks. Such tasks vary in their difficulty. Sometimes a task is so easy that everyone does well regardless of the conditions that are manipulated by the independent variable. This results in what is called a **ceiling effect**—the independent variable appears to have no effect on the dependent measure only because subjects quickly reach the maximum performance level. The opposite problem occurs when a task is so difficult that hardly anyone can perform well, which is called a **floor effect.**

The need to consider sensitivity of measures is nicely illustrated in the Freedman et al. (1971) study of crowding mentioned in Chapter 3. The study

Table 8-1
Some self-report scales

Example 1: A graphic rating scale. On a graphic rating scale, a check mark is made on a continuous line.

How would you rate the movie you just saw?

Very
unenjoyable

Very
enjoyable

√

A ruler placed on this 100-mm line would show the score to be 84. Scores in the case could range from 0 to 100.

Example 2: A measure of interpersonal attraction. In a large number of studies, Byrne (1971) has used 7-point scales such as the following to measure liking for someone:

Personal feelings (check one)
_____ I feel that I would probably like this person very much.
_____ I feel that I would probably like this person.
_____ I feel that I would probably like this person to a slight degree.
_____ I feel that I would probably neither particularly like nor particularly dislike this person.
_____ I feel that I would probably dislike this person to a slight degree.
_____ I feel that I would probably dislike this person.
_____ I feel that I would probably dislike this person very much.

Example 3: A comparative rating scale. Sometimes it is useful to provide respondents with a frame of reference so that all ratings are made against some standard comparison. For example, a measure of student ratings of an instructor could ask the following question.

In comparison with other teachers at this university, how would you rate this instructor?

_____   _____   _____   _____   _____

Outstanding   Good   Average   Below   Poor
                                average

Example 4: Semantic differential scale. The semantic differential is a measure of the meaning of concepts that was developed by Osgood and his associates (Osgood, Suci, & Tannenbaum, 1957). Respondents rate any concept on a series of bipolar adjectives with 7-point scales. An example is the following rating of your local state senator, Ed Norton.

Ed Norton

Good   _____:_____:_____:_____:_____:_____:_____: Bad
Foolish _____:_____:_____:_____:_____:_____:_____: Wise
Strong _____:_____:_____:_____:_____:_____:_____: Weak
Slow   _____:_____:_____:_____:_____:_____:_____: Fast
Active _____:_____:_____:_____:_____:_____:_____: Passive

126

Table 8-1
(continued)

Research on the semantic differential shows that virtually anything may be measured using this technique. Respondents' ratings of specific things (e.g., marijuana, foreign cars), places (library, classroom), people (the president, one's mother), ideas (communism, abortion), or behaviors (going to church, riding a bus) can be measured. Research on the semantic differential has shown that ratings of concepts are along three basic dimensions: (1) *evaluation* (e.g., good-bad, wise-foolish, beautiful-ugly, kind-cruel), (2) *activity* (e.g., active-passive, slow-fast, excitable-calm), and (3) *potency* (e.g., weak-strong, large-small, hard-soft). Many researchers use evaluative adjectives only to measure attitude toward a concept (cf. Fishbein & Ajzen, 1975).

Example 5: A measure for children. Young children may not be able to comprehend many items and scales devised for adults. Nevertheless, they may be given self-report measures like this one:

Point to the face that shows how you feel about the toy.

examined the effect of crowding on various measures of cognitive task performance and found that crowding did not impair performance. You could conclude that crowding has no effect on performance; however, it is also possible that the measures were either too easy or too difficult to detect an effect of crowding. Subsequent research showed that the tasks may have been too easy; when subjects were asked to perform more complex tasks, crowding did result in lower performance (Paulus, Annis, Seta, Schkade, & Matthews, 1976).

Multiple measures

It is often desirable to measure subjects on more than one dependent variable. One reason to use multiple measures stems from the fact that a variable can be measured in a variety of concrete ways (recall the discussion of operational definitions in Chapter 3). In a study on health-related behaviors, for example, researchers measured the number of work days missed because of ill health, number of doctor visits, and use of aspirin and tranquilizers (Matteson & Ivancevich, 1983). Physiological measures might have been taken as well. If the independent variable has the same effect on several measures of the same dependent variable, our confidence in the results is increased. It is also useful to know if the same independent variable affects some measures but not others. For example, an independent variable designed to affect liking might

127

have an effect on some measures of liking (for example, desirability as a person to work with) but not others (for example, desirability as a dating partner). Researchers are also interested in studying the effects of an independent variable on several different behaviors. For example, an experiment on the effects of a new classroom management technique might examine academic performance, interaction rates among classmates, and teacher satisfaction.

Making multiple measurements in an experiment is valuable when it is feasible to do so. However, it may be necessary to conduct a series of experiments to explore the effects of an independent variable on various behaviors.

Computer response recording

We should mention again that computers are being used more and more in psychological research. Subjects can be asked to answer questions at a computer terminal rather than by using the traditional paper-and-pencil method, the computer can be used to record response times, and observers can use computers to record behaviors. They are also used as an interface to record physiological measures. Computers can make it easier to measure behavior, and they can also facilitate the statistical analyses of the results of the experiment.

Cost of measures

Another consideration is cost—some measures may be more costly than others. Paper-and-pencil self-report measures are generally inexpensive while other measures that require trained observers or expensive equipment can become quite costly. A researcher studying nonverbal behavior, for example, might have to have a camera and videorecorder to obtain a record of each subject's behaviors in a situation. Two or more observers would then have to view the tapes to code behaviors such as eye contact, smiling, or self-touching (two observers are needed to make sure that the observations are reliable); thus, there would be expenses for both equipment and personnel. Physiological recording devices are also expensive. Researchers need resources from the university or outside agencies to carry out such research.

Ethics

Ethical concerns can also be important. Subject anonymity must be protected in all research, and researchers must also be extremely careful when invasion of privacy is a possibility. These issues are explored fully in Chapter 12.

ADDITIONAL CONTROLS

The basic experimental design has two groups: in the simplest case, an experimental group that receives the manipulation and a control group that does not. Use of a control group makes it possible to eliminate a variety of alternative explanations based on history, maturation, statistical regression, and so on. Sometimes additional control procedures may be necessary to address other types of alternative explanations. Two general control issues concern expectancies on the part of both subjects and experimenters.

Controlling for subject expectations

Demand characteristics We noted earlier that experimenters do not wish to inform subjects about the specific hypotheses being studied or the purpose of the research. The reason for this lies in the problem of **demand characteristics** (Orne, 1962). A demand characteristic is any feature of the experiment that might inform subjects of the purpose of the study. The concern is that when subjects form expectations about the hypothesis of the study, they will then do whatever is necessary to confirm the hypothesis; they will try to be cooperative. Orne conducted research to demonstrate that subjects are in fact cooperative. For example, he had subjects add up numbers on a sheet of paper. When they had finished, they picked up a card from a large stack for further instructions. Each instruction card told the subject to tear the sheet into 32 pieces and to go to the next page of numbers. Thus, the subjects repeatedly destroyed their work and continued this ridiculous task for several hours! While you can probably think of situations in which the subjects would try to be uncooperative, Orne's conception of the cooperative subject seems to be generally correct.

One way to control for demand characteristics is to use deception. Care can be taken to make sure subjects think that the experiment is studying one thing when actually it is studying something else. The experimenter may use elaborate cover stories to explain the purpose of the study and to disguise what is really being studied. The researcher may also attempt to disguise the dependent measure by using an unobtrusive measure or by placing the measure among a set of unrelated "filler-items" on a questionnaire. Another approach is to simply assess whether demand characteristics are a problem by asking subjects about their perceptions of the purpose of the research. It may be that subjects do not have an accurate view of the purpose of the study; or if some subjects do guess the hypotheses of the study, their data may be analyzed separately.

Demand characteristics may be eliminated when subjects are not aware that there is an experiment or that their behavior is being observed. Thus, experiments conducted in field settings and observational research in which the observer is concealed or unobtrusive measures are used minimize the problem of demand characteristics.

Placebo groups A special kind of subject expectation arises in research on the effects of drugs. Consider a drug experiment that is investigating whether a drug reduces depression in mental patients. One group of patients receives the drug and the other group does not. Now suppose that the drug group shows an improvement. We don't know whether the improvement was

129

caused by the properties of the drug or by the subjects' expectations about the effect of the drug—what is called the placebo effect. In other words, just the administration of a pill or an injection may be sufficient to cause an observed improvement in behavior. To control for this possibility, a **placebo group** can be added. Subjects in the placebo group receive a pill or injection containing a harmless substance—for example, a "sugar pill"—but do not receive the drug given to subjects in the experimental group. If the improvement results from the active properties of the drug, the subjects in the experimental group should show greater improvement than those in the placebo group. If the placebo group improves as much as the experimental group, the improvement is a placebo effect.

Sometimes subjects' expectations are the primary focus of an investigation. For example, Marlatt and Rohsenow (1980) conducted research to determine which behavioral effects of alcohol are due to alcohol itself as opposed to the psychological impact of believing one is drinking alcohol. The experimental design to examine these effects had four groups: (1) expect no alcohol—receive no alcohol, (2) expect no alcohol—receive alcohol, (3) expect alcohol—receive no alcohol, and (4) expect alcohol—receive alcohol. Their research suggests that the belief that one has received alcohol is a more important determinant of behavior than the alcohol itself. That is, people who believe they have received alcohol (groups 3 and 4) behaved very similarly, although those in the third group were not actually given any alcohol.

Controlling for experimenter expectancies

Experimenters are usually aware of the purpose of the study and may thus develop expectations about how subjects should respond. These expectations can in turn bias the results. This general problem is called **experimenter bias** or **expectancy effects** (Rosenthal, 1966, 1967, 1969).

Expectancy effects may occur whenever the experimenter knows which condition subjects are in. There are two potential sources of experimenter bias. First, the experimenter might unintentionally treat subjects differently in the various conditions of the study. For example, certain words might be emphasized when reading instructions to subjects in one group but not the other, or the experimenter might smile more when interacting with subjects in one of the conditions. The second source of bias can occur when experimenters record the behaviors of subjects; there may be subtle differences in the way the experimenter interprets and records the subjects' behavior.

Research on expectancy effects   Expectancy effects have been studied in a variety of ways. Perhaps the earliest demonstration of the problem is the case of Clever Hans, a horse whose brilliance was shown by Pfungst (1911) to be an illusion. Robert Rosenthal describes Clever Hans:

> Hans, it will be remembered, was the clever horse who could solve problems of mathematics and musical harmony with equal skill and grace, simply by tapping out the answers with his hoof. A committee

of eminent experts testified that Hans, whose owner made no profit from his horse's talents, was receiving no cues from his questioners. Of course, Pfungst later showed that this was not so, that tiny head and eye movements were Hans' signals to begin and to end his tapping. When Hans was asked a question, the questioner looked at Hans' hoof, quite naturally so, for that was the way for him to determine whether Hans' answer was correct. Then, it was discovered that when Hans approached the correct number of taps, the questioner would inadvertently move his head or eyes upward—just enough that Hans could discriminate the cue, but not enough that even trained animal observers or psychologists could see it.[1]

If a clever horse can respond to subtle cues, it is reasonable to suppose that clever humans can, too. Research has shown that experimenter expectancy can be communicated to humans by both verbal and nonverbal communication (Duncan, Rosenberg, & Finklestein, 1969; Jones & Cooper, 1971).

An example of more systematic research on expectancy effects is a study by Rosenthal (1966). In this experiment, graduate students trained rats that were described as coming from either "maze bright" or "maze dull" genetic strains. The animals actually came from the same strain and had been randomly assigned to the bright and dull categories; however, the "bright" rats *did* perform better than the "dull" rats. Subtle differences in the ways the students treated the rats or recorded their behavior must have caused this result. A generalization of this particular finding is called "teacher expectancy." Research has shown that telling a teacher that a pupil will bloom intellectually over the next year results in an increase in the pupil's IQ score (Rosenthal & Jacobson, 1968). Teachers' expectations can influence students' performance.

The problem of expectations influencing ratings of behavior is nicely illustrated in an experiment by Langer and Abelson (1974). Clinical psychologists were shown a videotape of an interview in which the person interviewed was described as either an applicant for a job or a patient—in fact, all saw the same tape. The psychologists later rated the person as more "disturbed" when they thought the person was a patient than when the person was described as a job applicant.

Solutions to the expectancy problem   Clearly expectancies can influence the outcomes of research investigations. How can this problem be solved? Fortunately, there are a number of ways of minimizing expectancy effects. First, experimenters should be well trained and should practice so that their behavior is consistent for all subjects. The benefit of training was illustrated in the Langer and Abelson study with clinical psychologists. The bias of rating the "patient" as disturbed was much less among behavior-oriented than among traditional therapists. Presumably, the training of the behavior-ori-

---

1. From Rosenthal, R. (1967). Covert communication in the psychological experiment. *Psychological Bulletin, 67*, 356–367. Copyright 1967 by the American Psychological Association. Reprinted by permission.

ented therapists led them to focus more on the actual behavior of the person, and so they were less influenced by the expectations stemming from the label of "patient."

Another solution is to run subjects in all conditions simultaneously so that the experimenter's behavior is the same for all subjects. This solution is feasible only under certain circumstances, however, generally only when the study can be carried out with the use of printed materials and the experimenter's instructions to subjects can be the same for everyone.

Expectancy effects are also minimized when the procedures are automated. As noted above, it may be possible to manipulate independent variables and record responses using computers, and with automated procedures, it is unlikely that the experimenter's expectations can influence the results.

A final solution is to use experimenters who are unaware of the hypothesis being investigated. In these cases, the person conducting the study or making observations is blind regarding either what is being studied or which condition the subject is in. This procedure originated in drug research using placebo groups. In a *single-blind* experiment, the subject is unaware of whether a placebo or the actual drug is being administered; in a *double-blind* experiment, neither the subject nor the experimenter knows whether the placebo or actual treatment is being given. To use a procedure in which the experimenter or observer is unaware of either the hypothesis or the group the subject is in, you must hire others to conduct the experiment and make observations.

Because researchers are now aware of the problem of expectancy effects, solutions such as the ones just described are usually incorporated into the procedures of the study. Most research you read about will not be plagued with this problem.

DEBUGGING THE STUDY

So far, we have discussed several of the factors that a researcher considers when planning a study. Actually conducting the study and analyzing the results is a time-consuming process. Before beginning the research, the investigator wants to be as sure as possible that everything will be done right. How can a researcher do this? There are a number of ways of eliminating the bugs from a study before it starts.

Research proposals

After putting considerable thought into planning the study, the researcher writes a research proposal. The proposal details why the research is being done—what questions it is designed to answer—and discusses the variables being studied. The details of the procedures that will be used to test the idea are then given. A research proposal is very similar to the introduction and method sections of a journal article.

Such proposals are required as part of applications for research grants, and they are a useful part of the planning process for any type of research project. Just putting thoughts into words helps to organize and systematize ideas. In addition, the proposal can be shown to friends, colleagues, professors, and other interested parties who can provide useful feedback about the adequacy of your procedures. They may see problems that you didn't recognize, or they may offer ways of improving the study.

Pilot studies

When the researcher has finally decided on all the specific aspects of the procedure, it is possible to conduct a pilot study, in which the researcher does a "trial run" with a small number of subjects. The pilot study will reveal whether subjects understand the instructions, whether the total experimental setting seems plausible, whether any confusing questions are being asked, and so on. This provides the researcher with an opportunity to make any necessary changes in the procedure before doing the entire study. Also, a pilot study allows the people who are collecting the data to become comfortable with their roles and to standardize their procedures.

Manipulation checks

The pilot study also provides an opportunity for a **manipulation check:** an attempt to directly measure whether the independent variable manipulation has the intended effect on subjects. If you were manipulating anxiety, a manipulation check could tell you whether subjects in the high-anxiety group really were more anxious than subjects in the low-anxiety condition. The manipulation check might involve a self-report of anxiety, a behavioral measure (such as number of arm and hand movements), or a physiological measure. If the manipulation was the physical attractiveness of someone, the manipulation check could determine whether subjects do rate the highly attractive person as more physically attractive. Manipulation checks can be included in the actual experiment, although you may want to avoid a check in the actual experiment if you are trying to disguise the purpose of the experiment.

A manipulation check has two advantages. First, if the check shows that your manipulation was not effective, you have saved the expense of running the actual experiment. You can turn your attention to changing the manipulation to make it more effective. For instance, if the manipulation check showed that neither the low- nor the high-anxiety group was very anxious, you could change your procedures to increase the anxiety in the high-anxiety condition.

Second, a manipulation check is advantageous if you get nonsignificant results—that is, if the results indicate that there is no relationship between the independent and dependent variables. A manipulation check can identify

133

whether the nonsignificant results are due to a problem in manipulating the independent variable. If your manipulation is not successful, it is only reasonable that you will obtain nonsignificant results. If both groups are equally anxious after you manipulate anxiety, anxiety can't have any effect on the dependent measure. What if the check shows that the manipulation was successful, but you still get nonsignificant results? Then you know at least that the results were not due to a problem with the manipulation; the reason for not finding a relationship lies elsewhere. You may have had a poor dependent measure, or perhaps there really is no relationship between the variables.

DEBRIEFING

After all the data are collected, there is usually a **debriefing** session. During debriefing, the researcher explains the purpose of the study and tells subjects what kinds of results are expected; the practical implications of the results may also be discussed. In some cases, it may be possible to contact subjects later in order to inform them of the actual results of the study. This is the educational purpose of debriefing.

If subjects have been deceived in any way, debriefing is necessary for ethical reasons—the researcher needs to explain why the deception was necessary. If the research altered the subject's physical or psychological state in some way—as in an experiment on the effects of stress—the researcher must make sure that the subject has "calmed down" and is comfortable about having participated. The subjects should be able to leave the experiment without any ill feelings toward the field of psychology, and they may even leave with some new information about their own behavior.

The researcher may ask the subjects to refrain from discussing the study with others. Such requests are made when more subjects will be participating and it is possible that the subjects will talk to each other in classes or residence halls. Subjects who have already participated are aware of the general purposes and procedures; it is important that these subjects not provide expectancies about the study to potential future subjects.

ANALYZING AND INTERPRETING RESULTS

After the data have been collected, the next step is to analyze them. Statistical analyses of the data are carried out to allow the researcher to examine and interpret the pattern of results obtained in the study. The statistical analysis helps the researcher decide whether there really is a relationship between the independent and dependent variables, for example. The logic underlying the use of statistical tests is discussed in the next chapter. It is not the purpose of this book to teach statistical methods; however, the calculations involved in several statistical tests are provided in Appendix B.

WRITING THE RESEARCH REPORT

The last step is to write a report that details why you conducted the research, how you obtained your subjects, the procedures you used, and what you found. A description of how to write such reports is included in Appendix A. After you have written the report, what do you do with it? How do you communicate the findings to others?

Research findings are most often submitted as journal articles or as papers to be read at scientific meetings. In either case, the submitted paper is reviewed by two or more knowledgeable reviewers, who decide whether the paper is acceptable for publication or presentation at the meeting.

Professional meetings

An important opportunity for presenting research findings is provided by conventions sponsored by professional associations. In psychology, the two major professional societies in the United States are the American Psychological Association (APA) and the American Psychological Society (APS). There is also a national psychological association in Canada. APA includes both scientific researchers and practitioners in clinical psychology and other areas of applied psychology, publishes some of the major journals in psychology, and influences public policy by advising on legislation and court cases. APS focuses on basic research in all areas of psychology. Both APA and APS hold national conventions each year.

Several regional associations, such as the Eastern Psychological Association (EPA), sponsor meetings for the presentation of research. Such meetings provide excellent opportunities for students to become involved with psychology as a profession, because the meetings are close and involve little travel expense. You can find out about recent research studies at either paper sessions in which researchers present a brief talk or poster sessions in which researchers prepare visual displays of their results and are available to speak individually with you. You can also attend talks given by major figures in the field, and at some conventions, there may be discussions and workshops on issues and techniques of therapy. If you continue your studies, you might even find yourself giving a talk or poster session at one of these meetings. Your professors can tell you more about the specifics of these meetings and ways that students can become members of professional associations.

There are also many professional societies in specialized areas of research, and these organizations also sponsor meetings. Developmental psychologists may belong to the Society for Research in Child Development, experimental psychologists may attend the Psychonomic Society meeting, and social psychologists may be members of the Society for Experimental Social Psychology. These and other specialized professional organizations provide ways for researchers to communicate with one another, share ideas, and familiarize themselves with recent developments in their fields.

135

Journal articles

As we noted in Chapter 2, there are many journals in which research papers are published. Nevertheless, the number of journals is small compared to the number of reports written; thus, it isn't easy to publish research. When a researcher submits a paper to a journal, two or more reviewers read the paper and recommend acceptance (often with the stipulation that revisions be made) or rejection. As many as 75 to 90 percent of papers submitted to the more prestigious journals are rejected. Many rejected papers are submitted to other journals and eventually accepted for publication, but much research is never published. This isn't necessarily bad; it simply means that selection processes separate high-quality research from that of lesser quality.

As you become familiar with research presented at professional meetings and in journals, you may notice that most studies report results that are statistically significant. The papers present positive findings that demonstrate relationships between variables—it is very rare to read about research that reports negative results in which there was no support of the hypothesis being investigated. This situation does not arise because research results always support the hypothesis but rather, there are two reasons why negative results are not often published: First, space in journals is limited, and, as we noted, many papers are rejected even if the results were significant; second, negative results are puzzling. A nonsignificant result may occur because there really is no relationship between the variables that were investigated. However, there is also the possibility that there were problems with the planning and execution of the study or with the manipulation of the independent variable, or perhaps the dependent variables were not sufficiently reliable or sensitive. It is likely that you will read about nonsignificant results in a journal only when a series of well-designed studies have demonstrated that there is no relationship between the variables. This problem of interpreting nonsignificant results will be discussed further in the next chapter after we explore the concept of statistical significance in more detail.

STUDY QUESTIONS

1. Discuss the considerations involved in deciding how to manipulate an independent variable.

2. Distinguish between the general types of dependent variables.

3. What is meant by the sensitivity of a measure? What are ceiling and floor effects?

4. Discuss the ways that computers can be used in conducting an experiment.

5. What are demand characteristics? Describe ways to minimize demand characteristics.

6. What is the reason for a placebo group?

7. What are experimenter expectancy effects? What are some solutions to the experimenter bias problem?

8. What methods can be used to debug an experiment?

9. What is a pilot study?

10. What is a manipulation check? How does it help the researcher interpret the results of an experiment?

11. What does a researcher do with the findings after completing a research project?

ACTIVITY QUESTION

Dr. Baker studied the relationship between age and reading comprehension, specifically predicting that older subjects will show lower comprehension than younger subjects. Dr. Baker was particularly interested in comprehension of material that is available in the general press. Groups of subjects who were 20, 30, 40, and 50 years of age read a chapter from a book by physicist Stephen W. Hawking (1988) titled *A Brief History of Time: From the Big Bang to Black Holes* (the book was on the best-seller list at the time). After reading the chapter, subjects were given a comprehension measure. The results showed that there was no relationship between age and comprehension scores; all age groups had equally low comprehension scores. Identify reasons why no relationship was found. (*Hint:* In addition to obvious reasons you may identify, remember to consider sensitivity of measures.)

CHAPTER

9

Understanding Research Results

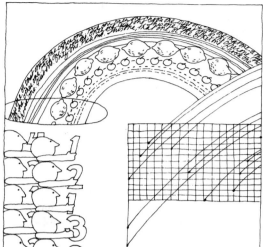

Research data are analyzed through the use of statistics. There are two reasons for using statistics. First, statistics are used to describe the data collected in the study. Second, statistics are used to make inferences, on the basis of sample data, about a population. The discussion here is quite general. The focus is on the underlying logic and general procedures for statistical decision making. Specific calculations for a variety of statistics are provided in Appendix B.

Let's start with some fictitious data from a hypothetical experiment on modeling and aggression. The 20 subjects were 6-year-old children selected from the students at an elementary school. The children were randomly assigned to one of two groups: The experimental group witnessed an aggressive adult (a model); the control group was not exposed to the model. The children then played alone in a room containing a number of toys. Observers watched each child and rated the child on the dependent variable, aggression. The children's scores on the aggression measure are shown in Table 9-1. These data will be used in discussing the analysis of research results.

SAMPLES AND POPULATIONS

One should first note that the results of the experiment are based on data obtained from samples of subjects. Researchers rarely if ever study entire populations; their findings are based on sample data.

Descriptive statistics provide a description of the sample. However, we are usually not interested in simply describing the sample; we want to make statements about populations. Would the results hold up if the experiment were conducted over and over again, each time with a new sample of subjects? **Inferential statistics** are used to determine whether we can, in fact, make statements that the results reflect what would happen if we were to test the entire population of children who do or do not witness an aggressive model. In essence, we are asking whether we can infer that the difference in the sample means shown in Table 9-1 reflects a true difference in the population means.

You may be familiar with the basic issue here if you have paid attention to polling data reported in newspapers. The poll might tell you that 57 percent prefer the Republican candidate for an office while 43 percent favor the Democratic candidate. The report then says that these results are accurate within 5 percentage points with a 95 percent confidence level. This means that the researchers are very confident that, if they were able to study the entire population rather than a sample, the actual percentage who prefer the Republican candidate would be between 62 and 52 percent, while the percentage preferring the Democrat would be between 48 and 38 percent. Inferential statistics allow us to arrive at such conclusions on the basis of sample data.

139

Table 9-1
Scores on aggression measure in a hypothetical experiment on modeling and aggression

Model group	No-model group
3	1
4	2
5	2
5	3
5	3
5	3
6	4
6	4
6	4
7	5
$\Sigma X = 52$	$\Sigma X = 31$
$\overline{X} = 5.20$	$\overline{X} = 3.10$
$s^2 = 1.288$	$s^2 = 1.433$
$s = 1.135$	$s = 1.197$
$n = 10$	$n = 10$

FREQUENCY DISTRIBUTIONS

When analyzing results it is useful to start by constructing a frequency distribution from the data. A **frequency distribution** indicates the number of subjects who receive each possible score on a variable. Frequency distributions of exam scores are familiar to most college students—they tell how many students received each score on an exam.

Frequency polygons

Frequency distributions can be depicted in a graph such as Figure 9-1, which presents the data from the modeling experiment. These two **frequency polygons**—one for each group—show how many people received each score on the aggression measure. The solid line represents the no-model group, and the dotted line stands for the model group.

Histograms

Histograms, or bar graphs, are an alternative method of presenting a frequency distribution (this method is frequently used to report data in newspapers and magazines). In a histogram, a bar is drawn for each score on the measure; the length of the bar depicts the number of persons who received that score. Figure 9-2 illustrates a histogram for the no-model group only.

It is obvious that the frequency distributions for the two groups in the experiment are not identical. However, a researcher wants to make precise

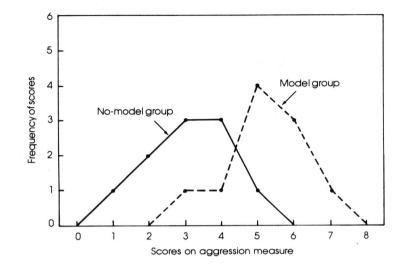

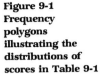

**Figure 9-1
Frequency
polygons
illustrating the
distributions of
scores in Table 9-1**

Note: Each frequency
polygon is anchored at
scores that were not
obtained by anyone (0
and 6 in the no-model
group; 2 and 8 in the
model group).

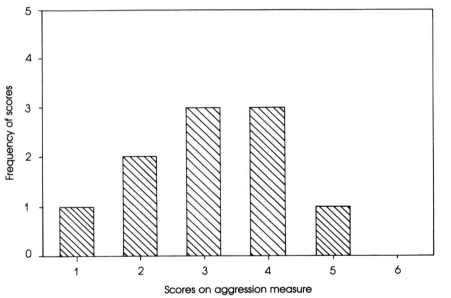

**Figure 9-2
Histogram
showing the
distribution of
scores in the no-
model group**

statements about the data. Two statistics are needed to describe the data. A single number can be used to describe the central tendency, or how subjects scored overall. Another number describes how much variability there is in the scores, or how widely the distribution of scores is spread. These two numbers summarize the information contained in a frequency distribution.

141

DESCRIPTIVE STATISTICS

Central tendency

A **central tendency** statistic tells us what the sample as a whole, or on the average, is like. The most common central tendency statistic is the **mean,** which is symbolized as $\overline{X}$. The mean of a set of scores is obtained by taking the sum of all scores and dividing by the number of scores. In Table 9-1, the mean score in the no-model group is 3.10, and the mean of the model group is 5.20.

There are measures of central tendency other than the mean. The **median** is the score that divides the group in half (with 50 percent scoring below and 50 percent scoring above the median). The **mode** is the most frequent score. The median of the model group is 5 and the mode is also 5. The median of the no-model group is 3; here there are two modal values—3 and 4 are equally frequent. The median or mode can be a better indicator of central tendency than the mean if there are a few unusual scores that bias the mean. For example, the median family income of a county or state is usually a better measure of central tendency than the mean; because of a relatively small number of individuals with extremely high income, using the mean would make it appear that the "average" person makes more money than is actually the case.

Variability

We can also determine how much variability exists in a set of scores. A measure of variability is a number that characterizes the amount of spread in a distribution of scores. One such measure is the **standard deviation,** symbolized as s, which indicates the average deviation of scores from the mean. It is derived by first calculating the variance, symbolized as s^2 (the standard deviation is the square root of the variance). In the model group, the standard deviation is 1.135, which tells us that most subjects' scores lie 1.135 units above and below the mean—that is, between 4.065 and 6.335. Thus, the mean and the standard deviation provide a great deal of information about the distribution.

Another measure of variability is the range, which is simply the difference between the highest score and the lowest score. The range in both the model and no-model groups is 4.

GRAPHING MEANS

At this point, we will review graphs of relationships between variables (see Figure 3–1). The most common way to graph relationships between variables is to use a line graph similar to the frequency polygons just discussed. Figure

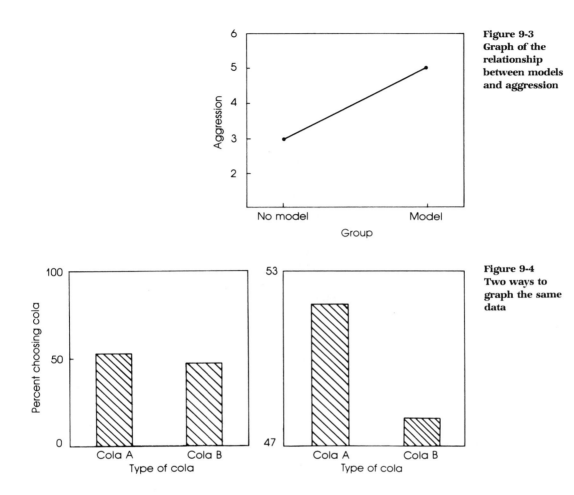

**Figure 9-3
Graph of the
relationship
between models
and aggression**

**Figure 9-4
Two ways to
graph the same
data**

9-3 illustrates the graphing of the means in the model and no-model groups. A point is placed representing the means in each group, and a line is drawn to connect the points.

As an alternative to the line graph, a bar graph could be prepared. A bar would be drawn for each group up to the point that represents the mean of each group.

It is interesting to note a common trick that is sometimes used by scientists and all too commonly used by advertisers. The trick is to exaggerate the distance between points on the measurement scale to make the results appear more dramatic than they really are. Suppose, for example, that a cola company (Cola A) conducts a taste test that shows that 52% of the subjects prefer Cola A and 48 percent prefer Cola B. How should the cola company present these results? Figure 9-4 shows the most honest method as well as one that

143

is considerably more dramatic. It is wise to look carefully at the numbers on the scales depicted in graphs.

INFERENTIAL STATISTICS

The use of descriptive statistics showed that the no-model mean score is 3.10, and the model group mean is 5.20. Thus, the independent variable seems to have had an effect on aggression. Children who viewed the aggressive model were more aggressive than children who didn't witness the model. These statements are based on sample data. Can we infer, on the basis of these data, that this difference between groups holds true in the population?

Much of the previous discussion of experimental design centered on the importance of making sure that the groups are equivalent in every way except the independent variable manipulation. Equivalency of groups is achieved by experimentally controlling all other variables or by randomization. The assumption is that if the groups are equivalent, any differences in the dependent variable must be due to the effect of the independent variable.

This assumption is usually valid. However, it is also true that the difference between any two groups will almost never be zero. In other words, there will be some difference in the sample means, even when all of the principles of experimental design are utilized. This is true because we are dealing with samples rather than populations. Random or chance error may affect the results. For example, random assignment to groups cannot absolutely ensure equivalency of groups. As a result of the way we obtained our no-model and model group samples, the groups in the experiment may not have been equivalent to begin with.

The point is that the difference in the sample means reflects a true difference in the population plus any random error. Inferential statistics allow researchers to make inferences about the true difference in the population on the basis of the sample data. Specifically, inferential statistics give the probability that the difference between means reflects random error rather than a real difference.

One way of thinking about inferential statistics is to use the concept of reliability that was introduced in Chapter 3. Recall that reliability refers to the stability or consistency of scores; a reliable measure will yield the same score over and over again. Inferential statistics allow researchers to assess whether the results of a study are reliable: Would the same results be obtained if the study were repeated over and over again? You could of course repeat your study many times, each with a new sample of subjects. However, this is not practical. Instead, inferential statistics are used to tell you the probability that your results would be obtained if you repeated the study on numerous occasions.

NULL HYPOTHESIS

When a researcher uses inferential statistics, he or she begins by stating a null hypothesis and a research (or alternative) hypothesis. The **null hypothesis** is simply that the population means are equal—the observed difference is due to random error. The **research hypothesis** is that the population means are in fact not equal. The null hypothesis states that the independent variable had no effect; the research hypothesis states that the independent variable did have an effect. In the modeling experiment, the null and research hypotheses are:

H_0 (null hypothesis):   The population mean of the no-model group is equal to the population mean of the model group.

H_1 (research hypothesis):   The population mean of the no-model group is not equal to the population mean of the model group.

The logic of the null hypothesis is this: If we can determine that the null hypothesis is incorrect, then we accept the research hypothesis as correct. Acceptance of the research hypothesis means that the independent variable had an effect on the dependent variable.

The null hypothesis is used because it is a very exact statement—the population means are exactly equal. This permits us to know precisely the probability of the outcome of the study occurring if the null hypothesis is correct. Such precision isn't possible with the research hypothesis, so we infer that the research hypothesis is correct only by rejecting the null hypothesis. The null hypothesis is rejected when there is a very low probability that the obtained results could be due to random error. This is what is meant by **statistical significance:** A significant result is one that has a very low probability of occurring if the population means are actually equal. More simply, significance indicates that there is a low probability that the difference between the obtained sample means was due to random error. Significance, then, is a matter of probability.

PROBABILITY AND SAMPLING DISTRIBUTIONS

Probability is the likelihood of the occurrence of some event or outcome. We all use probabilities frequently in everyday life. If you say that there is a high probability that you will get an A in this course, you mean that it is likely that this outcome will occur. Your probability statement is based on specific information, such as your grades on examinations. The weather forecaster says there is a 10 percent chance of rain today; this means that the likelihood of rain is very low. A gambler gauges the probability that a particular horse will win a race on the basis of the past records of that horse.

145

Probability in statistical inference is used in much the same way. We want to specify the probability that an event (a difference between means in the sample) will occur if there is no difference in the population. The question is, "What is the probability of obtaining this result if only random error is operating?" If this probability is very low, we reject the possibility that only random or chance error is responsible for the obtained difference in means.

The use of probability in statistical inference can be understood intuitively from a simple example. Suppose that a friend claims to have ESP (extrasensory perception) ability. You decide to test your friend by using a set of five cards that have been used in ESP research. A different symbol is presented on each card. In the ESP test, you look at each card and think about the symbol, and your friend, the subject, tells you which symbol you are thinking about. In your actual experiment, you have 10 trials; each of the five cards is presented two times in a random order. Your task is to know whether your friend's answers reflect random error (guessing) or whether the answers indicate that something more than random error is occurring. The null hypothesis in your study is that only random error is operating. The research hypothesis is that the number of correct answers shows more than just random or chance guessing. (Note, however, that accepting the research hypothesis could mean that your friend has ESP ability, but it could also mean that the cards were marked, that you had somehow cued your friend when thinking about the symbols, and so on.)

You can easily determine the number of correct answers to expect if the null hypothesis is correct. Just by guessing, the subject should get one out of five correct (20 percent). On 10 trials, two correct answers are expected under the null hypothesis. If, in the actual experiment, more (or less) than two correct answers are obtained, would you conclude that the obtained data reflect random error, or would you conclude that the data reflect something more than just random guessing?

Suppose that your subject gets three correct. Then you would probably conclude that only guessing is involved, because you would recognize that there is a high probability that the subject would get three correct *even though only two correct are expected under the null hypothesis*. You expect that exactly two out of 10 answers would be correct in the long run, if you conducted this experiment with this subject over and over again. However, small deviations away from the expected two are highly likely in a sample of 10 trials.

Suppose, though, that your subject gets seven correct—you might conclude that the results indicate more than random error in this one sample of 10 observations. This conclusion would be based on your intuitive judgment that an outcome of 70 percent correct when only 20 percent is expected is very unlikely. At this point, you would decide to reject the null hypothesis and state that the result is significant. A significant result is one that is very unlikely if the null hypothesis is correct.

How unlikely does a result have to be before we say it is significant? The most common probability used is .05. The outcome of the study is considered significant when there is a .05 probability or less of obtaining the re-

Number of correct answers	Probability
10	.00000 +
9	.00000 +
8	.00007
7	.00079
6	.00551
5	.02642
4	.08808
3	.20133
2	.30199
1	.26844
0	.10737

Table 9-2
Exact probability of each possible outcome of the ESP experiment with 10 trials

sults—that is, there are only 5 chances out of 100 that the results were due to random error in one sample from the population. If it is very unlikely that random error is responsible for the obtained results, the null hypothesis is rejected.

Sampling distributions

You may have been able to judge intuitively that obtaining seven correct on the 10 trials is very unlikely. Fortunately, we don't have to rely on intuition to determine the probabilities of different outcomes. Table 9-2 shows the probability of actually obtaining each of the possible outcomes in the ESP experiment with 10 trials and a null hypothesis expectation of 20 percent correct. An outcome of two correct answers has the highest probability of occurrence. Also, as intuition indicates, an outcome of three correct is highly probable, but an outcome of seven correct has a very low likelihood of occurrence.

The probabilities shown in Table 9-2 were derived from a probability distribution called the binomial distribution; all of our statistical significance decisions are based on probability distributions such as this one. Such distributions are called *sampling distributions*. The sampling distribution is based on the assumption that the null hypothesis is true; in the ESP example, the null hypothesis is that the subject is only guessing and should therefore get 20 percent correct. Such a distribution assumes that if you were to conduct the study with the same number of observations over and over again, the most frequent finding would be 20 percent. However, because of the random error possible in each sample, there is a certain probability associated with other outcomes. Outcomes that are close to the expected null hypothesis value of 20 percent are very likely. However, outcomes farther from the expected result are less and less likely, if the null hypothesis is correct. When your obtained results are very unlikely if you are in fact sampling from the distribution specified by the null hypothesis, you conclude that the null hypothesis is incorrect. Instead of concluding that your sample results reflect a random

147

deviation from the long-run expectation of 20 percent, you decide that the null hypothesis is incorrect. That is, you conclude that you have not sampled from the sampling distribution specified by the null hypothesis. Instead, in the case of the ESP example, you decide that your data are from a different sampling distribution in which, if you were to test the person over and over again, most of the outcomes would be near your obtained result of seven correct answers.

All statistical tests rely on sampling distributions to determine the probability that the results are consistent with the null hypothesis. When it is very unlikely that the null hypothesis is correct (usually a .05 probability or less), the researcher decides to reject the null hypothesis and therefore accept the research hypothesis.

Sample size

The ESP example also illustrates the importance of sample size, the total number of observations, on determinations of statistical significance. Suppose you had tested your friend on 100 trials instead of 10, and you observed 30 correct answers. Just as you had expected two correct answers in 10 trials, you would now expect 20 of 100 answers to be correct. However, 30 out of 100 has a much lower likelihood of occurrence than 3 out of 10. This is because with more observations sampled, you are more likely to obtain an accurate estimate of the true population value. Thus, as the size of your sample increases, you are more confident that your outcome is actually different from the null hypothesis expectation.

EXAMPLE: THE *t*-TEST AND *F* TEST

Different statistical tests allow us to use probability to decide whether to reject the null hypothesis. In this section, we will examine the *t*-test and the *F* test. The *t*-test is most commonly used to examine whether two groups are significantly different from one another. In the hypothetical experiment on the effect of a model on aggression, a *t*-test is appropriate because we are asking whether the mean of the no-model group is different from the mean of the model group. The *F* test is a more general statistical test that can be used to ask whether there is a difference among three or more groups, or to evaluate the results of the factorial designs discussed in Chapter 7.

To use a statistical test, you must first specify the null hypothesis and the research hypothesis that you are evaluating. The null and research hypotheses for the modeling experiment were described earlier. You must also specify the significance level that you will use to decide whether to reject the null hypothesis. As noted, researchers generally use a significance level of .05.

t-test

A value of t is calculated from the obtained data and evaluated in terms of the sampling distribution of t that is based on the null hypothesis. If the obtained t has a low probability of occurrence (.05 or less), then the null hypothesis is rejected. The t value is a ratio of two aspects of the data, the difference between the group means and the variability within groups. The ratio may be described as follows:

$$t = \frac{\text{group difference}}{\text{within-group variability}}$$

The group difference is simply the difference between your obtained means; under the null hypothesis, you expect this difference to be zero. The value of t increases as the difference between your obtained sample means increases. You should note that the sampling distribution of t assumes that there is no difference in the population means; thus, the expected value of t under the null hypothesis is zero. The within-group variability is the amount of variability of scores about the mean. The denominator of the t formula is essentially an indicator of the amount of random error in your sample. Recall that s, the standard deviation, and s^2, the variance, are indicators of how much scores deviate from the group mean.

A concrete example of a calculation of a t-test should help clarify these concepts. The formula for the t-test for two groups of subjects with equal or nearly equal numbers of subjects in each group is:

$$t = \frac{\overline{X}_1 - \overline{X}_2}{\sqrt{\dfrac{s_1^2}{N_1} + \dfrac{s_2^2}{N_2}}}$$

The numerator of the formula is simply the difference between the means of the two groups. In the denominator, we first divide the variance (s^2) of each group by the number of subjects in the group and add these together. We then find the square root of the result. This yields an estimate of the overall amount of variability within the groups.

When this formula is applied to the data in Table 9-1, we find:

$$t = \frac{5.2 - 3.1}{\sqrt{\dfrac{1.288}{10} + \dfrac{1.433}{10}}}$$

$$= \frac{2.1}{\sqrt{.1288 + .1433}}$$

$$= \frac{2.1}{.522}$$

$$= 4.023$$

149

Thus, the t value calculated from the data is 4.023. Is this a significant result? A computer program analyzing the results would immediately tell you the probability of obtaining a t value of this size with a total sample size of 20. Without such a program, however, you can refer to a table of critical values of t, such as Table C-4 in Appendix C. We will discuss the use of the appendix tables in detail in Appendix B. Before going further, you should know that the obtained result is significant. Using a significance level of .05, the critical value from the sampling distribution of t is 2.101. Because our obtained value is larger than the critical value, we can reject the null hypothesis and conclude that the difference in means obtained in the sample reflects a true difference in the population.

Degrees of freedom

You are probably wondering how the critical value was selected from the table. To use the table, you must first determine the degrees of freedom for the test. When comparing two means, the degrees of freedom are equal to $N_1 + N_2 - 2$, or the total number of subjects in the groups minus the number of groups. In our experiment, the degrees of freedom would be $10 + 10 - 2 = 18$. The degrees of freedom are the number of scores free to vary once the means are known; for example, if the mean of a group is 6.0 and there are five subjects in the group, there are 4 degrees of freedom; once you have any four scores, the fifth score is known because the mean must remain 6.0.

One-tailed versus two-tailed tests

In the table, you must choose a critical t for either (1) the situation in which your research hypothesis specified a direction of difference between the groups (e.g., group 1 will be greater than group 2) or (2) the situation in which you did not specify a predicted direction of difference (e.g., group 1 will differ from group 2). Somewhat different critical values of t are used in the two situations: The first situation is called a one-tailed test, and the second situation is called a two-tailed test. The issue can be visualized by looking at the sampling distribution of t values for 18 degrees of freedom, as shown in Figure 9-5. As you can see, a value of 0.00 is expected most frequently. Values greater than or less than 0 are less likely to occur. The first distribution shows the logic of a two-tailed test. We used the value of 2.101 for the critical value of t with a .05 significance level because a direction of difference was not predicted. This critical value is the point beyond which 2.5 percent of the positive values lie and 2.5 percent of the negative values of t lie (hence, a total probability of .05 combined from the two "tails" of the sampling distribution). The second distribution illustrates a one-tailed test. If a directional difference had been predicted, the critical value would have been 1.734. This is the value beyond which 5 percent of the values lie in only one "tail" of the

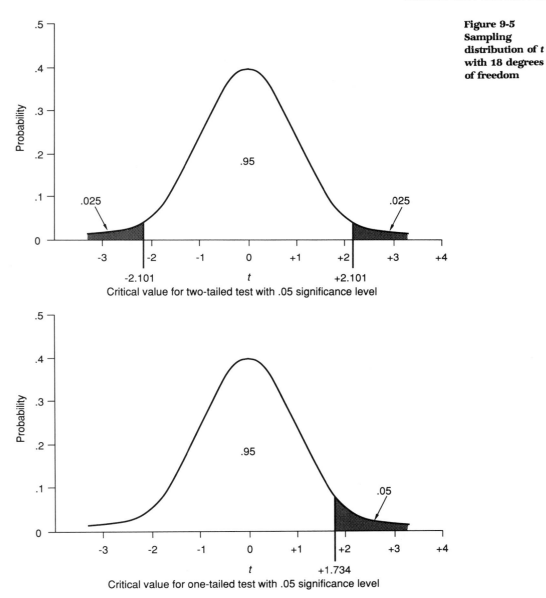

**Figure 9-5
Sampling
distribution of *t*
with 18 degrees
of freedom**

distribution. Whether to specify a one-tailed or two-tailed test will depend on whether you originally designed your study to test a directional hypothesis.

F test

The **analysis of variance,** or **F test,** is an extension of the *t*-test. The analysis of variance is a more general statistical procedure than the *t*-test. When a

151

study has only one independent variable with two groups, F and t are virtually identical—the value of F equals t^2 in this situation. However, analysis of variance is also used when there are more than two levels of an independent variable, and with factorial designs in which there are several independent variables. Thus, the F test is appropriate for the simplest experimental design as well as the more complex designs discussed in Chapter 7. The t-test was presented because the formula allows us to demonstrate easily the relationship of the group difference and the within-group variability to the outcome of the statistical test. However, in practice, analysis of variance is the more common procedure. The calculations necessary to conduct an F test are provided in Appendix B.

The F statistic is a ratio of two types of variance (hence the term "analysis of variance"): systematic variance and error variance. **Systematic variance** is the deviation of the group means from the grand mean, which is the mean score of all subjects in all groups. Systematic variance is small when the difference between group means is small and increases as the group mean differences increase. **Error variance** is the deviation of the individual scores in each group from their respective group means. Terms that you may see in research instead of systematic and error variance are between-group variance and within-group variance: Systematic variance is the variability of scores between groups, and error variance is the variability of scores within groups. The larger the F ratio, the more likely it is that the results are significant.

Summary

The logic underlying the use of statistical tests rests upon statistical theory. There are some general concepts, however, that should help you understand what you are doing when you conduct a statistical test. First, the goal of the test is to allow you to make a decision about whether your obtained results are reliable; you want to be confident that you would obtain similar results if you conducted the study over and over again. Second, the significance level you choose indicates how confident you wish to be when making the decision. A .05 significance level says that you are 95 percent sure of the reliability of your findings; however, there is a 5 percent chance that you could be wrong. There are few certainties in life! Third, you are most likely to obtain significant results when you have a large sample size, because larger sample sizes provide better estimates of true population values. Finally, you are most likely to obtain significant results when differences between groups are large and variability of scores within groups is small.

In the remainder of the chapter, we will expand on these issues. We will examine the implications of making a decision about whether results are significant, how to determine a significance level, and how to interpret non-significant results. We will then provide some guidelines for selecting the appropriate statistical test in various research designs.

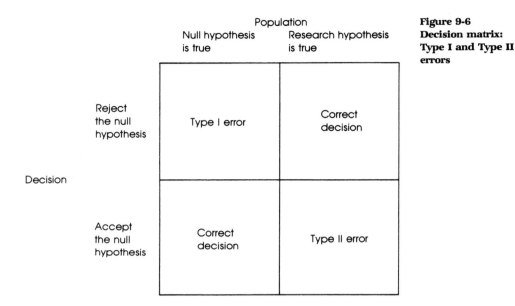

Figure 9-6
**Decision matrix:
Type I and Type II
errors**

TYPE I AND TYPE II ERRORS

The decision to reject the null hypothesis is based on probabilities rather than on certainties. The decision is made without direct knowledge of the true state of affairs in the population. Thus, the decision might not be correct; there may be errors resulting from the use of inferential statistics.

A decision matrix is shown in Figure 9-6. Notice that there are two possible decisions: We can (1) reject the null hypothesis or (2) accept the null hypothesis. There are also two possibilities that may be true in the population: (1) The null hypothesis is true or (2) the research hypothesis is true. You can see from this decision matrix that there are two kinds of correct decisions and two kinds of errors.

Correct decisions

One correct decision occurs when we reject the null hypothesis and the research hypothesis is true in the population. Our decision is to say that the population means are not equal, and in fact this is true in the population. The other correct decision is to accept the null hypothesis, and the null hypothesis is true in the population: The population means are in fact equal.

Type I errors

A **Type 1 error** is made when we reject the null hypothesis but the null hypothesis is actually true. Our decision is that the population means are not

153

equal when they actually are equal. Type I errors occur when, just by chance, we obtain a large value of t or F. For example, even though a t value of 4.023 is highly improbable if in fact the population means are equal (less than five chances out of 100), it *can* happen. When we obtain such a large t value by chance, we *incorrectly* decide that the independent variable had an effect.

The probability of making a Type I error is determined by the choice of significance level. When the significance level for deciding whether to reject the null hypothesis is .05, the probability of a Type I error is .05. If the null hypothesis is rejected, there are five chances out of 100 that the decision is wrong. The probability of making a Type I error can be changed by changing the significance level. If we use a significance level of .01, for example, there is less chance of making a Type I error. With a .01 significance level, the null hypothesis is rejected only when the probability of obtaining the results is .01 or less if the null hypothesis is correct.

Type II errors

A **Type II error** occurs when the null hypothesis is accepted although in the population the research hypothesis is true. The population means are not equal, but the results of the experiment do not lead to a decision to reject the null hypothesis.

The probability of making a Type II error is not directly specifiable, although the significance level is an important factor. If we set a very low significance level to decrease the chances of a Type I error, we increase the chances of a Type II error. In other words, if we make it very difficult to reject the null hypothesis, the probability of incorrectly accepting the null hypothesis goes up.

The everyday context of Type I and Type II errors

The decision matrix used in statistical analyses is really only one example of the kinds of decisions people frequently make. For example, consider the decision made by a juror in a criminal trial. As is the case with statistics, a decision must be made on the basis of evidence: Is the defendant innocent or guilty? However, the decision is the juror's and does not necessarily reflect the true state of affairs: that the person really is innocent or guilty.

The juror's decision matrix is illustrated in Figure 9-7. To draw the parallel to the statistical decision, assume as the null hypothesis that the defendant is innocent (i.e., the dictum that a person is innocent until proven guilty). Thus, rejection of the null hypothesis is to decide that the defendant is guilty, and acceptance of the null hypothesis is to decide that the defendant is innocent. The decision matrix also shows that the null hypothesis may actually be true or false. There are two kinds of correct decisions and two kinds of errors like those described in statistical decisions. A Type I error is to find the defendant guilty when the person is really innocent; a Type II error is deciding

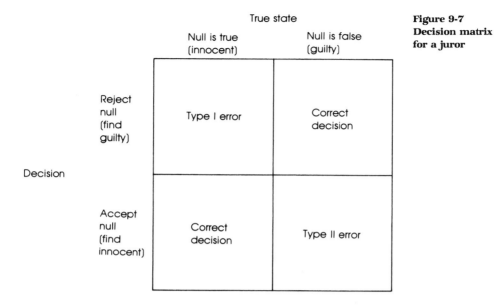

Figure 9-7
**Decision matrix
for a juror**

the defendant is innocent when the person is actually guilty. In our society, it is generally felt that Type I errors by jurors are more serious than Type II errors. Thus, before the juror finds someone guilty, the juror is asked to make sure that the person is guilty "beyond a reasonable doubt," or to consider that "it is better to have a hundred guilty persons go free than to find one innocent person guilty."

The decision that a doctor makes to operate or not operate on a patient provides another example of our decision matrix. The matrix is shown in Figure 9-8. Here the null hypothesis is that no operation is necessary. The decision is whether to reject the null hypothesis and perform the operation or to accept the null hypothesis and not perform surgery. In reality, the physician is faced with two possibilities: Either the surgery is unnecessary (the null hypothesis is true) or the patient will die without the operation (a dramatic case of the null hypothesis being false). Which error is more serious in this case? Most doctors would feel that not operating on a patient who really needs the operation—making a Type II error—is more serious than making the Type I error of performing surgery on someone who does not really need it.

One final example of a decision matrix is the important decision to marry someone. If the null hypothesis is that the person is "wrong" for you, and the true state is that the person is either "wrong" or "right," you must decide whether to go ahead and marry the person. You might try to construct a decision matrix for this particular problem. Which error is more costly: a Type I error or a Type II error?

155

Figure 9-8
Decision matrix
for a doctor

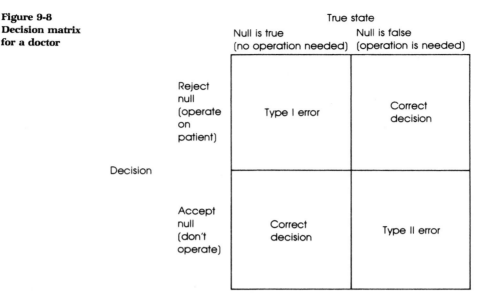

CHOOSING A SIGNIFICANCE LEVEL

Researchers have traditionally used either a .05 or a .01 significance level in the decision to reject the null hypothesis. If there is less than a .05 or a .01 probability that the results occurred because of random error, the results are said to be significant. However, there is nothing magical about a .05 or a .01 significance level. The significance level chosen merely specifies the probability of a Type I error if the null hypothesis is rejected. The significance level chosen by the researcher is usually dependent on the consequences of making a Type I versus a Type II error. As previously noted, for a juror, a Type I error is more serious than a Type II error; for a doctor, however, a Type II error is more serious.

Researchers usually feel that the consequences of making a Type I error are more serious than the consequences of a Type II error. If the null hypothesis is rejected, the researcher might publish the results in a journal and the results might be reported by others in textbooks or in newspaper or magazine articles. Researchers don't want to mislead others or risk damaging their reputations by publishing results that aren't true and cannot be replicated. Thus, they want to guard against the possibility of making a Type I error by using a very low significance level (.05 or .01). In contrast to the consequences of publishing false results, the consequences of a Type II error are not seen as being very serious.

Thus, researchers want to be very careful to avoid Type I errors when their results may be published. However, there are circumstances in which a Type I error is not serious. For example, if you are engaged in pilot or exploratory research, your results are used primarily to decide whether it is worthwhile to pursue your research ideas. In this situation, it would be a mistake to overlook potentially important data by using a very conservative significance level. In exploratory research, a significance level of .25 may be more appropriate for deciding whether to do more research. Remember, the significance level chosen and the consequences of a Type I or a Type II error are determined by what the results will be used for.

INTERPRETING NONSIGNIFICANT RESULTS

Although "accepting the null hypothesis" is convenient terminology, it is important to recognize that researchers are not generally interested in accepting the null hypothesis. Research is designed to show that a relationship between variables does exist, rather than to demonstrate that variables are unrelated.

More important, there are problems with a decision to accept the null hypothesis when the study doesn't show significant results, because negative or nonsignificant results are difficult to interpret. First, it isn't possible to specify the probability that you could be wrong in the decision to accept the null hypothesis. Also, a single study might not show significant results, even when there is a relationship between the variables in the population. For example, a researcher might obtain nonsignificant results by making the instructions to subjects incomprehensible, by having a very weak manipulation of the independent variable, or by using a dependent measure that is unreliable and insensitive. When nonsignificant results are obtained, the researcher must reexamine all aspects of the procedures to try to discover if something went wrong.

Nonsignificant results can also be obtained by using a very low significance level. If the researcher uses a significance level of .001 in deciding whether to reject the null hypothesis, there isn't much chance of a Type I error. However, a Type II error is possible, because the researcher has decreased the chances of wrongly rejecting the null hypothesis. In other words, a meaningful result is more likely to be overlooked when the significance level is very low.

A small sample size also might cause a researcher to be wrong in accepting the null hypothesis. A general principle is that the larger the sample size, the greater the likelihood of obtaining a significant result. This is because large sample sizes give more accurate estimates of the actual population than do small sample sizes. In any given study, it is possible that the sample size is too small to permit detection of a significant result.

This is not meant to imply that researchers should always use huge samples. A very large sample size (for example, 200 subjects in each group)

157

might enable the researcher to find a significant difference between means. This difference, however, even though it is statistically significant, might have very little *practical* significance. For example, if an expensive new psychiatric treatment technique significantly reduces hospital stay from 60 days to 58 days, it might not be practical to use the technique even though there is evidence for its effectiveness.

The general point of this discussion is that *you should not always accept the null hypothesis just because the results are nonsignificant*. Before a researcher accepts the null hypothesis, the experiment must be conducted again with refined procedures and possibly a larger sample. But if repeated evidence from well-designed studies with adequate sample sizes shows no relationship between the variables, then you are justified in concluding that there is in fact no relationship.

SCALES OF MEASUREMENT

Whenever a variable is measured, the measure uses one of four kinds of measurement scales: nominal scales, ordinal scales, interval scales, and ratio scales. The scale that is used determines the type of statistical test that will be appropriate when the results of a study are analyzed. Also, the conclusions one draws about the meaning of a particular score on a variable depend on which type of scale was used for measuring the variable. The properties and implications of the various scales of measurement are described in the following subsections.

Nominal scales

Nominal scales have no numerical or quantitative properties. An obvious example is the variable of sex, or gender. A person is classified as either male or female. Being male does not imply a greater amount of "sexness" than being female; the two levels of the sex variable are merely different. This is called a nominal scale because we simply assign names to different categories. Another example is the classification of undergraduates according to major. A psychology major would not be entitled to a higher number than a history major, for instance. Even if you were to assign numbers to the different categories, the numbers would be meaningless, except for identification.

Ordinal scales

Ordinal scales are a bit more sophisticated than nominal scales because they involve quantitative distinctions. Ordinal scales allow us to rank order people or objects on the variable being measured.

One example of an ordinal scale is provided by the movie rating system used in the television section of the *Los Angeles Times*. Movies on television are given one, two, three, or four checks. The ratings are described like this:

√√√√   New or old, a classic
  √√√   First-rate
    √√   Flawed; may have moments
     √   Desperation time

The rating system is not a nominal scale because the number of checks is meaningful in terms of a continuum of quality. However, the checks allow us only to rank order the movies. A four-check movie is better than a three-check movie; a three-check movie is better than a movie with two checks; and so on. Although we have this quantitative information about the movies, we cannot say that the difference between a one-check and a two-check movie is always the same or that it is equal to the difference between a two- and a three-check movie. No particular value is attached to the intervals between the numbers used in the rating scale.

Interval scales

In an interval scale, the difference between the numbers on the scale is meaningful. Specifically, the intervals between the numbers are equal in size. The difference between 1 and 2 on the scale, for example, is the same as the difference between 2 and 3.

A household thermometer (Fahrenheit or Celsius) measures temperature on an interval scale. The difference between 40° and 50° is equal to the difference in temperature between 70° and 80°. However, there is no absolute zero on the scale that would indicate the absence of temperature. The zero on any interval scale is only an arbitrary reference point. The implication of this property of interval scales is that we cannot form ratios of the numbers. That is, we cannot say that one number on the scale represents twice as much (or three times as much, and so forth) temperature as another number. You cannot say, for example, that 60° is twice as warm as 30°.

An example of an interval scale in the behavioral sciences might be a personality measure of a trait such as extraversion. If the measurement is an interval scale, we cannot make a statement such as "the person who scored 20 is twice as extraverted as the person who scored 10," because there is no absolute zero point that indicates an absence of the trait that is being measured.

In the behavioral sciences, it is often difficult to know precisely whether an ordinal or an interval scale is being used. However, it is often useful to assume that the variable is being measured on an interval scale, because interval scales allow more sophisticated statistical treatments than are allowed with ordinal scales. Of course, if the measure is a rank ordering (for example, a rank ordering of students in a class on the basis of popularity), it is obvious that an ordinal scale is being used.

Ratio scales

Ratio scales do have an absolute zero point that indicates the absence of the variable being measured. Examples include many physical measures, such

159

as length, weight, or time. With a ratio scale, it is possible to make such statements as "a person who weighs 220 pounds weighs twice as much as a person who weighs 110 pounds."

Ratio scales are used in the behavioral sciences when variables that involve physical measures are being studied—particularly time measures such as reaction time. However, most variables in the behavioral sciences are less precise and so use nominal, ordinal, or interval scale measures.

SELECTING THE APPROPRIATE TEST

Many statistical tests have been developed for different research designs. The appropriateness of a particular test of significance depends on the design used and the type of measurement scale employed when obtaining scores from subjects. This section will not provide guidelines for selecting a test in all situations; rather, only the appropriate tests for some of the more common designs will be listed.

Measures of central tendency

Nominal scale data With nominal scale data, the only appropriate measure of central tendency is the mode, the most frequent score. Most commonly, the researcher reports the number or percentage of individuals that falls into each of the nominal categories.

Ordinal scale data The median or midpoint should be used with ordinal scale data (although the mode can also be used).

Interval or ratio scale data The mean is usually the best measure of central tendency for interval or ratio scale data. It is useful, however, to also determine the median and the mode. If these measures are substantially different from the mean, the distribution of scores may have unusual characteristics (recall the discussion of family income data).

One independent variable—two groups only

Nominal scale data When subjects have been measured using a nominal scale, the appropriate test is a Chi-square test. Chi-square tests are used with all nominal data. Check a statistics book for the formula for your application.

Ordinal scale data If an independent groups design was used, the Mann–Whitney U test is appropriate. This test is described in Appendix B. For a repeated measures or matched design, Wilcoxon's T or the sign test is used. The procedures for these tests may be found in many statistics texts (see Siegel & Castellan, 1988).

Interval or ratio scale data For independent groups designs, the t-test described in this chapter or a one-way analysis of variance is used. The analysis of variance calculations are given in Appendix B. With repeated measures or matched groups designs, a t-test with a slightly different calculational procedure or a repeated measures analysis of variance should be employed. The calculations for a repeated measures analysis of variance are shown in Appendix B.

One independent variable—three or more groups

Nominal scale data   A Chi-square test is used in this situation.

Ordinal scale data   The Kruskal–Wallace H test is appropriate for an independent groups design. For repeated measures designs, the Friedman T test is appropriate. Consult a statistics text for details on calculating these tests.

Interval or ratio scale data   A one-way analysis of variance is used. The procedures to calculate this test for both independent groups and repeated measures designs are provided in Appendix B.

Two or more independent variables

Nominal scale data   Again, a Chi-square test is appropriate for nominal scale data. The formula for a Chi-square in which subjects are classified on two variables, both with nominal scale properties, is provided in Appendix B.

Ordinal scale data   No appropriate statistical test is available.

Interval or ratio scale data   A two-way analysis of variance is used for factorial designs with two independent variables. Analysis of variance can be extended to designs with any number of independent variables—it is appropriate for independent groups, repeated measures, or combined independent groups and repeated measures factorial designs.

Measuring subjects on two variables

In many studies, there are no "groups" of subjects. Instead, the data consist of scores on two or more variables. For example, if you are interested in the relationship between church attendance and income, you might sample 150 subjects and simply ask them their income and how many times they attended church during the previous year. Suppose you then have church attendance scores ranging from 0 to 55 and income ranging from $5,000 to $83,000. Since you don't have "groups" of subjects, how do you determine if there is a relationship? You could divide them into groups—for example, a low-attendance group and a high-attendance group—and perform one of the statistical tests just described. However, a better procedure is available: The appropriate statistic is called a correlation coefficient, which is discussed in Chapter 10.

STUDY QUESTIONS

1. What is a frequency distribution?

2. Be able to distinguish between and construct a frequency polygon and a histogram.

3. What is a measure of central tendency? Distinguish between the mean, median, and mode.

4. What is a measure of variability? Distinguish between the standard deviation and the range.

5. Why are inferential statistics necessary?

6. Distinguish between the null hypothesis and the research hypothesis. When does the researcher decide to reject the null hypothesis?

7. What is meant by statistical significance?

8. What factors are most important in determining whether obtained results will be significant?

9. Distinguish between a Type I and a Type II error. Why is your significance level the probability of making a Type I error?

10. What factors are involved in choosing a significance level?

11. What is the difference between statistical significance and practical significance?

12. Discuss the reasons why a researcher might obtain nonsignificant results.

13. Distinguish between nominal, ordinal, interval, and ratio scales.

ACTIVITY QUESTION

In an experiment, one group of subjects were given 10 pages of material to proofread for errors. Another group of subjects proofread the same material on a computer screen. The dependent variable was the number of errors detected in a 5-minute period. A .05 significance level was used to evaluate the results.

1. Is the dependent variable measured on a nominal, ordinal, interval, or ratio scale?

2. What statistical test would you use?

3. What is the null hypothesis? What is the research hypothesis?

4. What is the Type I error? What is the Type II error?

5. What is the probability of making a Type I error?

CHAPTER 10

Correlation Coefficients

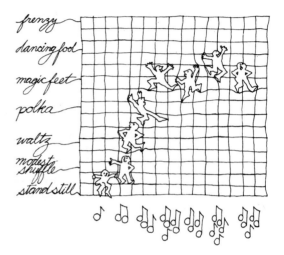

The concept of *correlation* is a fundamental one in the behavioral sciences. Correlation means that variables are systematically related to one another. This chapter discusses the use of correlation coefficients in behavioral research. A **correlation coefficient** is a statistic that indicates how strongly two variables are related.

FUNDAMENTAL PROCEDURES

Data collection procedures must involve making pairs of observations on each subject. Thus, each subject has two scores, one on each of the variables. Table 10-1 shows fictitious data for 10 subjects who were measured on the variables of classroom seating pattern and exam grade. Students in the first row receive a seating score of 1, those in the second row receive a 2, and so on. Once we have made our observations, we can see if the two variables are related. Do the variables go together in a systematic fashion?

INDEXING THE STRENGTH OF A RELATIONSHIP

To determine whether two variables are related, a descriptive statistic called a correlation coefficient is used. There are a number of different types of correlation coefficients (see Appendix B). One of the most frequently used is the *Pearson product-moment correlation coefficient*, which is referred to as r.

The values of r can range from $+1.00$ to -1.00. The plus and minus signs indicate whether there is a positive linear or negative linear relationship between the two variables. The absolute size of r is an index of the strength of the relationship: The nearer r is to 1.00 (plus or minus), the stronger the relationship. Indeed, a 1.00 correlation is sometimes called a perfect relationship, because the two variables go together in a perfect fashion.

Data from studies examining similarities of intelligence test scores illustrate the connection between the magnitude of a correlation coefficient and the strength of a relationship. The relationship between scores of identical twins is very strong ($r = +.86$), demonstrating a strong similarity of test scores in these pairs of individuals. The correlation for fraternal twins reared together is less strong ($r = +.60$). The correlation among nontwin siblings raised together is $+.47$, and the correlation among nontwin siblings reared apart is only $+.24$ (cf. Bouchard & McGue, 1981).

Correlation coefficients can be visualized in scatterplots in which each subject's pair of scores is plotted as a single point in a diagram. Figure 10-1 shows scatterplots for a perfect positive relationship ($+1.00$) and for a perfect negative relationship (-1.00). (Such relationships in actual research are rare.) You can easily see why these are perfect relationships. For all subjects, the scores on the two variables fall on a straight line that is on the diagonal of the diagram. Each subject's score on one variable goes perfectly with his

Subject identification number	Seating	Exam score
01	2	95
02	5	50
03	1	85
04	4	75
05	3	75
06	5	60
07	2	80
08	3	70
09	1	90
10	4	70

Table 10-1
Pairs of scores for 10 subjects on seating pattern and exam score (fictitious data)

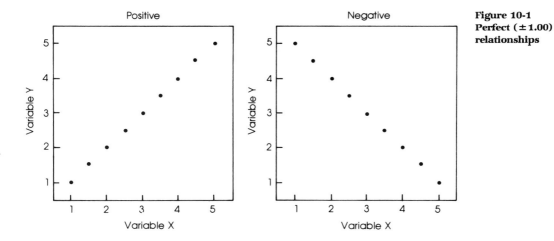

Figure 10-1
Perfect (± 1.00) relationships

or her score on the other variable. If we know a subject's score on one of the variables, we can predict exactly what his or her score will be on the other variable.

The diagrams in Figure 10-2 show patterns of correlation you are likely to encounter in exploring research findings. The first diagram shows data that yield a correlation of + .65; the second shows a negative relationship, − .77. The data points in these two scatterplots show a general pattern of either a positive or negative relationship, but the relationships are not perfect. You can make a general prediction in the first diagram, for instance, that the higher the score on one variable, the higher the score on the second variable. However, if you know a subject's score on the first variable, you can't *perfectly* predict what that person's score will be on the second variable. To confirm this, take a look at value 1 on variable X (the horizontal axis) in the positive scatterplot. Looking up, you will see that two subjects had a score of 1. One

Figure 10-2
Scatterplots

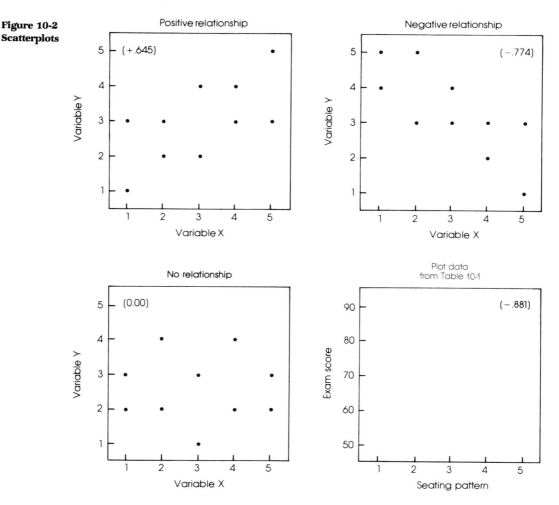

of these subjects had a score of 1 on variable Y (the vertical axis), and the other subject had a score of 3. The data points do not fall on the perfect diagonal. Instead, there is a variation (scatter) from the perfect diagonal line.

The third diagram shows a scatterplot in which there is absolutely no correlation ($r = 0.00$). The points fall all over the diagram, and there is no pattern. Scores on variable X are not related to scores on variable Y.

The fourth diagram has been left blank, so that you can plot the scores from the data in Table 10-1. The X (horizontal) axis has been labeled for the seating pattern variable, and the Y (vertical) axis has been labeled for the exam score variable. To complete the scatterplot, you will need to plot the scores for each of the 10 subjects. For each subject, find the score on the seating pattern variable, then go up until you reach that subject's exam score.

A point there will describe the subject's score on both variables. There will be 10 points on the finished scatterplot.

The correlation coefficient calculated from these data shows that there is a negative relationship between the variables ($r = -.88$). As the seating distance from the front of the class increases, the exam score decreases. Although these data are fictitious, they are consistent with actual research findings (Brooks & Rebata, 1991).

It is always important to remember that results based on the correlational method have the problems of direction of cause-and-effect and of uncontrolled third variables. It is possible that sitting close to the front causes good grades, but it is also possible that good exam scores received earlier cause people to sit at the front of the class. Uncontrolled third variables may also be responsible for the correlation. Highly motivated students may arrive early to get front seats and may study harder to get good grades. If this is true, seating pattern and grades are not directly related. Instead, the third variable is actually responsible for the apparent correlation.

IMPORTANT CONSIDERATIONS

Restriction of range

It is important that the researcher sample from the full range of possible values of both variables. If the range of possible values is restricted, the magnitude of the correlation coefficient is reduced. For example, if the range of seating pattern scores had been restricted to the first two rows, you would not get an accurate picture of the relationship between seating pattern and exam score. In fact, the correlation between the two variables when only scores of subjects sitting in the first two rows are considered is exactly 0.00.

The problem of restriction of range occurs when the subjects in your sample are very similar or *homogeneous*. If you are studying age as a variable, for instance, testing only 6- and 7-year-olds will reduce your chances of finding age effects. Likewise, trying to study the correlates of intelligence will be almost impossible if your subjects are all very similar in intelligence (e.g., the senior class of a prestigious private college).

Curvilinear relationship

The Pearson product-moment correlation coefficient (r) is designed to detect only linear relationships. If the relationship is curvilinear, as in the scatterplot shown in Figure 10-3, the correlation coefficient will not indicate that there is a relationship. The correlation coefficient calculated from the data in Figure 10-3 shows an r of 0.00, although it is clear that the two variables are related.

When the relationship is curvilinear, special correlational techniques are necessary to determine the strength of the relationship. Because a relationship may be curvilinear, it is important to construct a scatterplot in addition to

167

**Figure 10-3
Scatterplot of a
curvilinear
relationship
(Pearson product-
moment
correlation
coefficient = 0.00)**

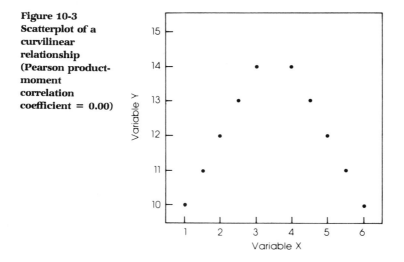

looking at the magnitude of the correlation coefficient. The scatterplot is valuable because it gives a visual indication of the shape of the relationship.

Significance of a correlation coefficient

The correlation coefficient is a descriptive statistic—it describes the strength of the relationship between the variables in the sample of subjects studied. Researchers are also interested in learning whether the obtained correlation coefficient is large enough to infer that there is a relationship between the variables in the population. Thus, null hypothesis testing procedures can be used to see whether the correlation coefficient in the population is 0.00. Table C-7 in Appendix C shows the size of the obtained r that is necessary for rejection of the null hypothesis at the .05 level. By rejecting the null hypothesis, we infer that the population correlation is *not* 0.00.

The importance of sample size in making inferences from the sample to the population can be seen in Table C-7. When the sample size is four, an obtained r of at least .950 (plus or minus) is necessary to reject the null hypothesis at the .05 level. However, the obtained r must be .444 (plus or minus) or larger when the sample size is 20. For much research in the behavioral sciences, a sample size of between 50 and 100 is necessary to reach a .05 significance level.

RELIABILITY AND CORRELATION COEFFICIENTS

The concept of reliability was discussed in Chapter 3. Recall that any measurement contains two components: a true score component and a measurement error component. A reliable measure contains little measurement error. We cannot directly observe the true score and error components of an actual score on the measure, however. Instead, correlational techniques are used to give an estimate of the extent to which the measure reflects true score rather than measurement error. There are several ways of estimating reliability, each involving correlation coefficients.

Test-retest and alternate forms reliability

Test-retest reliability and **alternate forms reliability** measure the same individuals at two points in time. For example, the reliability of a test of intelligence could be assessed by giving the measure to a group of subjects on one day and again a week later. We would then have two scores for each subject, and a correlation coefficient could be calculated to determine the relationship between the test score and the retest score. High reliability is indicated by a high correlation coefficient. It is difficult to say how high the correlation should be before we accept the measure as reliable, but for most measures the correlation should probably be at least +.80.

Test-retest reliability involves giving the same test twice, and this could create a problem—the correlation might be artificially high because the sub-jects might remember how they responded the first time. Alternate forms reliability is sometimes used to avoid this problem. Alternate forms reliability involves administering two different forms of the same test to the same subjects at two points in time.

Intelligence is a variable that can be expected to stay relatively constant over time, thus; we expect the test-retest reliability for intelligence to be very high. Test-retest and alternate forms reliability should be used for variables that remain stable over time, such as intelligence and achievement. However, some variables may be expected to change from one test period to the next. A mood scale designed to measure a person's current mood state is an exam-ple of a measure that might easily change from one test period to another. Methods to assess reliability without two testings are presented in the follow-ing section.

Split-half, odd-even, and item-total reliability

It is possible to assess reliability by measuring subjects at only one point in time. We can do this because most psychological measures are made up of a number of different items. For example, an intelligence test might have 100 items; a subject's test score would be based on the total of his or her scores on all items. Thus, methods to assess reliability at only one point in time are referred to as internal consistency measures of reliability. **Split-half reliabil-ity** is the correlation between the subject's total score on the first half of the test and his or her total score on the second half of the test. **Odd-even reliability** involves finding the correlation between total score on the odd-numbered items and the total score on the even-numbered items. A third method is **item-total reliability,** in which a correlation between the score on each item of a measure and the total score is calculated. If there are 10 items in the measure, 10 correlation coefficients are obtained. Reliability is the average of the correlations. In all cases, if the test is reliable, the correlation coefficients will be high.

CORRELATION COEFFICIENTS AND THE CORRELATIONAL METHOD

There is a very confusing aspect of the term *correlation* as it has been used over many years by researchers in the behavioral sciences. We have reviewed the distinction between the experimental and correlational methods of studying relationships between variables. We have seen that correlation coefficients function as indices of the strength of relationships between variables. One might expect that researchers use correlation coefficients only when using the correlational method since the term *correlation* is common to both, but unfortunately, that is not correct. The term *correlational method* refers to a nonexperimental study, and *correlation coefficient* refers to an index of the strength of relationship between two variables *irrespective of whether the experimental or correlational method was used*.

This confusion arises because historically the results of studies using the correlational method have been analyzed using Pearson correlation coefficients. However, it has become increasingly clear to researchers that correlation coefficients are always used as an index of strength of relationships in both correlational and experimental research.

The result is that more and more researchers are reporting correlation coefficients in both correlational and experimental research. Special types of correlation coefficients can be calculated for all types of research designs. An example is ω^2 (omega-squared), which is used to calculate the strength of a relationship in an experiment that is analyzed with the F test, or analysis of variance.

REGRESSION EQUATIONS

Regression equations are calculations used to predict a person's score on one variable when that person's score on another variable is already known. They are essentially "prediction equations" that are based on known information about the relationship between the two variables. For example, after discovering that seating pattern and exam score are related, a regression equation may be calculated that predicts anyone's exam score based only on information about where the person sits in the class.

The general form of a regression equation is

$$Y = a + bX$$

where Y is the score we wish to predict, X is the known score, a is a constant, and b is a weight that is multiplied by X. In our seating-exam score example, the following regression equation is calculated from the data:

$$Y = 99 + (-8)X$$

Thus, if we know a person's score on X (seating), we can insert that into the equation and predict what that person's score on Y (exam score) will be. If the person's X score is 2, we can predict that $Y = 99 + (-16)$, or that the person's exam score will be 83.

It is through the use of regression equations such as these that colleges use SAT scores to predict college grades, or that employers use tests to decide whether to hire someone.

When researchers are interested in predicting some future behavior (called the **criterion variable**) on the basis of a person's score on some other variable (called the **predictor variable**), it is first necessary to demonstrate that there is a reasonably high correlation between the criterion and predictor variables. The regression equation then provides the method for making predictions on the basis of the predictor variable score only.

MULTIPLE CORRELATION

Thus far we have focused on the correlation between two variables at a time. Researchers recognize that a number of different variables may be related to a given behavior. A technique called **multiple correlation** is used to combine a number of predictor variables to increase the accuracy of prediction of a given criterion variable.

A multiple correlation is the correlation between a combined set of predictor variables and a single criterion variable. When all of the predictor variables are taken into account, it is usually possible to achieve greater accuracy of prediction than if any single predictor is considered alone. For example, applicants to graduate school in psychology could be evaluated on a combined set of predictor variables using multiple correlation. The predictor variables might be (1) college grades, (2) scores on the Graduate Record Exam Aptitude Test, (3) scores on the Graduate Record Exam Psychology Test, and (4) favorability of letters of recommendation. No one of these factors is a perfect predictor of success in graduate school, but a prediction based on this combination of variables can be more accurate than a prediction based on only one of them. The multiple correlation is usually higher than the correlation between any one of the predictor variables and the criterion variable.

In actual practice, researchers would use an extension of the regression

171

equation technique discussed above. A multiple regression equation can be calculated that takes the following form:

$$Y = a + b_1X_1 + b_2X_2 + \ldots + b_nX_n$$

where Y is the criterion variable, X_1 to X_n are the predictor variables, a is a constant, and b_1 to b_n are weights that are multiplied by scores on the predictor variables. For example, a regression equation for graduate school admissions would be: predicted grade point average $= a + b_1$ (college grades) $+ b_2$ (score on Graduate Record Exam) $+ b_3$ (score on Graduate Record Psychology Exam) $+ b_4$ (favorability of recommendation letters).

More and more researchers in all areas of research are using multiple correlation and regression analysis to study research problems. For example, Ajzen and Fishbein (1980) have developed a model that uses multiple correlation and regression to predict specific behavioral intentions (e.g., to attend church on Sunday, buy a certain product, or join an alcohol recovery program) on the basis of two predictor variables. These are (1) attitude toward the behavior and (2) perceived normative pressure to engage in the behavior. In one study, these researchers demonstrated that the multiple correlation between the intention to buy a brand of beer and the combined predictors of attitude and norm was $+.79$. The regression equation was as follows:

$$\text{Intention} = .76(\text{Attitude}) + .27(\text{Norm})$$

The weight for the attitude predictor is higher than the weight for the norm predictor; this shows that, in this case, attitudes are more important as a predictor of intention than are norms. However, for other behaviors it may be found that attitudes are less important than norms.

It is also possible to visualize the regression equation. In the beer purchase example, the relationships among variables could be diagrammed as follows:

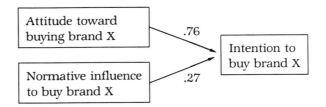

PARTIAL CORRELATION AND THE THIRD-VARIABLE PROBLEM

Researchers face the third-variable problem in correlational research when it is possible that some uncontrolled third variable is responsible for the relationship between the two variables of interest. The problem doesn't exist in experimental research, because all extraneous variables are controlled either by keeping the variables constant or by the use of randomization. A

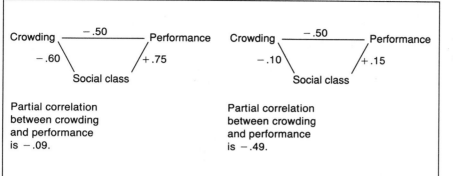

Figure 10-4
Two partial
correlations
between crowding
and performance

technique called **partial correlation** provides a way of statistically controlling third variables. A partial correlation is a correlation between the two variables of interest, with the influence of the third variable removed, or partialled out, of the original correlation.

Suppose that a researcher finds that the correlation between residential crowding and performance on a test is − .50. The researcher suspects that a third variable may be operating. Social class, for example, could influence both crowding and performance. The use of partial correlations involves measuring subjects on the third variable in addition to the two primary variables. Thus, the researcher has to measure subjects on all the variables: crowding, performance, and social class.

When a partial correlation between crowding and performance, with social class partialled out, is calculated, we can determine whether the original correlation is substantially reduced. Is our original correlation of − .50 lowered very much when the influence of social class is removed? Figure 10-4 shows two different partial correlations—in both, there is a − .50 correlation between crowding and performance. However, the first partial correlation drops to − .09 when social class is statistically controlled, and the second partial correlation remains high even when the influence of social class is removed. The outcome of the partial correlation depends on the magnitude of the correlations between the third variable and the two variables of primary interest.

STRUCTURAL MODELS

Recent advances in statistical theory and methods have resulted in techniques for testing **structural models** of relationships among variables using the correlational method. Although these methods are beyond the scope of this book, you should be aware that they exist (see James, Mulaik, & Brett, 1982; Coovert, Penner, & MacCallum, 1990; Tanaka, Panter, Winborne, & Huba,

**Figure 10-5
Example of a
causal or
structural model**

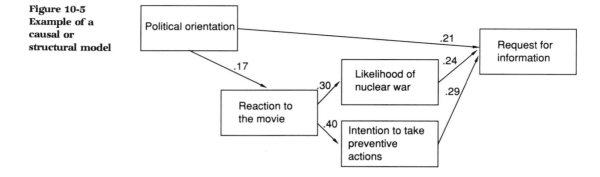

1990). A structural model is an expected pattern of relationships among a
set of variables. The proposed pattern is based upon a theory of how the
variables are causally related to one another. Thus, a popular term for conducting the statistical analysis is *causal modeling*; however, a more general
term is *structural modeling* because the techniques really allow researchers
to test how well obtained data fit a theoretical "structure" among variables.
(Also, the mathematical operations underlying the technique are based upon
structural equations.)

The diagram shown earlier for attitudes and intentions is a very simple
structural model. An example of a more complex model is shown in Figure
10-5. King (1985) developed the model from a study of reactions to viewing
a television movie titled "The Day After" (Oskamp, King, Burn, Konrad,
Pollard, & White, 1985). The movie depicted the events that might follow a
nuclear attack on the United States and was regarded as a film that contained
an antinuclear message. The model in Figure 10-5 shows the relationships
among variables leading to a behavioral request to receive information from
an antinuclear war group. The variables in the model, in addition to the
request for information, are political orientation (conservative-liberal), reaction to the movie (negative-positive), rated likelihood of nuclear war (low-
high), and intention to take preventive actions concerning nuclear war (low-
high).

Arrows leading from one variable to another depict obtained paths that
relate the variables in the model. The coefficients are similar to the weights
derived in the regression equations described previously. Focus your attention
on the request for information variable. There are three arrows or paths to
this variable: These are direct influences on the variable. The direct influences
are political orientation, rated likelihood of nuclear war, and intention to take
preventive actions. Reaction to the movie has an indirect effect on requests for
information by directly influencing subjects' rated likelihood of nuclear attack
and intentions to take preventive actions. Research that develops structural
models such as this enables researchers to better understand complex networks of relationships among variables.

174

STUDY QUESTIONS

1. What is a correlation coefficient? What do the size and sign of the correlation coefficient tell us about the relationship between variables?

2. What is a scatterplot? Construct a scatterplot like the one in Figure 10-1 or 10-2, using data from Table 10-1.

3. What happens when a scatterplot shows the relationship to be curvilinear?

4. Distinguish between test-retest and alternate forms reliability, and split-half and odd-even reliability.

5. What is the difference between correlation coefficients and the correlational method?

6. What is a regression equation? How might an employer use a regression equation?

7. How does multiple correlation increase accuracy of prediction?

8. What is the purpose of partial correlation?

9. What is a structural model?

ACTIVITY QUESTION

Hill (1990) studied the correlations between final exam score in an Introductory Sociology course and several other variables, such as number of absences. The following correlations with final exam score were obtained:

Overall college GPA	.72
Number of absences	− .51
Hours spent studying on weekdays	− .11 (not significant)
Hours spent studying on weekends	.31

Describe each correlation and draw graphs depicting the general shape of each relationship. Why might hours spent studying on weekends be correlated with grades while weekday studying is uncorrelated with grades?

11

Generalizing Results

In this chapter we will consider the problem of generalization of research findings. Can the results of a completed research project be generalized to other subject populations, to other age groups, to other ways of manipulating or measuring the variables? **Internal validity** refers to the adequacy of the procedures and design of the research. **External validity** is the extent to which the findings may be generalized. Internal validity is of primary importance; ideally, however, a study should have external validity as well.

GENERALIZING TO OTHER SUBJECT POPULATIONS

Even though a researcher randomly assigns subjects to experimental conditions, rarely are subjects randomly selected from the general population. As we noted in Chapters 4 and 8, subjects for psychological research are usually selected because they are available, and the most available subject population consists of college students—or more specifically, students who are usually sophomores enrolled in the introductory psychology course to satisfy a general education requirement. They may also be primarily from a particular college or university, may be volunteers, or may be mostly males or mostly females.

College students

Smart (1966) found that college students were the subjects in over 70 percent of the studies published between 1962 and 1964 in the *Journal of Experimental Psychology* and the *Journal of Abnormal and Social Psychology*. Sears (1986) reported similar percentages in 1980 and 1985 in a variety of social psychology journals. The potential problem is that such studies use a highly restricted subject population. Sears points out that most of the students are freshmen and sophomores taking the introductory psychology class. They therefore tend to be very young and possess the characteristics of late adolescents: a sense of self-identity that is still developing, social and political attitudes that are in a state of flux, a high need for peer approval, and unstable peer relationships. They also are intelligent, have high cognitive skills, and know how to win approval from authority (having done well enough in a school environment to get into college). Thus, what we know about "people in general" may actually be limited to a highly select and unusual group.

The problem of unrepresentative subjects is not confined to human research. A great deal of research with animals relies solely on the infamous white rat. Why? In part because, as Beach (1950) points out, "Rats are hardy, cheap, easy to rear, and well adapted to laboratory existence." Thus, like sophomores, they are easy to obtain on a college campus.

Volunteers

Researchers usually must ask people to volunteer to participate in the research. At many colleges, the introductory psychology students are required to either volunteer for experiments or complete an alternative project. If you are studying populations other than college students, you are even more dependent upon volunteers—for example, asking people at a PTA meeting to participate in a study of marital interaction. Research indicates that volunteers differ in various ways from nonvolunteers (Rosenthal & Rosnow, 1975). Volunteers tend to be more highly educated, higher in need of approval, and more social; and they tend to have a higher socioeconomic background.

It is also true that different kinds of people volunteer for different kinds of experiments. Again, in colleges there may be a subject signup board with the titles of many studies listed. Different types of people may be drawn to the study titled "problem solving" than to the one titled "interaction in small groups." Available evidence indicates that the title does influence who signs up (cf. Hood & Back, 1971).

Gender

Sometimes researchers use either males or females (or a very disproportionate ratio of males to females) simply because this is convenient or the procedures seem better suited to either males or females. Because males and females may differ, it is possible that the results of such studies cannot be generalized (Denmark, Russo, Frieze, and Sechzer, 1988). Denmark et al. provide an example of studies on contraception practices that use only females because of stereotypical assumptions that only females are responsible for contraception. They also point out several other ways that gender bias may arise in psychological research, including confounding gender with age or job status. Their paper offers several suggestions for avoiding such biases. Denmark et al. (1988) also note that the problems they raise regarding gender apply to other potential biases, including race and ethnicity.

Locale

Subjects in one locale may differ from subjects in another locale. Students at UCLA may differ from students at a nearby state university, and these students may differ from those at a community college. People in Iowa may differ from people in New York City. Thus, a finding obtained with the students in one type of educational setting or in one geographic region may not generalize to people in other settings or regions. One interesting approach to this problem was demonstrated in a study that was done simultaneously at seven different campuses (Cialdini et al., 1974). The researchers reported that it was surprisingly easy to coordinate their efforts.

Generalization as a statistical interaction

The problem of generalization can be thought of as an interaction in a factorial design (see Chapter 7). An interaction occurs when there is a relationship between variables under one condition but not another, or the nature of the

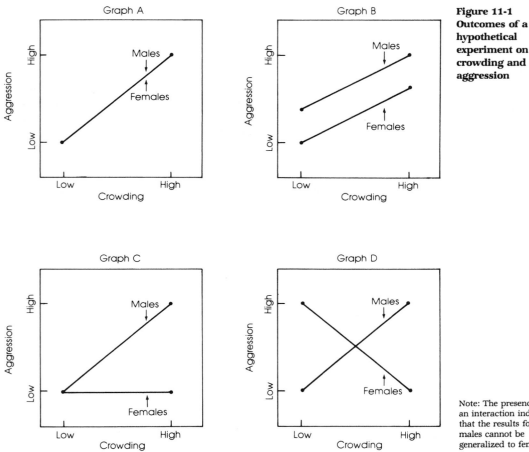

Figure 11-1
Outcomes of a hypothetical experiment on crowding and aggression

Note: The presence of an interaction indicates that the results for males cannot be generalized to females.

relationship is different in one condition than it is in another. Thus, if you question the generalizability of a study that used only males as subjects, you are suggesting that there is an interaction between gender and the treatment that was manipulated. Suppose, for example, that a study examines the relationship between crowding and aggression among male subjects and reports that crowding is associated with higher levels of aggression. You might then question whether the results are generalizable to females.

Figure 11-1 shows four potential outcomes of a study that tested both males and females. In each graph, the relationship between crowding and aggression for males has been maintained. In Graph A, there is no interaction—the behavior of males and females is virtually identical. Thus, the results of the original all-male study could be generalized to females. In Graph B, there is also no interaction; the effect of crowding is identical for males and females. However, in this graph males are more aggressive than

179

females. Although such a difference is interesting, it is not a factor in generalization because the overall relationship between crowding and aggression is present for both males and females.

Graphs C and D do show interactions. In both, the original results with males cannot be generalized to females. In Graph C, there is no relationship between crowding and aggression for females. The answer to the generalization question, "Is this true for females?" is "No!" In Graph D, the interaction tells us that there is a positive relationship between crowding and aggression for males, but a negative relationship exists for females. As it turns out, Graph D describes the results of several studies (cf. Freedman, Levy, Buchanan, & Price, 1972).

Researchers can address generalization issues that stem from the use of different subject populations by including subject type as a variable in the study. By including variables such as gender, age, or ethnic group in the design of the study, the results may be analyzed to determine whether there are interaction effects like the ones illustrated in Figure 11-1.

In defense of college students and rats

It is easy to criticize research on the basis of subject characteristics, yet simply because we can raise the criticism does not mean that the research is in fact flawed. Although we need to be concerned about the potential problems of generalizing from special populations such as college students (cf. Sears, 1986), there are two things to keep in mind when thinking about this issue. First, criticisms of the use of any particular type of subject, such as college students, in a study should be backed with good reasons why a relationship would not be found with other types of subjects. College students, after all, *are* human, and researchers should not be blamed for not worrying about generalization to a particular type of subject if there is no good reason to do so. Second, it should be remembered that replication of research studies provides a safeguard against limited generalizability. Studies are replicated at other colleges using different mixes of students, and many findings first established with college student subjects are later applied to other subject populations, such as children, aging adults, or hospital patients. Also, you might note that rats are in fact hardy and cheap, but the value of using rats as subjects has been demonstrated by research that applies findings to human problems (e.g., research on reinforcement using rats and pigeons has been applied to behavior modification, understanding personality, and studying choice behavior in humans).

GENERALIZING TO OTHER EXPERIMENTERS

The person who actually conducts the experiment is the source of another generalization problem. In most research, only one experimenter is used, and rarely is much attention paid to the personal characteristics of the experimenter (McGuigan, 1963). The main goal is to make sure that any influence the experimenter has on subjects is constant throughout the experiment. There is always the possibility, however, that the results are generalizable only to certain types of experimenters.

Some of the important characteristics of experimenters have been discussed by Kintz and his colleagues (1965). These include the experimenter's personality and gender and the amount of practice she or he has had as an experimenter. A friendly, warm experimenter will almost certainly produce different results from those of an unfriendly, cold experimenter. Subjects may behave differently with male and female experimenters. It has even been shown that rabbits learn faster when trained by experienced experimenters (Brogden, 1962)! The influence of the experimenter may also depend on the characteristics of the subjects. For example, subjects seem to perform better when tested by an experimenter of the opposite sex (Stevenson & Allen, 1964).

One solution to the problem of generalizing to other experimenters is to use two or more experimenters, preferably both male and female, to conduct the research. Ideally, several of each sex would be used. A fine example of the use of multiple experimenters is a study by Rubin (1975), who sent several male and female experimenters to the Boston airport to study self-disclosure. The experimenters revealed different kinds of information about themselves to passengers of both sexes and recorded the passengers' return disclosures.

PRETESTS AND GENERALIZATION

Researchers are often faced with the decision of whether to give a pretest. Intuitively, pretesting seems to be a good idea. The researcher can be sure that the groups are equivalent on the pretest, and it is often more satisfying to see that individuals changed their scores than it is to look only at group means on a posttest. Pretesting, however, may limit the ability to generalize to populations that did not receive a pretest. In the real world people are rarely pretested—attitudes are not measured prior to listening to a political speech or viewing an advertisement, for example (cf. Lana, 1969).

The major problem with pretests stems from demand characteristics, as discussed in Chapters 5 and 8. Pretests may sensitize subjects to the hypothesis being investigated and they may behave quite differently than they would if there had not been a pretest. If there is a reason to believe that this could be a problem in the study, the researcher might try to disguise the pretest. Sometimes researchers will directly examine whether pretests are a problem for their research by studying the effects of pretesting. Half the subjects are given the pretest; the other half receive the posttest only. The researcher can then examine whether there is an interaction between the independent variable and the pretest variable; that is, are posttest scores on the dependent variable different depending on whether the pretest was given? This procedure is sometimes referred to as a Solomon four group design (Solomon,

1949). If it is not feasible to do this in a single experiment, the study can be replicated without the pretest.

GENERALIZING FROM LABORATORY SETTINGS

Research conducted in a laboratory setting has the advantage of allowing the experimenter control over most extraneous variables. The question arises, however, whether the artificiality of the laboratory setting limits the ability to generalize what is observed in the laboratory to real-life settings. Field experiments, discussed in Chapter 3, represent one method of counteracting laboratory artificiality. In a field experiment, the researcher manipulates the independent variable in a natural setting—a factory, a school, or a street corner, for example.

Mundane and experimental realism

Aronson et al. (1985) point out that even field experiments can be contrived and artificial, having little real-world relevance. They propose a better distinction, termed **mundane realism** versus **experimental realism.** Mundane realism refers to whether the experiment bears similarity to events that occur in the real world. Experimental realism refers to whether the experiment has an impact on the subjects, involves them, and makes them take the experiment seriously. Aronson et al. point out that experimental and mundane realism are separate, independent dimensions. An experiment may have considerable mundane realism (thus be very similar to real life) but be totally boring and uninvolving and thus lacking experimental realism. Consider two examples.

Example 1. In a helping study, an experimenter drops some pencils outside a building on campus and waits to see whether anyone stops to help pick up the pencils. The dependent variable is the helping by observers of the "accident." This study would possess considerable mundane realism but little experimental realism.

Example 2. In another helping experiment, subjects are seated in individual cubicles that are interconnected via an intercom system. During the course of the study, the subject hears another (supposed) subject having an epileptic seizure and must decide whether or not to help the person (Darley & Latané, 1968). This study has relatively little mundane realism but a great deal of experimental realism.

Other experimental procedures, in both lab and field settings, may rate high on both mundane and experimental realism or low on both dimensions. The main point is that laboratory experiments are not automatically artificial; even when an experiment lacks mundane realism, it may be very realistic in terms of experimental realism.

182

Mutual benefits of lab and field research

Aronson et al. (1985) also point out that it is unwise to consider laboratory or field experiments in isolation. Conducting research in both laboratory and field settings provides the greatest opportunity for advancing our understanding of behavior. Recall the Langer and Rodin (1976) study on the effects of giving elderly nursing home residents greater control over decisions in their lives (see Chapter 3). This field experiment was part of a research tradition that includes laboratory studies of control over stressors using both animal and human subjects, the effects of stress in natural settings, and field experiments on the general effects of perceived control. Aronson et al. also point to research on the "jigsaw" technique to reduce conflict among different ethnic and racial groups in a school setting (Aronson, Stephan, Sikes, Blaney, & Snapp, 1978). In the "jigsaw" classroom, each student in a group learns a portion of a larger lesson. In order for all the students in the group to learn the lesson, they must work together cooperatively to teach each other the material. The effectiveness of the technique in reducing intergroup conflict has been demonstrated in both laboratory and field settings. These studies have also led to laboratory investigations of the exact processes that occur to produce the effect.

THE IMPORTANCE OF REPLICATIONS

Throughout this chapter, replication has been stressed as a way of overcoming any problems of generalization that occur in a single study. There are two types of replications to consider: exact replications and conceptual replications.

Exact replications

An **exact replication** is an attempt to replicate exactly the procedures of a study to see if the same results are obtained. A researcher who obtains an unexpected finding will frequently attempt a replication to make sure that the finding is reliable. If you are starting your own work on a problem, you may try to replicate a crucial study to make sure that you understand the procedures and can obtain the same results. Often, exact replications occur when a researcher builds on the findings of an earlier study. For example, suppose you were intrigued by the Tversky and Kahneman (1983) study on the judgments of probabilities of single and joint events. In your research, you might replicate the procedures used in the original study while expanding on the original research. For example, you might study whether people who have had a course in statistics or probability respond differently to the problems, what happens when a third joint event is added, or whether it makes a difference if the events could actually happen to the subjects. In all of these replication situations, confidence in the generalizability of the findings is

183

increased because they were obtained with different subjects and often in a different locale with different experimenters.

Sometimes a researcher will be unable to replicate a previous finding. A single failure to replicate doesn't reveal much, though; it is unrealistic to assume, on the basis of a single failure to replicate, that the previous research is invalid. Failures to replicate share the same problems as nonsignificant results, discussed in Chapter 9. A failure to replicate *could* mean that the original results are invalid, but it could also mean that the replication attempt was flawed. For example, if the replication is based on the procedure as reported in a journal article, it is possible the article omitted an important aspect of the procedure. For this reason, it is usually a good idea to write the researcher to obtain detailed information on all of the materials that were used in the study.

A single failure to replicate is not adequate cause for discarding the original research finding. Repeated failures, however, do lead to reconsideration of the original findings. Eventually, we may conclude that the original results were a fluke—a Type I error was made—which is especially likely when unsuccessful attempts to replicate employ not only the original procedures but different procedures as well.

Conceptual replications

The use of different procedures to replicate a research finding is called a **conceptual replication.** Conceptual replications are even more important than exact replications in furthering our understanding of behavior.

In most research, the goal is to discover whether there is a relationship between conceptual variables. Thus, Tversky and Kahneman (1983) were interested in the effects of single versus conjoint events on probability judgments; the specific method of operationalizing the variable was to have subjects make judgments about the probability of a flood versus the probability of an earthquake *and* a flood. Or consider the Petty et al. (1981) study of the effect of issue involvement on attitude change. Here involvement was manipulated by having subjects think either that a new graduation requirement would affect them or that it would instead only affect students who would graduate in ten years. The specific manipulations are operational definitions of the conceptual variables of interest. The same general point can be made about the operational definitions of dependent variables as well.

In a conceptual replication, the same independent variable is manipulated in a different way (and possibly the dependent variable is measured in a different way also). Such conceptual replications are extremely important in the social sciences because the specific manipulations and measures are usually operational definitions of complex variables. A crucial generalization question is whether the relationship holds when other ways of manipulating or measuring the variables are studied. Do different types of single and conjoint probability problems lead to the same result? Does issue involvement result in the same conclusion when it is manipulated in different ways?

When conceptual replications produce similar results, our confidence in the generalizability of relationships between variables is greatly increased.

This discussion should also alert you to an important way of thinking about research findings. The findings represent relationships between conceptual variables but are grounded in specific operations. You may read about the specific methods employed in a study conducted 20 years ago and question whether the study could be replicated today. Or the specific method may seem narrowly focused on one particular issue and setting (e.g., issue involvement manipulated by having college seniors think that a proposal to institute a comprehensive examination as a graduation requirement might affect them). These concerns are not as serious when placed within the context of conceptual replications. It is true that a specific method from a study conducted at one time might not be effective today, given changes in today's political and cultural climate. A conceptual replication of the manipulation, however, would demonstrate that the relationship between the conceptual theoretical variables is still present. Similarly, the narrow focus of a particular study is less problematic if the general finding is replicated with different procedures.

EVALUATING GENERALIZATIONS VIA LITERATURE REVIEWS AND META-ANALYSIS

Researchers have traditionally drawn conclusions about the generality of research findings by conducting literature reviews. In a literature review, a number of studies that address a particular topic are read and the reviewer organizes a paper summarizing findings that are strongly supported by the research (e.g., obtained across numerous conceptual replications), findings that are less strongly supported (e.g., reported by only a few researchers), and findings that are puzzling because of contradictory results (e.g., results obtained in some studies but not others). Literature reviews provide valuable information because they organize many studies on a topic and point to areas in which there are well-established findings and others in which more research needs to be done.

The conclusions in a traditional literature review are based on the subjective impressions of the reviewer. There is nothing wrong with this procedure, but another technique for comparing a large number of studies in an area has emerged in recent years. This technique is termed **meta-analysis** (Rosenthal, 1984). Meta-analysis is being used more and more by researchers as an alternative to the traditional literature review, and you are likely to see references to meta-analysis studies as you become more familiar with research in psychology.

In a meta-analysis, the researcher combines the actual results of a number of studies. The analysis consists of a set of statistical procedures that allows the researcher to estimate the strength of a given finding across many different studies. Instead of relying on subjective judgments obtained in a

185

traditional literature review, statistical conclusions can be drawn. The statistical procedures need not concern you; the main point to remember is that meta-analysis is a method for determining the reliability of a finding by examining the results from many different studies.

An example of a meta-analysis is a study by Smith and Glass (1977) on the effectiveness of psychotherapy techniques as reported in 375 studies. The researchers examined the reported effects of different modes of therapy (e.g., behavioral, psychodynamic, and client-centered therapies) across many different studies that used several different outcome measures (e.g., anxiety reduction, self-esteem). They then applied appropriate statistical techniques to be able to combine and compare the different results. Their research allowed them to conclude that therapy does have a beneficial effect. In fact, they concluded that the "typical therapy client is better off than 75% of untreated controls."

They were also able to make general statements that applied to different types of therapies. For example, some therapies, such as systematic desensitization, produce very large changes in behavior compared to others; however, overall there was no difference between the "behavioral" types of therapies and the "traditional" ones. The information obtained from a meta-analysis such as the one conducted by Smith and Glass is very informative. In a traditional literature review, it would be very difficult to provide the type of general conclusion that was reached with the meta-analysis. Anyone would find it difficult to easily integrate the results of so many studies with different experimental designs, subject types, and measures. In fact, if you read all the studies and someone asked you the simple question "Does psychotherapy work?" you might proceed to spend a day telling the person about all the specific studies and the complexities you noted in reading the literature. This would be the result of information overload and the fact that it is difficult to integrate information from diverse sources.

An interesting study by Cooper and Rosenthal (1980) actually demonstrated that researchers are more likely to draw strong conclusions about a set of findings when using meta-analysis than when using traditional subjective judgments. In this study, researchers read only seven articles on gender differences in task persistence; still, the researchers who used meta-analysis were more likely to conclude that females do show greater task persistence than do males. Beaman (1991) has also favorably compared meta-analysis with traditional reviews. It is interesting to note as well that meta-analyses are also able to show that some findings are less robust than we previously thought them to be—for example, the physical attractiveness stereotype that "what is beautiful is good" (Eagly, Ashmore, Makhijani, & Longo, 1991).

GIVING PSYCHOLOGY AWAY

In a presidential address to the American Psychological Association, George Miller (1969) discussed the topic of "psychology as a means of promoting human welfare." He spoke of "giving psychology away." Miller was addressing the broadest issue of generalizability, taking what we know about human behavior and allowing it to be applied by many people in all areas of everyday life. Perhaps the strongest evidence for the generalizability of research findings is to view what has happened to psychology in the years since Miller urged us to give psychology away. The impact of psychological research can be seen in the fields of health (programs to reduce stress and promote health-related behaviors), the environment (designing work spaces that promote worker satisfaction and productivity; providing energy companies with ways of encouraging conservation), law (providing data on the effects of 6- versus 12-person juries; showing how the testimony of eyewitnesses can be biased), and education (providing methods for encouraging academic performance or reducing conflict among different ethnic groups). These are only a few of the ways that basic research has been applied to help promote human welfare. Despite all the potential problems of generalizing research findings that were highlighted in this chapter, the evidence suggests that we can generalize our findings to many aspects of our lives.

STUDY QUESTIONS

1. Why should a researcher be concerned about generalizing to other subject populations? What are some of the subject population generalization problems that a researcher might confront?
2. What is the source of the problem of generalizing to other experimenters? How can this problem be solved?
3. Why is pretesting a problem for generalization?
4. Distinguish between mundane and experimental realism.
5. Distinguish between an exact replication and a conceptual replication. What is the value of a conceptual replication?
6. What is a meta-analysis? Find a meta-analysis published in *Psychological Bulletin*; what conclusions were drawn from the meta-analysis?

ACTIVITY QUESTION

A researcher reports that there is an interaction between extraversion-introversion and memory for different types of faces: Extraverts remember smiling faces better than faces with neutral expressions, while introverts remember both types of faces equally well. Why does this interaction relate to the issue of generalization?

12

Ethical Concerns

At numerous points throughout this book, ethical concerns and their impact on research have been mentioned. In this chapter, we will explore in detail the nature of ethical problems that arise in research, and we will examine some guidelines for dealing with these problems.

MILGRAM'S OBEDIENCE EXPERIMENT

Stanley Milgram conducted a series of experiments (1963, 1964, 1965) to study the phenomenon of blind obedience to an authority figure. He placed an ad in the local newspaper in New Haven, Connecticut, offering to pay $4.50 to men to participate in a "scientific study of memory and learning" being conducted at Yale University. Men who read the ad and wished to take part in the experiment reported to Milgram's laboratory at Yale, where they met a scientist dressed in a lab coat and another subject—a middle-aged man named Mr. Wallace. Mr. Wallace was a confederate of the experimenter, but the subject didn't know this. The scientist explained that the study would examine the effects of punishment on learning. One subject would be the "teacher" who would administer the punishment, and the other subject would be the "learner." Mr. Wallace and the subject then drew slips of paper to determine who would be the teacher and who would be the learner. The drawing was rigged, and the true subject was always the teacher.

The scientist attached electrodes to Mr. Wallace and placed the real subject in front of an impressive-looking shock machine. The shock machine had a series of levers that the subject was told would deliver shocks to Mr. Wallace when pressed. The first lever was labeled 15 volts, the second, 30 volts, the third, 45 volts, and so on up to 450 volts. The levers were also labeled "Slight Shock," "Moderate Shock," and so on up to "Danger: Severe Shock," followed by red X's above 400 volts.

Mr. Wallace was instructed to learn a series of word pairs. Then he was given a test to see if he could identify which words went together. Every time Mr. Wallace made a mistake, the teacher was to deliver a shock as punishment. The first mistake was supposed to be answered by a 15-volt shock, the second by a 30-volt shock, and so on. Each time a mistake was made, the learner received a greater shock. The learner, Mr. Wallace, never actually received any shock, but the real subject didn't know that. In the experiment, Mr. Wallace made mistake after mistake. When the teacher shocked him about 120 volts, Mr. Wallace began screaming in pain and eventually yelled that he wanted out. What if the teacher wanted to quit? This happened—the real subjects became visibly upset by the pain that Mr. Wallace was experiencing. The scientist told the teacher that he could quit but urged him to continue, using a series of prods that stressed the importance of continuing the experiment.

Milgram's study purported to be an experiment on memory and learning, but he was really interested in learning whether subjects would continue to obey the experimenter by administering higher and higher levels of shock to the learner. What happened? Approximately 65 percent of the subjects continued to deliver shock all the way to 450 volts. Milgram's study received a great deal of publicity, and the results challenged many of our views of our ability to resist authority. Such results have implications for real situations, such as Nazi Germany, the My Lai massacre in Vietnam, and the Jonestown mass suicide (see Miller, 1986). But what about the ethics of the Milgram study? What aspects of the experimental procedure might we find objectionable?

STRESS AND PSYCHOLOGICAL HARM

The first problem concerns the stress that subjects experienced while delivering intense shocks to an obviously unwilling learner. A film that Milgram made shows subjects protesting, sweating, and even laughing nervously while delivering the shocks. You might ask whether subjecting people to such a stressful experiment is justified, and you might wonder whether the experience had any long-range consequences. For example, did subjects who obeyed the experimenter feel continuing remorse or begin to see themselves as cruel, inhumane people? A defense of Milgram's study follows, but first let's consider some potentially stressful research procedures.

Milgram's study required the subject to deliver electric shock to someone else, but in some experiments, the subject might be on the receiving end of a shock machine. Such a procedure would involve actual physical stress, and, of course, great care would have to be taken to make it ethically acceptable.

More common than physical stress is psychological stress. For example, a subject might be told he or she will receive some extreme-intensity electric shocks. The subject never actually receives the shock—it is the fear or anxiety during the waiting period that is the variable of interest. Research by Schachter employing a procedure like this showed that the anxiety produced a desire to affiliate with others during the waiting period (Schachter, 1959).

In another procedure that produces psychological stress, subjects are given unfavorable feedback about their personalities or abilities. Researchers interested in self-esteem have typically given a subject a personality test, followed by an evaluation that lowers or raises the subject's self-esteem. One study went even further. After raising or lowering a male subject's self-esteem, the researcher then gave the subject evidence that he had possible homosexual tendencies (Bramel, 1962).

You can see by now that some procedures used in research involve physical or psychological stress. Whether such research should be conducted is a difficult question that we'll grapple with a little later.

DECEPTION AND THE PRINCIPLE OF INFORMED CONSENT

The Milgram experiment also illustrates the use of deception. Subjects in the Milgram experiment agreed to participate in a study of memory and learning, but they actually took part in a study on obedience. Who would imagine that a memory and learning experiment (that title does sound tame, after all) would involve delivering high-intensity, painful shock to another person? Subjects in the Milgram experiment didn't know what they were letting themselves in for. The procedure lacked what is called **informed consent.** Informed consent means that the subject is given an accurate perception of the risks involved before he or she consents to participate in the experiment.

The problem of deception is not limited to laboratory research; procedures in which observers conceal their purposes, presence, or identity are also deceptive. For example, Humphreys (1970) studied the behavior of male homosexuals who frequent public restrooms (called "tearooms"). Humphreys did not participate in any homosexual activities, but he served as a lookout who would warn the others of possible intruders. In addition to observing the activities in the tearoom, Humphreys wrote down license plate numbers. Later, he obtained the addresses of the men, disguised himself, and visited their homes to interview them. Humphreys' procedure is certainly one way of finding out about homosexuality, but it employs considerable deception.

Herbert Kelman (1967) noted several problems with the use of deception. First, deception is unethical. Kelman wrote:

> In our other interhuman relationships, most of us would never think of doing the kinds of things that we do to our subjects—exposing others to lies and tricks, deliberately misleading them about the purposes of the interaction or withholding pertinent information, making promises or giving assurances that we intend to disregard. We would view such behavior as a violation of the respect to which all fellow humans are entitled and of the whole basis of our relationship with them. Yet we seem to forget that the experimenter-subject relationship . . . is a real interhuman relationship, in which we have responsibility toward the subject as another human being whose dignity we must preserve.[1]

A second problem noted by Kelman is that deception may fail to achieve its intended goals. The primary justification for deceiving subjects is that knowledge of the purpose of an experiment would contaminate the results. If the subject is unaware of the real purpose, he or she will behave more naturally. Kelman feels, however, that subjects are aware of psychologists' tricks and that they come to experimental situations expecting to be lied to. Thus, they take nothing the researcher says at face value. Instead, subjects simply respond to the demand characteristics present in the situation. This may be an extreme statement of the problem, but it is a possibility to be concerned about.

---

1. From Kelman, H. C. (1967). Human use of human subjects: The problem of deception in social psychological experiments. *Psychological Bulletin, 67,* 1–11. Copyright 1967 by the American Psychological Association. Reprinted by permission.

Another problem with deception has been noted by Rubin (1970) and by Ring (1967). These authors point not only to the possible harmful effects of deception but also to the motivation of some researchers who use deception. Rubin refers to "jokers wild in the lab," and Ring talks about a "fun and games" approach to research. The official justification for deception is that it is a way to make sure that the subjects behave naturally and spontaneously, so that researchers get a better picture of real behavior. This justification is based on scientific grounds and so has some merit. Observers such as Rubin and Ring note, however, that some researchers are motivated by the desire to devise clever and elaborate experimental manipulations that are sure to capture the attention of others. Ring (1967) states that "there is a distinctly exhibitionist flavor to much current experimentation, while the experimenters often seem to equate notoriety with achievement."

Rubin (1970) describes the following research procedure: The subject sits behind a large machine and is shown how to operate it by pushing the proper buttons. He is then told, "All my research money is tied up in this contraption and I'll never get my master's degree if it doesn't function properly." However, there is an explosion and the machine begins to erupt with smoke. The experimenter now says, "I'll never get my master's now . . . . (choke) . . . What did you do to the machine? . . . (sob) . . . Well, I guess that ends the experiment . . . . (long pause and then, solemnly) . . . The machine is broken."[2] The The real purpose of the experiment is to see if this experience will increase the likelihood that the subject will sign a petition being circulated by the experimenter (it does). The description of this little drama staged by the experimenter makes for amusing reading, but how amused was the subject? Deception perpetrated solely for the amusement of others or to make yourself known must certainly be termed unethical behavior.

It was previously stated that the use of deception deprives the subject of informed consent—of the right to all information that might influence a decision to participate in a research project. If the subjects in Milgram's experiment had participated only after giving informed consent, they would first have been told that obedience was being studied and that they would be required to inflict painful shocks on another person. Informed consent is intended to eliminate the problem of deception, or at least to diminish it.

Obviously, informed consent is not a completely satisfactory solution to the deception problem. First, knowledge that the research is designed to study obedience is bound to alter the subjects' behavior. Few of us like to think of ourselves as obedient, and we would probably go out of our way to prove that we are not obedient. In this situation, even limited informed consent would distort the results obtained. Research indicates that the procedure of providing informed consent may in fact bias subjects' responses. For example, research on stressors such as noise or crowding has shown that a feeling of

---

2. From Rubin, Z. (1970, December). Jokers wild in the lab. *Psychology Today*, pp. 18ff. Copyright © 1970 by Ziff-Davis Publishing Company. All rights reserved.

"control" over a stressor reduces its negative impact. If you know that you can terminate a loud, obnoxious noise, the noise produces less stress than when the noise is uncontrollable. Studies by Gardner (1978) and Dill, Gilden, Hill, and Hanslka (1982) have demonstrated that informed consent procedures do increase perceptions of control in stress experiments and therefore can affect the conclusions drawn from the research.

A final problem with informed consent is that it may bias the subject sample. In Milgram's experiment, it is possible that if subjects had prior knowledge that they would be asked to give severe shocks to the other person, certain subjects would not agree to be in the experiment. Therefore, we might limit our ability to generalize the results only to those "types" who agreed to participate. If this were true, anyone could say that the obedient behavior seen in the Milgram experiment occurred simply because the subjects were sadists in the first place.

DEBRIEFING

The traditional solution to the problem of deception is to thoroughly debrief subjects after the experiment. Debriefing has become a standard part of experimental procedure, even when there is no stress and virtually no possibility of harm to subjects. Researchers feel that participation should be an educational experience, so they communicate their ideas about human behavior to the subjects. Is debriefing sufficient to remove any negative effects when stress and elaborate deception are involved? Let's turn again to Milgram's research.

Milgram went to great lengths to provide a thorough debriefing session. Subjects who were obedient were told that their behavior was normal in that they had acted no differently from most other subjects. They were made aware of the strong situational pressure that was exerted on them, and efforts were made to reduce any tension they felt. Subjects were assured that no shock was actually delivered, and there was a friendly reconciliation with the confederate, Mr. Wallace. Milgram also mailed a report of his research findings to his subjects and at the same time asked about their reactions to the experiment. The responses showed that 84 percent were glad that they had participated, and 74 percent said they had benefitted from the experience. Only 1 percent said they were sorry they had participated. When subjects were interviewed by a psychiatrist a year later, no ill effects of participation could be detected. We can only conclude that debriefing did have its intended effect. Other researchers who have conducted further work on the ethics of Milgram's study reached the same conclusion (Ring, Wallston, & Corey, 1970).

Other research on debriefing has also concluded that debriefing is effective as a way of dealing with deception in experiments (Smith, 1983; Smith & Richardson, 1983). However, deception remains a controversial issue (see

193

Rubin, 1985; Smith & Richardson, 1985). You may be wondering, then, whether there are alternatives to deception.

ALTERNATIVES TO DECEPTION

After criticizing the use of deception in research, Kelman (1967) called for the development of alternative procedures. One procedure Kelman suggests is role-playing.

Role-playing

In one role-playing procedure, the experimenter describes a situation to subjects and then asks them how they would respond. Sometimes subjects are asked to say how they themselves would behave in the situation; sometimes they are asked to predict how real participants in such a situation would behave. It isn't clear whether these two instructions produce any differences in results.

Role-playing is not generally considered to be a satisfactory alternative to deception (Freedman, 1969; Miller, 1972). One problem is that simply reading a description of a situation does not involve the subjects very deeply—they are not part of a real situation. Also, role-playing procedures seem particularly vulnerable to the problem of demand characteristics. Because the experimenter gives the subjects a complete description of the situation, the experimenter's hypothesis may be obvious to the subjects.

The most serious defect of role-playing is that, no matter what results are obtained, a critic can always say that the results would have been different if the subjects had been in a real situation. This criticism is based on the assumption that people aren't always able to accurately predict their own behavior or the behavior of others. This would be particularly true when undesirable behavior—such as conformity, obedience, or aggression—is involved. For example, if Milgram had used a role-playing procedure, how many people do you think would have predicted that they would be completely obedient? Milgram asked a group of psychiatrists to predict the results of his study and found that even these experts could not accurately anticipate what would happen. A similar problem would arise if people were asked to predict whether they would help someone in need. Most of us would probably overestimate our altruistic tendencies.

One potential use of role-playing may be to gather evidence about subjects' perceptions of a possible experiment. If the role-playing subjects indicate that they would participate in the experiment, at least one objection to deception has been addressed (cf. Berscheid, Baron, Dermer, & Libman, 1973).

Simulation studies

A different type of role-playing involves simulation of a real-world situation. A simulation study that impressed Kelman (1967) is the Inter-Nation Simulation in which subjects role-play being leaders of nations and the researchers observe processes of negotiation, problem solving, and so on. Such simulations can create high degrees of involvement, as anyone who has played an all-night game of Monopoly will appreciate.

Even with simulations, there may be ethical problems. A dramatic example is the Stanford Prison Experiment conducted by Zimbardo (1973). Zimbardo set up a simulated prison in the basement of the psychology building at Stanford University. He then recruited college students who were paid $15 per day to play the role of either a prisoner or guard for a period of two weeks. Guards were outfitted in uniforms and given sunglasses and clubs. Prisoners were assigned numbers and wore nylon stocking caps to simulate prison haircuts and reduce feelings of individuality. The subjects became deeply involved in their roles, so much so that Zimbardo had to stop the simulation after six days because of the cruel behavior of the "guards" and the stressful reactions of the "prisoners." This was only a simulation—subjects knew that they were not really prisoners or guards—yet they became so involved in their roles that the experiment produced levels of stress that were higher than almost any other experiment one can imagine. Fortunately, the Zimbardo experiment is an unusual case—most simulation studies do not raise the ethical issues seen in this particular study.

Honest experiments

Rubin (1973) described what he called "honest" experimental strategies, none of which involve role-playing. The first strategy is one in which the subjects are made completely aware of the purposes of the research. In a study by Byrne, Ervin, and Lamberth (1970), the researchers told subjects that they were interested in the effectiveness of computer dating. They used a computer program to match male and female students who held either similar or dissimilar attitudes. Each couple had a brief date on campus, and then the researchers measured how much the members of each couple liked one another. Couples who were similar were more attracted to each other than couples who were dissimilar. The study involved no deception nor misrepresentation of the purposes of the research.

A second honest strategy is used in situations in which there are explicit programs to change people's behavior. Examples cited by Rubin include educational programs, health appeals, charity drives, political campaigns, and solicitations for volunteers. In such situations, people are aware that someone is trying to change their behavior. For instance, people may voluntarily expose themselves to an appeal to quit smoking. Researchers can then investigate the effectiveness of such an appeal while manipulating variables such as the amount of fear aroused (Leventhal, 1970).

Rubin also stated that many field experiments involve honest procedures. Recall from Chapter 3 that field experiments introduce the experimental manipulation in a natural context. Rubin cites a study in which an experimenter stared at drivers of cars while they were waiting for a red light to change

195

(Ellsworth, Carlsmith, & Henson, 1972). These drivers crossed the intersection faster than did drivers in a control condition in which there was no staring experimenter. This particular experiment does not seem particularly unethical—we have all experienced being stared at. The researchers merely applied experimental methods in order to systematically study this situation. Much research in field settings is indeed honest. Researchers are observing the behavior of people in public places and everyday situations. However, just because an experiment is conducted in the field does not mean that there are no ethical issues. For example, what are the ethical (and legal) implications of taking the time of auto salespersons while posing as a customer in order to study different types of price offers, or exposing subway passengers to a person who collapses between stations (cf. Silverman, 1975)?

The last honest strategy discussed by Rubin involves situations in which a naturally occurring event presents an opportunity for research: "Nature, fate, government, and other unalterable forces often impose their will on people in random or nonsystematic ways." For example, researchers were able to study the effects of crowding when a shortage of student housing forced Rutgers University to assign entering students randomly to crowded and uncrowded dormitory rooms (Aiello, Baum, & Gormley, 1981). Baum, Gachtel, and Schaeffer (1983) studied the stressful effects of living near the Three Mile Island nuclear plant disaster by comparing people who lived near Three Mile Island with others who lived near an undamaged nuclear plant or a conventional coal-fired power plant. Such natural experiments occur frequently enough so that they are worthwhile sources of data.

Is deception still a problem?

It is obvious that psychologists have thought a great deal about the problems of deception since Milgram did his experiments in the 1960s. A reasonable question to ask is whether deception is still a problem in research, and the answer isn't easy. Deception has never been a major problem in many areas of experimental psychology, such as human perception, learning, memory, and motor performance. Even in these areas, however, the experimenter rarely tells subjects everything that will happen in the experiment, or researchers may use a cover story to make the experiment seem plausible and involving (e.g., telling subjects that they are reading actual newspaper stories for a study on readability when the true purpose is to examine memory errors or organizational schemes).

Traditionally, deception has been more problematic in social psychology and research on motivation and emotion. In these areas, researchers have used complex event manipulations designed to produce various emotions and other psychological states, or to simulate events such as an emergency in which someone needs help. Thus, machines break down to produce guilt, false feedback is given on a personality test, or a bookcase falls on a person in the next room. Gross and Fleming (1982) studied 691 social psychological studies published in the 1960s and 1970s. Although most research in the

1970s still used deception, the deception primarily involved false cover stories. There were many fewer questionable deceptions in which blatant lies were told or subjects were exposed to stressful events.

The impression one gets from reviewing current studies is that the trend noticed by Gross and Fleming has continued. In one recent issue of the *Journal of Personality and Social Psychology* (August 1991), 7 of 13 studies used judgment tasks or personality questionnaires to study behavior. In other studies, subjects interacted in a group decision-making task (two studies), were tested using hypnosis procedures (two studies), used a computer to simulate management of a business organization (one study), and were videotaped having conversations for later analysis of nonverbal behavior (one study). As you might expect, many of these studies did have false cover stories. Also, some included mild forms of deception—in a group discussion, for example, a confederate either agreed or disagreed with the rest of the group.

Thus, the answer to our original question is that there seem to be fewer problematic instances of deception in psychological research. There are three primary reasons for this change. First, more researchers have become interested in cognitive variables rather than emotions and so use methods that are similar to those used by researchers in memory and cognitive psychology. Second, the general level of awareness of ethical issues as described in this chapter has led researchers to study problems in other ways. Third, there is now greater review of proposed research by ethics committees at universities and colleges (ethics review boards are described in a later section).

OTHER ETHICAL ISSUES IN RESEARCH

Stress and deception are the two major sources of ethical concern in research. Several other ethical issues must be considered, however.

Privacy and confidentiality

Researchers must take care to protect the privacy of individuals. When studying topics such as sexual behavior, divorce, family violence, or drug abuse, researchers may sometimes need to ask subjects sensitive questions about their private lives. It is extremely important to make sure that responses to such questions are anonymous and confidential. The researcher may need to carefully plan ways of coding questionnaires and explaining the procedures to subjects so that there is no question concerning the anonymity of responses. The privacy of questionnaire responses is rarely an issue in psychological research.

A more problematic privacy issue concerns concealed observation of behavior. At several points in the book, observations of behavior in public places have been described. Observing people in shopping malls or in their cars at street corners does not seem to present any major ethical problems. But what if a researcher wishes to observe behavior in more private settings or in ways

197

in which an individual could not be reasonably expected to be observed (see Wilson & Donnerstein, 1976). For example, would it be ethical to examine a person's trash or watch people in restrooms? Middlemist, Knowles, and Matter (1976) measured length to onset of urination and duration of urination of males in restrooms at a college. The purpose of the research was to study the effect of personal space on a measure of physiological arousal (urination times). Subjects were observed while alone or with a confederate of the experimenter, who stood at the next stall or a more distant stall in the restroom. The presence and closeness of the confederate did have the effect of delaying urination and shortening the duration of urination. In many ways, this is an interesting study; also, the situation is one that males experience on a regular basis in their lives. However, one can question whether the invasion of privacy was justified (Koocher, 1977). The researchers can, in turn, argue that through pilot studies and talking to subjects they determined that ethical problems with the study were minimal (Middlemist et al., 1977). There are no easy answers to ethical dilemmas posed by some psychological research.

Special subject populations

Another ethical issue concerns the degree of voluntary subject participation. Most of us believe that college students are able to make free choices about whether to participate as a research subject or whether to walk out of research they consider unethical. But what about special subject populations such as children, mental patients, or prisoners? It seems clear that researchers must take special precautions when dealing with groups such as these. The Division of Developmental Psychology of the American Psychological Association and the Society for Research on Child Development have written their own guidelines for ethical research with child subjects.

Withholding beneficial treatments

Another issue arises when a researcher wishes to study the effect of a treatment that may benefit subjects. The issue in this situation is whether it is ethical to compare a group that receives the treatment with a control group that does not. To realize this problem, consider whether a researcher could ethically study the effect of a drug that very possibly could help AIDS patients. If the experimental drug is in short supply, it might be possible to randomly assign people to groups—an experimental treatment group and a waiting list control group. Otherwise, the researcher would need to use a quasi-experimental design to try to determine if the drug is effective (e.g., by comparing medical records of persons treated before the new drug was discovered with the records of current patients who all receive the drug). A similar issue arises when comparing the effectiveness of psychological therapies or training programs dealing with stress management or assertiveness. Again, a waiting list control group may be possible if all who want the program cannot receive it immediately.

Experimenters' obligations

Researchers make several implicit "contracts" with subjects during the course of a study. For example, if subjects agree to be present for a study at a specific time, the researcher should be there. The issue of punctuality is never mentioned by researchers, yet subjects mention it when asked about the obligations of the researcher (Epstein, Suedfeld, & Silverstein, 1973). Researchers may promise to send a summary of the results to subjects; if they do, the summary should be sent. If subjects are to receive course credit for participation, the researcher must immediately let the instructor know that the person took part in the study. These are "little details," but they are very important in maintaining trust between subjects and researchers.

FORMULATION OF ETHICAL PRINCIPLES

Psychologists recognize the ethical issues we have discussed, and the American Psychological Association (APA) has provided leadership in formulating ethical principles and guidelines. The Ethical Principles of Psychologists (American Psychological Association, 1990) and Ethical Principles in the Conduct of Research with Human Participants (American Psychological Association, 1982) are the primary sources. The first paragraph of the preamble to the Ethical Principles of Psychologists states:

> Psychologists respect the dignity and worth of the individual and strive for the preservation and protection of fundamental human rights. They are committed to increasing knowledge of human behavior and of people's understanding of themselves and others and to the utilization of such knowledge for the promotion of human welfare. While pursuing these objectives, they make every effort to protect the welfare of those who seek their services and of the research participants that may be the object of study. They use their skills only for purposes consistent with these values and do not knowingly permit their misuse by others. While demanding for themselves freedom of inquiry and communication, psychologists accept the responsibility this freedom requires: competence, objectivity in the application of skills, and concern for the best interests of clients, colleagues, students, research participants, and society. In the pursuit of these ideals, psychologists subscribe to principles in the following areas: 1. Responsibility, 2. Competence, 3. Moral and Legal Standards, 4. Public Statements, 5. Confidentiality, 6. Welfare of the Consumer, 7. Professional Relationships, 8. Assessment Techniques, 9. Research with Human Participants, and 10. Care and Use of Animals.

Thus, the principles address a variety of issues relating to general professional responsibility, clinical practice, and psychological assessment as well as research with both humans and animals. Of the 10 principles, we will be primarily concerned with the last two, which deal with the ethics of research.

199

RESEARCH WITH HUMAN PARTICIPANTS

The following is the complete text of principle 9, "Research with Human Participants":

The decision to undertake research rests upon a considered judgment by the individual psychologist about how best to contribute to psychological science and human welfare. Having made the decision to conduct research, the psychologist considers alternative directions in which research energies and resources might be invested. On the basis of this consideration, the psychologist carries out the investigation with respect and concern for the dignity and welfare of the people who participate and with cognizance of federal and state regulations and professional standards governing the conduct of research with human participants.

a. In planning a study, the investigator has the responsibility to make a careful evaluation of its ethical acceptability. To the extent that the weighing of scientific and human values suggests a compromise of any principle, the investigator incurs a correspondingly serious obligation to seek ethical advice and to observe stringent safeguards to protect the rights of human participants.

b. Considering whether a participant in a planned study will be a "subject at risk" or a "subject at minimal risk," according to recognized standards, is of primary ethical concern to the investigator.

c. The investigator always retains the responsibility for ensuring ethical practice in research. The investigator is also responsible for the ethical treatment of research participants by collaborators, assistants, students, and employees, all of whom, however, incur similar obligations.

d. Except in minimal-risk research, the investigator establishes a clear and fair agreement with research participants, prior to their participation, that clarifies the obligations and responsibilities of each. The investigator has the obligation to honor all promises and commitments included in that agreement. The investigator informs the participants of all aspects of the research that might reasonably be expected to influence willingness to participate and explains all other aspects of the research about which the participants inquire. Failure to make full disclosure prior to obtaining informed consent requires additional safeguards to protect the welfare and dignity of the research participants. Research with children or with participants who have impairments that would limit understanding and or communication requires special safeguarding procedures.

e. Methodological requirements of a study may make the use of concealment or deception necessary. Before conducting such a study, the investigator has a special responsibility to (i) determine whether the use of such techniques is justified by the study's prospective scientific, educational, or applied value; (ii) determine whether alternative procedures are available that do not use concealment or deception; and (iii) ensure that the participants are provided with sufficient explanation as soon as possible.

f. The investigator respects the individual's freedom to decline to participate in or to withdraw from the research at any time. The obligation to protect this freedom requires careful thought and consideration when the investigator is in a position of authority or influence over the participant. Such positions of authority include, but are not limited to, situations in which research participation is required as part of employment or in which the participant is a student, client, or employee of the investigator.

g. The investigator protects the participant from physical and mental discomfort, harm, and danger that may arise from research procedures. If risks of such consequences exist, the investigator informs the participant of that fact. Research procedures likely to cause serious or lasting harm to a participant are not used unless the failure to use these procedures might expose the participant to risk of greater harm, or unless the research has great potential benefit and fully informed and voluntary consent is obtained from each participant. The participant should be informed of procedures for contacting the investigator within a reasonable time period following participation should stress, potential harm, or related questions or concerns arise.

h. After the data are collected, the investigator provides the participant with information about the nature of the study and attempts to remove any misconceptions that may have arisen. Where scientific or humane values justify delaying or withholding this information, the investigator incurs a special responsibility to monitor the research and to ensure that there are no damaging consequences for the participant.

i. Where research procedures result in undesirable consequences for the individual participant, the investigator has the responsibility to detect and remove or correct these consequences, including long-term effects.

j. Information obtained about a research participant during the course of an investigation is confidential unless otherwise agreed upon in advance. When the possibility exists that others may obtain access to such information, this possibility, together with the plans for protecting confidentiality, is explained to the participant as part of the procedure for obtaining informed consent.

These principles stress the importance of informed consent as a fundamental part of ethical practice. However, fully informed consent may not always be possible, and deception may sometimes be necessary. In such cases, the researcher's responsibilities to the subject are increased. Obviously, decisions as to what should be considered ethical or unethical are not simple; there are no magic rules. Each piece of research has to be evaluated in terms of whether there are any ethical problems with the procedure, whether more ethical alternative procedures are available, and whether the importance of the study is such that the ethical problems are justified.

The principles also refer to "subject at risk" and "minimal risk." These terms are part of the federal Department of Health and Human Services (HHS) regulations for the protection of human research subjects (Department of Health and Human Services, 1981). Under these regulations, every institution that receives funds from the HHS must have an Institutional Review Board (IRB) that decides whether proposed research may be conducted. The IRB is composed of both scientists and nonscientists, members of the community, and legal specialists. The 1981 HHS regulations attempted to categorize research according to the amount of risk imposed on the subject. The rationale for doing this was that older regulations required the same type of review of a relatively harmless project and one that might involve physical or psychological harm (cf. Gergen, 1973).

The new regulations facilitate the ethical review of research by categorizing research in terms of the degree to which the subject is "at risk." Research in which there is no risk is exempt from review. The following are currently considered exempt research activities:

1. Research conducted in established or commonly accepted educational settings and involving normal educational practices, such as research on instructional strategies and the effectiveness of instructional techniques, curricula, or classroom management methods.

2. Research involving the use of educational tests (cognitive, diagnostic, aptitude, achievement), if subjects cannot be identified.

3. Research involving survey or interview procedures, except where all of the following conditions exist: (a) Responses are recorded in such a manner that the human subjects can be identified; (b) the subject's responses, if they become known outside the research, could reasonably place the subject at risk of criminal or civil liability or be damaging to the subject's financial standing or employability; and (c) the research deals with sensitive aspects of the subject's own behavior, such as illegal conduct, sexual behavior, or use of alcohol or drugs. All research involving survey or interview procedures is exempt, without exception, when the respondents are elected or appointed public officials or candidates for public office.

4. Research involving the observation of public behavior (including observation by participants), except where all the conditions identified in item 3 exist.

5. Research involving the collection or study of existing data, documents, records, pathological specimens, or diagnostic specimens if these sources are publicly available or if the information is recorded by the investigator in such a manner that subjects cannot be identified.

A second type of research activity is called "minimal risk." Minimal risk means that the risks of harm to subjects are no greater than risks encountered in daily life or in routine physical or psychological tests. When minimal-risk research is being conducted, there is less concern for elaborate safeguards and approval by the IRB is routine. Some of the research activities considered minimal risk are:

1. Recordings of data from subjects 18 years of age or older using noninvasive procedures routinely employed in clinical practice. This includes the use of physical sensors that are applied to the surface of the body or used at a distance and do not involve input of matter or significant amounts of energy into the subject or an invasion of the subject's privacy. It also includes such procedures as weighing, testing sensory acuity, electrocardiography, electroencephalography, radioactivity, diagnostic echography, and electroretinography. It does not include the exposure to electromagnetic radiation outside the visible range (e.g., x-rays, microwaves).

2. Voice recordings made for research purposes, such as investigations of speech defects.

3. Moderate exercise by healthy volunteers.

4. Research on individual or group behavior or characteristics of individuals, such as studies of perception, cognition, game theory, or test development, where the research investigator does not manipulate subjects' behavior and the research will not involve stress to subjects.

5. Collection of blood samples by venipuncture, in amounts not exceeding 450 milliliters in an eight-week period and no more often than two times per week from subjects 18 years of age or older who are in good health and not pregnant.

6. Research on drugs or devices for which an investigational new drug exemption or an investigational device exemption is not required.

Any research procedure that places the subject at greater than minimal risk is subject to thorough review by the IRB, and complete informed consent and other safeguards may be required before approval is granted.

We can conclude that, with the ethical principles of the American Psychological Association, the HHS regulations, and the review of research by the Institutional Review Board, the rights and safety of human subjects are well protected. We might note at this point that researchers and review board members tend to be very cautious in terms of what is considered ethical. In fact, several studies have shown that students who serve as subjects are more lenient in their judgments of the ethics of experiments than are researchers or IRB members (Epstein et al., 1973; Smith, 1983; Sullivan & Deiker, 1973). For example, subjects feel that deception is an acceptable part of experimentation.

ETHICS AND ANIMAL RESEARCH

Although this chapter has been concerned with the ethics of research with humans, you are well aware of the fact that psychologists sometimes conduct research with animal subjects. About 7 percent of the articles in *Psychological Abstracts* in 1979 used animal subjects (Gallup & Suarez, 1985). Animals are used for a variety of reasons. The researcher can carefully control the

203

environmental conditions of the animals, study the same animals for a long period of time, and monitor their behavior 24 hours a day if necessary. Animals are also used to test the effects of drugs and to study physiological and genetic mechanisms underlying behavior. Most commonly, psychologists work with rats and mice and, to a lesser extent, birds; according to one survey of animal research in psychology, over 95 percent of the animals in research were rats, mice, and birds (see Gallup & Suarez, 1985).

In recent years, groups opposed to animal research in medicine, psychology, biology, and other sciences have become more vocal and militant. For example, animal rights groups have staged protests at conventions of the American Psychological Association, and animal research laboratories in numerous cities have had animals stolen by members of these groups. The groups are also lobbying for legislation to prohibit all animal research.

Scientists argue that animal research benefits humans and point to many discoveries that would not have been possible without animal research (Miller, 1985). Also, it has been pointed out that animal rights groups have exaggerated the amount of research that involves any pain or suffering (Coile & Miller, 1984). Most important, there are strict laws and ethical guidelines that govern research with animals as well as teaching procedures in which animals are used. Such regulations deal with the need for proper housing, feeding, cleanliness, and health care. They specify that the research must avoid any cruelty in the form of unnecessary pain to the animal. In addition, institutions in which animal research is carried out must have an Institutional Animal Care and Use Committee (IACUC), composed of at least one scientist, one veterinarian, and a person from the community. The IACUC is charged with review of animal research procedures and ensuring that all regulations are adhered to (see Holden, 1987). American Psychological Association ethical principle 10, "Care and Use of Animals," states:

An investigator of animal behavior strives to advance understanding of basic behavioral principles and/or to contribute to the improvement of human health and welfare. In seeking these ends, the investigator ensures the welfare of animals and treats them humanely. Laws and regulations notwithstanding, an animal's immediate protection depends upon the scientist's own conscience.

a. The acquisition, care, use, and disposal of all animals are in compliance with current federal, state or provincial, and local laws and regulations.

b. A psychologist trained in research methods and experienced in the care of laboratory animals closely supervises all procedures involving animals and is responsible for ensuring appropriate consideration of their comfort, health, and humane treatment.

c. Psychologists ensure that all individuals using animals under their supervision have received explicit instruction in experimental methods and in the care, maintenance, and handling of the species being used. Responsibilities and activities of individuals participating in a research project are consistent with their respective competencies.

d. Psychologists make every effort to minimize discomfort, illness, and pain of animals. A procedure subjecting animals to pain, stress, or privation is used only when an alternative procedure is unavailable and the goal is justified by its prospective scientific, educational, or applied value. Surgical procedures are performed under appropriate anesthesia; techniques to avoid infection and minimize pain are followed during and after surgery.

e. When it is appropriate that the animal's life be terminated, it is done rapidly and painlessly.

A more complete set of detailed guidelines for researchers based on ethical principle 10 has also been developed (American Psychological Association, 1986). It is clear that psychologists are very concerned about the welfare of animals used in research, but nonetheless, this is likely to continue to be a controversial topic.

FRAUD

One final ethical problem should be mentioned: fraud. When a research finding is published, it is imperative that we have confidence that the research was actually conducted, that the procedures were accurately described, and that the results reported were actually obtained. We must believe the reported results of research or the entire foundation of the scientific method as a means of knowledge is in danger. In fact, although fraud may occur in many fields, it is probably true that fraud is most serious when it is discovered in two areas: science and journalism. This is because science and journalism are both fields in which written reports are assumed to be accurate descriptions of an event that has occurred. There are no independent accounting agencies to check on the activities of scientists and journalists.

Fortunately, instances of fraud have been rare in the field of psychology and are considered to be very serious (cf. Hostetler, 1987; Riordin & Marlin, 1987). Perhaps the most famous case is that of Sir Cyril Burt, who reported that the IQ scores of identical twins reared apart were highly similar. The data were used to support the argument that genetic influences on IQ were extremely important. However, Leon Kamin (1974) noted some irregular aspects of Burt's data: A number of correlations for different sets of twins were exactly the same to the third decimal place, virtually a mathematical impossibility. This observation led to the discovery that some of Burt's presumed co-workers did not work with him or were simply fabricated names made up by Burt. Ironically, though, Burt's "data" were close to what have been reported by other investigators who have studied the IQ scores of twins.

Burt's fraudulent data were not easy to detect. It took the careful eye of a skilled scientist to notice the unusual pattern of results and to suspect a problem with the data. The most common reason for suspecting fraud is when an important or unusual finding cannot be replicated. Fraud is not a great problem in science, probably because researchers know that others will read their research and conduct further studies, including replications. They know that their reputations and careers could be seriously damaged if other scientists concluded that the results were fraudulent.

205

Why do researchers sometimes commit fraud? For one thing, scientists sometimes find themselves in a job with extreme pressures to produce impressive results. However, this is not a sufficient explanation, because many researchers maintain high ethical standards under such pressures. Another reason is that researchers who feel a need to produce fraudulent data have an exaggerated fear of failure along with a great need for success and the admiration that comes with it. If you wish to explore further the dynamics of fraud and the controversies that still surround the Burt case, you might wish to begin with the books on Sir Cyril Burt by Hearnshaw (1979) and Joynson (1989).

We should make one final point: Allegations of fraud should not be made lightly. If you disagree with someone's results on philosophical, political, religious, or other grounds, it does not mean that they are fraudulent. Even if you cannot replicate the results, the reason may lie in aspects of the methodology of the study. Scientific rigor demands that we give careful consideration to all hypotheses. However, the fact that fraud could be a possible explanation of results stresses the importance of careful record keeping and documentation of the procedures and results.

These points are illustrated in a case in which fraud was suspected but not substantiated (see Marlatt, 1983). In the early 1970s, two psychologists (Sobell & Sobell, 1973) reported a study of the effectiveness of a controlled drinking treatment for alcoholics. Controlled drinking is a procedure designed to produce moderate social drinking, in contrast with the more traditional treatment that attempts to produce abstinence. The Sobells' finding is controversial, especially among antialcohol groups.

Later, another group of researchers (Pendery, Maltzman, & West, 1982) reported on the patients in the Sobells' controlled-drinking condition some 10 years later. These authors reported that the subjects of the study were in fact not helped, and they went on to describe the serious drinking problems of the persons that they interviewed. Two of the authors made statements to the press that their findings cast "grave doubt on the scientific integrity of the original research" and "beyond any reasonable doubt, it's fraud" (Marlatt, 1983). As a result of the Pendery study, a "blue-ribbon panel" of researchers and legal experts investigated the Sobells' original work. Fortunately, the Sobells had kept extensive records of their research activities, including audiotapes of interviews of the patients in a follow-up study. The panel concluded that there was "no reasonable cause to doubt the scientific or personal integrity" of the Sobells. In this case, careful record keeping by the researchers and a reasoned scientific examination of the original research and the later research by Pendery et al. prevented substantiation of a serious allegation of fraud.

We should note in conclusion that ethical guidelines and regulations are constantly evolving. Presently the American Psychological Association is circulating a draft of a proposed new APA Ethics Code (American Psychological Association, 1991); and federal, state, and local regulations may be revised periodically. You will need to always be aware of the most current policies and procedures.

STUDY QUESTIONS

1. Discuss the major ethical issues in behavioral research: physical and psychological harm, deception, debriefing, and informed consent. How can researchers weigh the need to conduct research against the need for ethical procedures?

2. Why is informed consent an ethical principle? What are the problems with full informed consent?

3. What alternatives to deception are described in the text?

4. Describe and compare the following experimental methods: laboratory deception experiments, field experiments, and role-playing experiments. What are the advantages and disadvantages of each?

5. Summarize the principles described in the Ethical Principles in the Conduct of Research with Human Participants.

6. What is the difference between "exempt" and "minimal-risk" research activities?

7. What is an Institutional Review Board?

8. Summarize the ethical procedures for research with animals.

9. What constitutes fraud, what are some reasons for its occurrence, and why doesn't it occur more frequently?

ACTIVITY QUESTION

Consider the following experiment, similar to one that was conducted by Smith, Lingle, and Brock (1978). Subjects interacted for an hour with another subject who was actually a confederate. After this interaction, each subject agreed to return one week later for another session with the same person. When subjects returned, they were informed that the person they had met the week before had died. The researchers then measured reactions to the death of the person.

1. Discuss the ethical issues raised by the experiment.

2. Would the experiment violate the guidelines articulated in APA ethical principle 9, Research with Human Participants? In what ways?

3. What alternative methods for studying this problem (reactions to death) might you suggest?

4. Would your reactions to this study be different if the subjects had played with an infant and then later had been told that the infant had died?

A

Writing Research Reports

INTRODUCTION

This appendix presents the information you will need to prepare a written report of your research for a course and for possible publication in a professional journal. We will consider the specific rules that should be followed in organizing and presenting research results. These rules are a great convenience for both the writer and the reader. They provide structure for the report and a uniform method of presentation, making it easier for the reader to understand and evaluate the report.

Specific rules vary from one discipline to another. A rule for presenting research results in psychology may not apply to the same situation in, for example, sociology research. Also, the rules may vary depending upon whether you are preparing the report for a class, a thesis, or submission to a journal. Fortunately, the variation is usually minor, and the general rules of presentation are much the same across disciplines and situations.

The format presented here for writing research reports is drawn from the *Publication Manual of the American Psychological Association* (third edition, 1983). The APA style is used in many journals in psychology, mental health, family relations, and education. If you are concerned about specific rules for a particular journal, consult a recent issue of that journal. You may purchase a copy of the *Publication Manual* through your bookstore or directly from the American Psychological Association (APA Book Order Department, P.O. Box 2710, Hyattsville, MD 20784). APA has also published a student workbook and training guide for the *Publication Manual* (Gelfand & Walker, 1990). Other useful sources for preparing papers are brief books by Rosnow and Rosnow (1992) and Sternberg (1988).

WRITING STYLE

In any format for preparing your report, writing style is important. A poorly written report that is difficult to understand is of no value (and almost certainly will bring you a poor grade!). Also, a good paper should be neatly typed and free of spelling and typographical errors.

Typing and word processing

You will eventually have to prepare a typed copy of your paper. In APA style, the paper should be *entirely double-spaced*. The margins for text should be $1\frac{1}{2}$ *inches* on all four sides of the page. All pages must be numbered except for figure pages at the end of the paper. Words should never be hyphenated at the end of a line; lines should be a little short or a little long rather than breaking a word. Such details used to be called typing rules; in the era of word processing, they become rules for printing.

Many students use word processing computer programs to prepare their papers: Through the use of the computer, it is possible to improve your writing and easier to submit a high-quality paper. If you are not already

209

using a word processor, you should strongly consider purchasing your own computer system or ask about access to word processing that you may have at your college. When you use a word processor, your writing is no longer typed copy but simply characters on a computer screen. Making corrections, revising material, and moving or deleting portions of text is no longer a chore; such changes are easily made on the computer screen using the word processing program. Writing several drafts of a paper is easy because you don't have to retype the paper each time you wish to make a change.

Many word processing programs also include a spelling check and thesaurus feature (if not, separate spelling and thesaurus programs can be used with the word processor). The spelling checker examines your paper for spelling errors and even suggests possible corrections for misspelled words; the thesaurus feature allows you to examine possible alternative words to express an idea. You can also use programs to analyze the grammar and readability of your paper; such programs look for sentences that are too long, words that might be difficult to understand, and simple grammatical mistakes. Finally, outlining programs facilitate the process of making an outline; the outline can then be used with the word processing program to help you write the actual paper.

Word processors also allow many advanced printing options, such as right justification of lines, different typestyles and type sizes, boldface, and other features that make the paper appear closer to an actual published report. There are many uses for such options. However, papers submitted for classes, or to a journal or professional meeting, should avoid these features. The final paper should look like a regular typed paper; it will simply be better because of the revisions, spelling checks, and other error corrections. Your final paper will have a neater appearance and in fact will be a better product.

Clarity

Clarity in writing is essential. Be precise and clear in presenting ideas. It is often a good idea to think about your intended audience. Usually it is best to direct your paper to an audience that is unfamiliar with your general topic and the methods you used to study the topic. At the same time, you should usually assume that the reader has a general familiarity with statistics and hypothesis testing. Thus, you want to eliminate jargon that most readers will not comprehend. Sometimes a researcher will develop an abbreviated notation for referring to a specific variable or procedure; such abbreviations may be convenient when communicating with others who are directly involved in the research project, but they are confusing to the general reader. At the same time, statistical outcomes can usually be presented without defining terms such as the mean, standard deviation, or significance. These are only general guidelines, however. Rosnow and Rosnow (1992) point out that when your intended audience is your instructor, you should pay close attention to what the instructor has to say about expectations for the paper! The entire report should have a coherent structure. Ideas should be presented in an orderly, logical progression to facilitate understanding. Again, if you write your report for someone who is just being introduced to your ideas and research findings for the first time, you will be more likely to clearly communicate with the reader.

One method for producing a more organized report is to use an outline. Many writers plan a paper by putting their thoughts and ideas into outline form; as noted above, there are computer programs that can facilitate outlining. The outline then serves as a writing guide. This method usually forces writers to develop a logical structure before writing the paper. Other writers prefer to use a less structured approach for the first draft. They then try to outline what has been written. If the paper does not produce a coherent outline, the organization needs to be improved.

After completing the first draft of your paper, it is a good idea to let it sit for a day or so and then reread it. After you make changes and corrections, and perhaps run it through a spelling checker, you may want to get feedback from others. Find one or more people who will read your report critically and suggest improvements. Be prepared, then, to write several drafts before you have a satisfactory finished product.

Acknowledging the work of others

It is extremely important to clearly separate your own words and ideas from those obtained from other sources. If you use a passage drawn from an article or book, make sure that the passage is presented as a direct quotation. There is nothing wrong with quoting another author as long as you acknowledge your source. Never present another person's idea as your own. This is plagiarism and is inexcusable. If you have any questions about how to properly include material from your source articles in your own paper, consult your instructor.

Sexist language

Avoid sexist language. Don't use *he*, *his*, *man*, *man's*, and so on when both males and females are meant. Sentences can usually be rephrased or specific pronouns deleted to avoid biases implied by sexist language. For example, "The worker is paid according to his productivity" can be changed to "The worker is paid according to productivity" or "Workers are paid according to their productivity." In the first case, the "his" was simply deleted; in the second case, the subject of the sentence was changed to plural. Do *not* try to avoid sexist language by simply substituting "s/he" whenever that might appear convenient. Other examples of how to avoid sexist language are provided in the APA *Publication Manual*.

ORGANIZATION OF THE REPORT

A research report is organized into five major parts: abstract, introduction, method, results, and discussion. References must be listed using a particular format. The report may also include tables and figures used in presenting the

211

results. We will consider the parts of the paper in the order prescribed by APA style. You should refer to the sample paper at the end of this appendix as you read the material that follows.

Title page

The first page of the paper is the title page. It is a separate page and is numbered as page 1. Primarily, it lists the title, the name of the author(s), and the name of the institution with which the authors are affiliated, all centered on the page on separate lines.

The title should be fairly short (usually no more than 12 to 15 words) and should inform the reader of the nature of your research. A good way to do this is to include the names of your variables in the title. For example, the following titles are both short and informative:

Effect of Anxiety on Mathematical Problem Solving
Memory for Faces Among Elderly and Young Adults

Sometimes a colon in the title helps to convey the nature of your research or even adds a bit of "flair" to your title, as in

Cognitive Responses in Persuasion: Affective
and Evaluative Determinants
Beautiful but Dangerous: Effects of Offender Attractiveness
and Nature of Crime in Juridic Judgments

Another method of titling a paper is to pose the question that the research addresses. For example:

Do Response Modality Effects Support Multiprocessor Models
of Divided Attention?
Does Sex-Biased Job Advertising "Aid and Abet" Sex Discrimination?

Now notice several other items that are found on the title page. A *short title*, usually consisting of the first two or three words of the title, is typed in the upper right-hand corner. The page number is typed one line below the short title (remember, all lines are double-spaced). The short title and page number are typed on all pages of the paper except figure pages. They appear *above* the 1½-inch margin where the text appears (i.e., only text is within the required 1½-inch margins on all sides of the page). The short title enables the reader to identify the paper in case pages get separated accidentally. If your word processing program will not allow the two lines needed for the short title and the page number (e.g., permitting only one line containing the short title and the page number), go ahead and use your program to take advantage of the benefits of word processing.

In addition, a *running head* must appear at the bottom of the title page with all letters capitalized. The running head is an abbreviated title and should be no more than 50 characters (letters, numbers, spaces) in length. If the paper is published in a journal, the running head is printed at the top of pages to help readers identify the article. Note that the running head is used for publication purposes while the short title is used by readers of your paper. In the sample paper, the short title is "Smell of Success"—a short description drawn from the first few words of the title of the paper. However, the running head is "EVALUATIONS OF JOB APPLICANTS": The running head is often longer than the short title and more descriptive of the content of the paper.

Abstract

The abstract is a brief summary of the research and is 100 to 150 words in length. It should describe the research problem that was studied, the method used to study the problem (including information on the type of subjects), the results, and the major conclusions.

The abstract should provide enough information so that the reader can decide whether to read the entire report, and it should make the report easier to comprehend when it is read. Although the abstract appears at the beginning of your report, you will probably want to wait until the body of the report is completed before you write the abstract.

The abstract is typed on a separate page and is numbered page 2. The word *Abstract* is centered at the top of the page. The abstract is always typed as a single paragraph in a "block" format with no paragraph indention.

Introduction

The introduction section begins on a new page (page 3), with the title of your report typed at the top of the page. This section introduces the reader to the problem being investigated, reviews past research and theory relevant to the problem, presents the predicted outcomes of the research, and gives the method used for testing the predictions. After reading the introduction, the reader should know why you decided to do the research and how you decided to go about doing it.

Bem (1981) has argued that, whenever possible, the introduction should begin with an opening statement of two or three sentences. The opening statement is intended to give the reader an appreciation of the broad context and significance of the topic being studied. This is worthwhile if it can be done: It helps readers, even those who are unfamiliar with the topic, to understand and appreciate why the topic was studied in the first place. Unfortunately, few articles in professional journals actually begin with an opening statement.

Following the opening statement, the introduction provides a description of past research and theory. This is called the literature review. An exhaustive review of past research is not necessary. Rather, you want to describe only the research and theoretical issues that are clearly related to your study. You should state explicitly how this previous work is logically connected to your research problem. This tells the reader why your research was conducted.

The final part of the introduction tells the reader exactly what hypothesis is being tested. Here you state what variables you are studying, what results you expect, and why you expect these results.

213

Method

The method section begins immediately after you have completed the introduction (on the same page, if space permits). This section provides the reader with detailed information about how your study was conducted. Ideally, there should be enough information in the method section to allow a reader to replicate your study.

The method section is typically divided into a number of subsections. The nature of the subsections is determined by the nature of the research you are describing. The subsections should be organized to present the method as clearly as possible. Some of the most commonly used subsections are discussed below.

Overview If the experimental design and procedures used in the research are complex, a brief overview of the method should be presented to help the reader understand the information that follows.

Subjects A subsection on subjects is always necessary. The number and nature of the subjects should be described. If the subjects were humans, gender and age should be given, along with any other relevant characteristics. State explicitly how the subjects were recruited for the study. The number of subjects per group also can be included here.

In animal research, it is common practice to report the species, strain number, and other information that specifically identifies the type of animal. The number of animals and the age and sex of each animal used should be indicated. If information about care, feeding, or handling conditions in the laboratory is relevant, it should be included here.

Apparatus An apparatus subsection may be necessary if special equipment was used in the experiment. The brand name and model number of the equipment may be specified; some apparatus may be described in detail.

Procedure The procedure subsection tells the reader exactly how the study was conducted. One way to report this information is to describe, step by step, what occurred in the experiment.

The procedure subsection should tell the reader what instructions were read to (human) subjects, how the independent variables were manipulated, and how the dependent variables were measured. The methods used to control extraneous variables also should be described. These would include randomization procedures, counterbalancing, and special means that were used to keep a variable constant across all conditions. Finally, the method of debriefing subjects should be described.

It is up to you to decide how much detail to include here. Use your own judgment to determine the importance of a specific aspect of the procedure and the amount of detail that is necessary if the reader is to clearly understand what was done in the study.

Other subsections Other subsections should be included if warranted by the nature of the experiment and needed for clear presentation of the method. For example, a subsection on "testing materials" might be necessary instead of an "apparatus" subsection.

214

Results

In the results section, you present the results as clearly as possible. When writing the results section, it is best to refer to your predictions as stated in the introduction. The order in which your results are presented should correspond to the order of your predictions. If a manipulation check measure was made, it should be presented before the major results are described.

The results should be stated in simple sentences. For example, the results of the modeling experiment described in Chapter 9 might be expressed as follows:

> As predicted, the model group was significantly more aggressive than the no-model group, $\underline{t}(18) = 4.023$, $\underline{p} < .01$. The mean aggression score in the model group was 5.20, and the no-model group mean was 3.10.

These two sentences inform the reader of the general pattern of the results, the obtained means, and the statistical significance of the results (note the placement of the results of the t-test, degrees of freedom, and significance level).

If the results are relatively straightforward, they can be presented entirely in sentence form. If the study involved a complex design, tables and figures may be needed to clarify presentation of the results.

Tables and figures Tables are generally used to present large arrays of data. For example, a table might be useful in a design with several dependent measures; the means of the different groups for all dependent measures would be presented in the table. Tables are also convenient when a factorial design has been used. For example, in a $2 \times 2 \times 3$ factorial design, a table could be used to present all 12 means.

Figures are used when a visual display of the results would help the reader understand the outcome of the study. Figures may be used to illustrate a significant interaction or show trends over time.

In APA style, tables and figures are not presented in the main body of the manuscript. Rather, they are placed at the end of the paper. Each table and figure appears on a separate page. A table or figure is noted in the text by describing the content of the table or figure and using the following notation to show the placement of the table in the printed article:

Insert Table 1 about here

When you are writing a research report for a purpose other than publication—for example, to fulfill a course or degree requirement—it may be more convenient to place each figure and table on a separate page within the main body of the paper. Because rules about the placement of tables and figures may vary, you should check on the proper format before writing your report.

Tables and figures are supplements to your written report of the results. They do not diminish your responsibility to clearly state the nature of the results in the text of your report. In fact, when tables or figures are used, you must also describe the important features of them.

Discussion of the results   It is usually *not* appropriate to discuss the implications of the results within the results section. However, the results and discussion section may be combined if the discussion is brief and greater clarity is achieved by the combination.

Discussion

The discussion section is the proper place to discuss the implications of the results. One way to organize the discussion is to begin by summarizing the original purpose and expectations of the study and then stating whether the results were consistent with your expectations. If the results do support your original ideas, you should discuss how your findings contribute to knowledge of the problem that you investigated. You will want to consider the relationship between your results and past research and theory. If you did not obtain the expected results, you will want to discuss possible explanations. The explanations would be quite different, of course, depending upon whether you obtained results that were the opposite of what you expected or the results were nonsignificant.

It is often a good idea to include your own criticisms of the study. Try to anticipate what a reader might find wrong with your methodology. For example, if you used the correlational method, you might point out problems of cause and effect and possible extraneous variables that might be operating. Sometimes there may be major or minor flaws that could be corrected in a subsequent study (if you had the time, money, and so on). You can describe such flaws and suggest corrections. If there are potential problems of generalizing your results, state the problems and give reasons why you think the results would or would not generalize.

The results will probably have implications for future research. If so, you should discuss the direction that research might take. It is also possible that the results have practical implications—for example, for child rearing or improving learning in the classroom. Discussion of these larger issues is usually placed at the end of the discussion section. Finally, you will probably wish to have a brief concluding paragraph that provides "closure" to the entire paper.

References

The list of references begins on a new page. The references must contain complete citations for all sources mentioned in your report. Do not omit any sources from the list of references; also, do not include any sources that are not mentioned in your report. The exact procedures for citing sources within the body of your report and in your list of references are described in detail below.

Appendix

An appendix is rarely provided in manuscripts submitted for publication. The APA *Publication Manual* notes that an appendix might be appropriate for such items as a new computer program used in the study, an unpublished test that was validated, a complex mathematical proof, or a detailed description of some equipment. An appendix (or several appendices) are much more appropriate for a student research project or a thesis. The appendix might include the entire questionnaire that was used or other materials employed in the study. Check with your instructor concerning the appropriateness of an appendix for your paper. If an appendix is provided, it begins on a new page with the word *Appendix* centered at the top.

Author notes

Author notes may be provided to acknowledge the help and assistance of others (for example, people who provided feedback on the manuscript or helped with the data collection). In journals, these notes are actually printed at the bottom of the first page of the article. Author notes are optional and will probably be unnecessary for class research reports.

Footnotes

Footnotes, if used, are not typed in the body of the text. Instead, all footnotes in the paper are typed on one page at the end of the paper. Avoid using footnotes unless they are absolutely necessary. They tend to be distracting to readers, and usually the information is best integrated into the actual body of the paper.

Tables

Each table should be on a separate page. As noted above, APA style requires placement of the table at the end of the paper, but for a class you may be asked to place your tables on separate pages within the body of the paper. A sample table is included in the example paper at the end of this appendix. In preparing your table, allow enough space so that the table does not appear cramped in a small portion of the page. Areas of the table are defined by typed horizontal lines (do not use vertical lines). Give some thought to the title so that it accurately and clearly describes the content of the table. You may wish to use an explanatory note in the table to show significance levels or the range of possible values on a variable. Before you make up your own tables, examine the tables in a recent issue of one of the journals published by the American Psychological Association (see Chapter 2).

Figures

There are two special APA style rules for the placement and preparation of figures: (1) Figures are placed after the tables in the papers, and (2) a separate page containing the figure captions is provided before the figures. Either or both of these rules may not be necessary for student reports or theses. You may be asked to place each figure on a separate page at the appropriate point in the body of the text, and you may not need a figure caption page (this is only for the convenience of typesetting and printing the paper). Also, if you are following true APA style, there is no page number or short title on the figure pages (the figure number is written on the back of the figure in pencil).

If you are preparing your figure by hand, it is a good idea to buy graph paper with lines that do not photocopy (a photocopy of the graph is turned in with your final report). Lines are drawn using black ink and a ruler (alternatively, you can use press-on type and rules, available at a graphics supply store). In deciding on the size of the figure, a good rule is that the horizontal axis should be about 5 inches wide and the vertical axis should be about $3\frac{1}{2}$ inches long. Both the vertical and the horizontal axes must be labeled. Dependent and criterion variables are placed on the vertical axis; independent and predictor variables are placed on the horizontal axis (see Chapter 3).

Instead of preparing your graphs by hand, you can use a computer graphics program. Graphics programs are becoming easier to use and can produce graphs on a variety of printers. They make preparation of graphs easier and ease the frustration that arises when you make mistakes.

Remember that the purpose of a figure is to increase your understanding of results by having a graphical display of data. If the graph is cluttered with information so that it confuses a reader, the graph is not serving its purpose. You will need to carefully plan your graphs to make sure that you are accurately and clearly informing the reader. If you become interested in the topic of how to display information in graphs and charts, a book by Tufte (1983) is recommended. Tufte explores a variety of ways of presenting data, factors that lead to clarity, and ways that graphs can deceive the reader.

To summarize, the organization of your paper is as follows:

1. Title page (page 1)
2. Abstract (page 2)
3. Pages of text (start on new page 3)
    a. Title at top of first page begins the introduction
    b. Method
    c. Results
    d. Discussion
4. References (start on new page)
5. Appendix (start on new page if included)
6. Author notes (start on new page if included)
7. Footnotes (start on new page if included)

8. Tables, with table captions (each on separate page)

9. Figure caption(s) (all together on one separate page)

10. Figures (each on separate page)

You should now have a general idea of how to structure and write your report. The remaining sections of this appendix will focus on some of the technical rules that may be useful as you prepare your own research report.

THE USE OF HEADINGS

Papers written in APA style use one to five levels of headings. Most commonly, you will use "level 2" and "level 4" headings, and you may need to use "level 5" headings as well. These are

(Level 2)   Centered Heading

(Level 4)   Margin Heading

     The text begins on a new line.

(Level 5)   Paragraph heading. The text begins on the same line.

Level 1 and level 3 headings will not be described because they are used only in very complex presentations.

Level 2, or centered, headings are used to head major sections of the report: Abstract, Title (on page 3), Method, Results, Discussion, References, and so on. Level 2 headings are typed with initial capitals and lowercase letters (i.e., the first letter of each major word is capitalized).

Level 4, or margin, headings are used to divide major sections into subsections. Level 4 headings are typed flush to the left margin. Like level 2 headings, they are initial capped and lowercase. They are also underlined. For example, the Method section is divided into at least two subsections: "Subjects" and "Procedure." The correct format is

Method

Subjects

     The description of the subjects begins on a new line.

Procedure

     The description of the procedure begins on a new line.

Level 5, or paragraph, headings are used to organize material within a subsection. Underlined headings will appear in italics in publications. Thus,

219

an italicized paragraph heading will "alert" the reader to the information in the subsequent paragraph(s).

Paragraph headings begin on a new line, indented five spaces. The first word begins with a capital letter; the remaining words are all typed in lower-case letters. The heading ends with a period and is underlined. All information that appears between a paragraph heading and the next heading (of any level) must be related to the paragraph heading. As an example, the Procedure subsection of the Method section may be organized with paragraph headings to emphasize the sequence of events, or operational definitions of the variables, sets of instructions, and so on.

CITING AND REFERENCING SOURCES

Citation style

Whenever you refer to information reported by other researchers, you *must* accurately identify the sources. APA journals use the author–date citation method: The author name(s) and year of publication are inserted at appropriate points. The citation style depends on whether the author name(s) are part of the narrative or are in parentheses.

One author When the author's name is part of the narrative, include the publication date in parentheses *immediately* after the name:

Dion (1972) found that adults judged the misbehavior of unattractive children to be more socially undesirable than the misbehavior of attractive children.

When the author's name is not part of the narrative, the name and date are cited in parentheses at the end of an introductory phrase or at the end of the sentence:

In one study (Dion, 1972) adults judged the misbehavior . . .

It has been reported that adults judge the misbehavior of unattractive children to be highly undesirable (Dion, 1972).

Two authors When the work has two authors, both names are included in each reference citation. The difference between narrative and parenthetical citations is in the use of the conjunction "and" or the ampersand "&." When the author's names are part of a sentence, use the word "and." When the complete citation is in parentheses, use the "&" symbol:

Hunt and Uzgiris (1975) developed a set of scales to measure sensorimotor development.

A set of scales to measure sensorimotor development has recently been developed (Hunt & Uzgiris, 1975).

Three to five authors When a report has three or more authors, all author names must be cited the first time the reference occurs. Thereafter, cite the first author's surname followed by the abbreviation "et al." ("and others") and the publication date. The abbreviation may be used in narrative and parenthetical citations:

First citation:
Dion, Berscheid, and Walster (1972) reported evidence of a physical attractiveness stereotype.

Evidence of a physical attractiveness stereotype has been reported (Dion, Berscheid, & Walster, 1972).

Subsequent citations:
Dion et al. (1972) found that attractive individuals are believed to lead happier lives than average-looking or unattractive individuals.

In this study (Dion et al., 1972), attractive individuals were believed to lead happier lives than unattractive individuals.

Another question about subsequent citations is whether to include the publication date each time an article is referenced. Within a paragraph, you do *not* need to include the year in subsequent citations as long as the study cannot be confused with other studies cited in your report.

First citation:
In a recent study of reaction times, Smith and Jones (1988) found . . .

Subsequent citations within a paragraph:
Smith and Jones also reported . . .

When subsequent citations are in another paragraph or in another section of the report, the publication date should be included.

Six or more authors   Occasionally you will reference a report with six or more authors. In this case, use the abbreviation "et al." after the first author's last name in *every* citation. Although you would not list all author names in the text, the citation in the references *list* should include the names of *all* authors.

References with no author   When an article has no author (e.g., a newspaper or popular magazine article), cite the first two or three words of the title in quotation marks, followed by the publication date:

Citation in reference list:
Study finds free care used more. (1982, September 5). *Los Angeles Times*, p. 14.

Citation in text:
In an article on free care ("Study Finds," 1982), data were reported to support . . .

Multiple works within the same parentheses   A convenient way to cite several studies on the same topic or several studies with similar findings is to reference them as a series within the same parentheses. When two or more works are by the same author(s), report them in order of year of publication, using commas to separate citations:

221

Hasam and Grammick (1981, 1982) found . . .

Past research (Hassam & Grammick, 1981, 1982) has indicated . . .

When two or more works by different authors are cited within the same parentheses, arrange them in alphabetical order and separate citations by semicolons:

Several studies (Doron & O'Neal, 1979; Mullaney, 1978; Talpers, 1981) have shown . . .

Memory for large amounts of information can be improved by visual imagery techniques (Bower & Clark, 1969; Jonides, Kahn, & Rozin, 1975; Paivio, 1971).

Style and grammar References within parentheses do not have a grammatical role in a sentence; thus, words in the sentence (such as pronouns) cannot refer to a citation within parentheses.

Incorrect:
Claiming that unattractive children are judged more harshly (Dion, 1972), she proposed . . .

Correct:
Unattractive children are judged more harshly, according to Dion (1972). She proposed . . .

Reference list style

The APA *Publication Manual* specifies different reference formats for journal articles, books, articles in books, technical reports, convention presentations, and so on. Only a few of these are presented here. When in doubt about how to construct a reference consult the APA manual (pages 118–133).

The general format for a reference list is

1. The references are listed in alphabetical order by first author's last name. *Do not* categorize references by type (i.e., books, journal articles, and so on).
2. The first line of each reference is typed flush with the left margin. Subsequent lines within a reference are indented *three* (not five) spaces.
3. Elements of a reference (authors' names, article title, publication data) are separated by periods.
4. Notice the spacing in typing of author's names in the examples below.

Format for journal articles Most journals are organized by volume and/ or year of publication (e.g., Volume 90 of the *Journal of Abnormal Psychology* consists of journal issues published in 1980). A common confusion is whether to include the journal issue number in addition to the volume number. The rule is simple: If the issues in a volume are paginated consecutively throughout the volume, *do not* include the journal issue number. If each issue in a volume begins on page *one*, the issue number should be included. Specific examples of journal article references are shown below.

In the reference list, both the name of the journal and the volume number are underlined. Also, note that only the first letter of the first word in article titles is capitalized (unless the title has a colon; then the first word after the colon is also capitalized).

1. *One author—no issue number:*

Paivio, A. (1975). Perceptual comparisons through the mind's eye. Memory and Cognition, 3, 635–647.

2. *Two authors—use of issue number:*

Becker, L. J., & Seligman, C. (1981). Welcome to the energy crisis. Journal of Social Issues, 37 (2), 1–7.

Format for books When a book is cited, the title of the book is underlined. Only beginning words are capitalized (however, proper nouns are also capitalized, as well as the first word after a colon). The city of publication and the publishing company follow the title. If the city is not well known, include the U.S. Postal Service two-letter abbreviation for the state (e.g., AZ, CA, NY, WA).

1. *One author:*

Chomsky, N. (1979). Language and responsibility. New York: Pantheon.

2. *One author—second or later edition:*

Aronson, E. (1984). The social animal (4th ed.). San Francisco: W. H. Freeman.

3. *Two authors—edited book:*

Letheridge, S., & Cannon, C. R. (Eds.). (1980). Bilingual education: Teaching English as a second language. New York: Praeger.

Format for articles in edited books For edited books, the reference begins with the names of the authors of the *article*, not the book. The title of the article follows. The name(s) of the book editor(s), the book title, the inclusive page numbers for the article, and the publication data for the book follow, in that order. Only the book title is underlined and only the first letters of article and book titles are capitalized. Here are some examples.

1. *One editor:*

Hartley, J. T., Harker, J. C., & Walsh, D. A. (1980). Contemporary issues and new directions in adult development of learning and memory. In L. W. Poon (Ed.), Aging in the 1980s: Psychological issues (pp. 239–252). Washington, DC: American Psychological Association.

223

2. *Two editors:*

Gurman, A. S., & Kniskern, D. P. (1981). Family therapy outcome research: Knowns and unknowns. In A. S. Gurman & D. P. Kniskern (Eds.), Handbook of family therapy (pp. 741–775). New York: Brunner/Mazel.

3. *Article from book in multivolume series:*

Berscheid, E., & Walster, E. (1974). Physical attractiveness. In L. Berkowitz (Ed.), Advances in experimental social psychology (Vol. 7, pp. 145–198). New York: Academic Press.

Format for "popular articles"   The reference style shown below should be used for articles from popular magazines and from newspapers. As a general rule, popular press articles are used sparingly (e.g., when no scientific articles on a topic can be found, or to provide an example of an event that is related to your topic).

1. *Magazine—continuous pages:*

Gardner, H. (1981, December). Do babies sing a universal song? Psychology Today, pp. 70–76.

2. *Newspaper—no author:*

Study finds free care used more. (1982, September 5). Los Angeles Times, p. 14.

3. *Newspaper—discontinuous pages:*

Lublin, J. S. (1980, December 5). On idle: The unemployed shun much mundane work, at least for awhile. The Wall Street Journal, pp. 1, 25.

Format for technical reports   A technical report is a document that is published by a specific institution and then made available to others who are interested in the research. References for technical reports are formatted like references for books. The main difference is the inclusion of the report number after the title. Two examples are given below.

1. *NEA (National Education Association) report:*

Birney, A. J., & Hall, M. M. (1981). Early identification of children with written language disabilities (Report No. 81-1502). Washington, DC: National Education Association.

2. *ERIC document:*

Gottfredson, L. S. (1980). How valid are occupational reinforcer pattern scores? (Report No. CSOS-R-292). Baltimore, MD: Johns Hopkins University, Center for Social Organization of Schools. (ERIC Document Reproduction Service No. ED 182 465)

ABBREVIATIONS

Abbreviations are not normally used in APA-style papers. They can be distracting because the reader must constantly try to translate the abbreviation into its full meaning. However, APA style does allow the use of abbreviations that are accepted as words by the dictionary (specifically, Webster's *New Collegiate Dictionary*). These terms include IQ, LSD, REM, and ESP.

Certain well-known terms may be abbreviated when it would make reading easier, but the term's full meaning should be given when it is first used. Some examples of commonly used abbreviations are:

Minnesota Multiphasic Personality Inventory (MMPI)

short-term memory (STM)

chronological age (CA)

reaction time (RT)

conditioned stimulus (CS)

intertrial interval (ITI)

consonant-vowel-consonant (CVC)

Statistical terms are sometimes used in their abbreviated or symbol form. These are always underlined in a manuscript. Examples include:

M	mean
SD	standard deviation
Mdn	median
df	degrees of freedom
n	number of subjects in a group
N	total number of subjects
p	probability level
SS	sum of squares
MS	mean square
F	value of F in analysis of variance
r	Pearson correlation coefficient
R	multiple correlation coefficient

Finally, certain abbreviations of Latin terms are regularly used in papers. Some of these abbreviations and their meanings are shown below.

cf.	compare
e.g.	for example
etc.	and so forth
i.e.	that is
viz.	namely
vs.	versus

SOME GRAMMATICAL CONSIDERATIONS

Transition words and phrases

One way to produce a clearly written research report is to pay attention to how you connect sentences within a paragraph and to how you connect paragraphs within a section. The transitions between sentences and paragraphs should be smooth and consistent with the line of reasoning. Some commonly used transition words and phrases and their functions are described in this section.

Adverbs   Adverbs can be used as introductory words in sentences. However, you must use them to convey their implied meanings.

Adverb	Implied meaning
(Un)fortunately	It is (un)fortunate that . . .
Similarly	In a similar manner . . .
Certainly	It is certain that . . .
Clearly	It is clear that . . .

One adverb that is frequently misused as an introductory or transition word is *hopefully*. Hopefully means "in a hopeful manner," *not* "it is hoped that . . ."

Incorrect:
Hopefully, this is not the case.
Correct:
I hope that this is not the case.

Words suggesting contrast   Some words and phrases suggest a contrast or contradiction between what was written immediately before and what is now being written:

Between sentences	Within sentences
By contrast	whereas
On the other hand	although
However	but
	however

The words in the left list refer to the previous sentence. The words in the right list connect phrases within a sentence; that is, they refer to another point in the same sentence.

Incorrect:
People typically state that physical appearance should not be considered when judging the guilt or innocence of someone. *Whereas* research suggests that in fact physical attractiveness plays a significant role in such judgments.
Correct:
People typically state that physical appearance should not be considered when judging the guilt or innocence of someone. *However*, research sug-

gests that in fact physical attractiveness plays a significant role in such judgments.

Words suggesting a series of ideas   Words and phrases that suggest that information after the transition word is related or similar to information in the previous sentence are

First	In addition	Last	Further
Second	Additionally	Finally	Moreover
Third	Then	Also	Another

Example:
The use of slang and popular expressions in scientific reports is inappropriate. *Also*, it is not proper to use contractions.

Words suggesting implication   These words and phrases indicate that the information following the transition word is implied by or follows from the previous information:

Therefore	If . . . then
It follows that	Thus
In conclusion	Then

Example:
Implicit in this reasoning is that the nature of the affective response, which influences whether kind or harsh treatment is recommended, is determined by the stimulus features associated with the target person. *Therefore*, when other things are equal, benefit accrues to the physically attractive (Sigall & Ostrove, 1975).

When you use transition words, be sure that they convey the meaning you intend. Sprinkling them around as a convenient way to begin sentences leads to confusion on the reader's part and thus defeats your purpose.

Troublesome words and phrases

"That" versus "which"   *That* and *which* are relative pronouns that introduce subordinate clauses and reflect the relationship of the subordinate clause to the main clause. *That* clauses (restrictive clauses) are essential to the meaning of the sentence; *which* clauses (nonrestrictive clauses) simply add more information. Note the different meanings of the same sentence using "that" and "which":

The monkeys that performed well in the first trial were used in the second trial.

The monkeys, which performed well in the first trial, were used in the second trial.

The first sentence states that only monkeys that performed well in the first trial were used in the second, whereas the second sentence means that all

227

monkeys were used in the second trial and they also happened to perform well in the first trial.

"While" versus "since"   *While* and *since* are subordinate conjunctions that also introduce subordinate clauses. To increase clarity in scientific writings, the APA manual suggests that *while* and *since* should be used only to refer to time. *While* is used to describe simultaneous events, and *since* is used to refer to a subsequent event:

Correct:

While the subjects viewed the words on the screen, they heard them being pronounced through headphones.

Correct:

Since the study by Dion (1972), many studies have been published in this area.

The APA manual suggests other conjunctions to use to link phrases that do not describe temporal events. *Although*, *whereas*, and *but* can be used in place of *while*; *because* should be substituted for *since*.

Incorrect:

While the study was well designed, the report was poorly written.

Correct:

Although the study was well designed, the report was poorly written.

Correct:

The study was well designed, *but* the report was poorly written.

Incorrect:

The data for two subjects were discarded *since* these subjects failed to attend the follow-up session.

Correct:

The data for two subjects were discarded *because* these subjects failed to attend the follow-up session.

"Effect" versus "affect"   A common error in student reports is the incorrect use of *effect* and *affect*. *Effect* is a noun that is used in scientific reports to mean "what is produced by a cause," as in the sentence: "The movie had a strong *effect* on me." *Affect* can be a noun or a verb. As a noun it means emotion, as in "The patient seemed depressed but she displayed very little *affect*." As a verb it means "to have an influence on," as in "The subjects' responses were *affected* by the music they heard."

Incorrect:

The independent variable *effected* the subject's behavior.

Correct:

The independent variable *affected* the subject's behavior.

Incorrect:

The independent variable had only a weak *affect* on the subject's behavior.

Correct:

The independent variable had only a weak *effect* on the subject's behavior.

Singular and plural   The following words are often misused. The left list contains singular nouns requiring singular verb forms. The right list contains plural nouns that must be used with plural verbs.

Singular	*Plural*
datum	data
stimulus	stimuli
analysis	analyses
phenomenon	phenomena
medium	media
hypothesis	hypotheses
schema	schemata

Probably the most frequently misused word from these lists is *data*.

Incorrect:
The data *was* coded for computer analysis.
Correct:
The data *were* coded for computer analysis.

REPORTING NUMBERS AND STATISTICS

Virtually all research papers report numbers: number of subjects, number of groups, the values of statistics such as t, F, or r. Should you use numbers (e.g., 43) or should you use words (e.g., forty-three)? The main rule is to use words when expressing the numbers zero through nine but use numbers for 10 and above. There are some important qualifications, however.

If you start a sentence with a number, you should use words even if the number is 10 or larger: *Eighty-five Introductory Psychology students served as subjects in the study*. Starting a sentence with a number is often awkward, especially with large numbers. Therefore, you should usually try to revise the sentence to avoid the problem: *The subjects were 85 students enrolled in Introductory Psychology classes*.

When numbers both above and below 10 are being compared in the same sentence, use numerals for both: *Subjects read either 8 or 16 paragraphs*. However, the following sentence contains an appropriate mix of numbers and words: *Subjects read eight paragraphs and then answered 20 multiple-choice questions*. The sentence is correct because the paragraphs and the questions are different and so are not being compared.

When reporting a percentage, always use numerals followed by a percent sign, except when beginning a sentence. This is true irrespective of whether the number is less than 10 (e.g., *Only 6% of the computer games appealed to females*) or greater than 10 (e.g., *When using this technique, 85% of the subjects improved their performance*).

Always use numbers when describing money (e.g., *The top scorer received*

229

either $1 or $5), ages (e.g., *5-year-olds*), points on a scale (e.g., a *3 on a 5-point scale*), and statistics (e.g., *the mean score in the no-model group was 3.10*). An odd but sensible exception to the word-number rule occurs when two different types of numbers must appear together. An example is: *Teachers identified the most aggressive fifteen 7-year-olds*. This sentence avoids an awkward juxtaposition of two numbers.

Finally, you need to know about presenting statistical results within your paper. As noted above, statistical terms are abbreviated and underlined (e.g., $\underline{M}$, $\underline{r}$, $\underline{t}$, $\underline{F}$). In addition, when reporting the results of a statistical significance test, provide the name of the test, the degrees of freedom, the value of the test statistic, and the probability level. Here are two examples of sentences that describe statistical results:

> As predicted, subjects in the high-anxiety condition took longer to recognize the words ($\underline{M}$ = 2.63) than did subjects in the low-anxiety condition ($\underline{M}$ = 1.42), $\underline{t}$(20) = 2.34, $\underline{p}$ < .05.

> Job satisfaction scores were significantly correlated with marital satisfaction, $\underline{r}$(50) = .38, $\underline{p}$ < .05.

If your printer cannot produce a particular symbol, you may draw it in with black ink. Pay attention to the way that statistics are described in the articles that you read. You will find that you can vary your descriptions of results to best fit your data and presentation and to give some variety in the way that the sentences are constructed.

CONCLUSION

When you have completed your research report, you should feel proud of your effort. You have considered past research on a problem, conducted a research project, analyzed the results, and reported the findings. Such a research effort may result in a publication or a presentation at a convention. This is not the most important part of your research, however. What is most important is that you have acquired new knowledge and that your curiosity has been aroused so you will want to learn even more.

SAMPLE PAPER

The following is a typed manuscript of a paper that was published in a professional journal. This is intended to be a useful guide when you write and organize your own reports in APA style. The margin notes point out important elements of APA style. Read through the manuscript, paying particular attention to the general format, and make sure you understand the rules concerning page numbering, section headings, citing references, and the format of tables and figures. Writing your first research report is always a difficult and challenging task. It will become easier as you read the research of others and practice by writing reports of your own.

The example article by Robert A. Baron was originally published in the *Journal of Applied Psychology*.[1] Certain modifications were made to illustrate various elements of APA style. Dr. Baron graciously gave his permission to reprint the paper in this form.

---

1. Baron, R. A. (1983). "Sweet smell of success"? The impact of pleasant artificial scents on evaluations of job applicants. *Journal of Applied Psychology*, 68, 709–713. Copyright 1983 by the American Psychological Association. Adapted by permission.

Each page is numbered. A short title is typed above each page number.

Smell of Success

1

Title page lists title, author, affiliation, and running head. It is usually no more than 15 words.

"Sweet Smell of Success"?   The Impact of Pleasant
Artificial Scents on Evaluations of Job Applicants

Robert A. Baron

Purdue University

Double space the entire paper.

Center each line of the title, author, and affiliation.

Running head is used by the typesetter as a short title at the top of each page of the printed article. It is 50 spaces maximum, and capitalized.

Running head: EVALUATIONS OF JOB APPLICANTS

Smell of Success

2

Abstract

Male and female subjects interviewed male or female applicants for an entry-level management position. Applicants were actually confederates of the researcher who wore or did not wear a measured amount of a popular perfume or cologne. Following the interview, subjects rated each applicant on a number of job-related dimensions (e.g., to what extent is this individual qualified for the job?) and personal characteristics (e.g., how friendly is this person?). Results indicated that sex of subject and the presence or absence of scent interacted in affecting ratings of the applicants. Males assigned lower ratings to these persons when they wore perfume or cologne than when they did not; females showed the opposite pattern. Moreover, this was true both for job-related and personal characteristics. These and other results are interpreted as reflecting greater difficulty on the part of males than females in ignoring extraneous aspects of job applicants' appearance or grooming.

Abstract begins on a new page.

The word "Abstract" is centered and not underlined.

There is no paragraph indentation in the abstract.

The abstract is usually 100 to 150 words in length.

The word "gender" is now used more commonly than "sex."

Page 3 begins the main body of the paper including method, results, and discussion.

Center the title and then begin introduction section. Do not give author's name.

Use author's last name and date for reference citations.

Use "&" symbol when authors' names are within parentheses. Use "and" when authors' names are part of text.

Give all authors' names in the first citation. When there are three or more authors, use "et al." for subsequent citations.

"Sweet Smell of Success"? The Impact of Pleasant

Artificial Scents on Evaluations of Job Applicants

Each year, manufacturers of clothing, cosmetics,

and other grooming aids spend huge sums in an effort to

convince consumers that use of their products will

yield important benefits. Interestingly, a large body

of research concerned with the impact of personal

attractiveness suggests that to some degree, these

claims may be justified (Berscheid & Walster, 1978).

For example, it has been found that individuals who are

attractive in personal appearance have an advantage

over those who are not in hiring decisions (Dipboye,

Arvey, & Terpstra, 1977). Similarly, attractive

persons are often perceived as possessing more positive

traits (e.g., greater potential for success) than

unattractive ones (e.g., Cash, Gillen, & Burns, 1977).

Additional evidence suggests that these advantages do

not exist in all situations or under all circumstances.

In particular, females may experience negative rather

than positive effects as a result of physical

attractiveness (e.g., Heilman & Saruwatari, 1979). Yet

the benefits of attractiveness appear to be general

enough in scope to suggest that efforts to enhance

one's personal appearance are often worthwhile.

Typically, people try to enhance their appeal to

others through appropriate dress, cosmetics, and various forms of personal grooming. In addition, they often adopt another tactic--the use of perfume or cologne. Advertisements for these artificial scents indicate that they can enhance one's attractiveness and so contribute to both personal happiness and career success. The millions of dollars spent on such products each year suggest that many consumers accept the accuracy of these claims.

But are these claims actually valid? Do perfumes and colognes yield the uniformly beneficial outcomes so often predicted? Surprisingly, no empirical evidence on these questions exists. While the behavioral impact of naturally occurring scents has been extensively studied (e.g., pheromones; Leshner, 1978), little research has focused on the effects of artificial aromas (Levine & McBurney, 1981). More to the point, no investigation has sought to determine the impact of such scents in work-related settings. The present research was designed to attain preliminary evidence on such effects. Specifically, it sought to determine whether wearing pleasant artificial scents can affect the ratings assigned to job candidates during employment interviews. Past research on related topics suggests that such effects might arise in two distinct ways.

First, because perfume and cologne are pleasant, they may induce positive moods among interviewers. These reactions, in turn, may enhance liking for interviewees (Clore & Byrne, 1974). Second, the use of artificial scents may lead interviewers to make negative attributions about the traits of people who use them (see Harvey & Weary, 1981). For example, individuals who wear perfume or cologne to a job interview may be perceived as overly concerned with their appearance or as manipulative. To the extent such perceptions occur, evaluations of job candidates may be reduced.

In the absence of directly relevant data, no firm predictions were offered concerning which of these two potential effects might predominate. However, because the results of one study (Baron, 1981) suggested that persons wearing perfume or cologne may evoke negative reactions even in purely social settings, it was tentatively predicted that the impact of such scents on evaluations of job candidates might be primarily unfavorable.

Method

Subjects

Forty-six undergraduates (19 males, 27 females)

Method section begins immediately after the introduction (no new page). The word "Method" is centered.

Subsection headings (e.g., Subjects) are flush to the left margin, underlined, and stand alone on the line.

enrolled in introductory psychology at Purdue
University participated in the study. Subjects took
part in the investigation in order to satisfy a course
requirement.

Design

A 2 x 2 x 2 factorial design based on the presence
or absence of perfume or cologne, sex of subjects
(interviewers), and sex of confederates (interviewees)
was employed. Subjects were randomly assigned to each
cell of this design as they appeared for their
appointments with one exception: Because of the
lingering qualities of the two scents employed, it was
necessary to conduct scent and no scent sessions on
alternate days. One male and one female undergraduate
served as confederates throughout the study.

Procedure

The employment interview. The study was described
as being concerned with the manner in which individuals
form first impressions of others. Within this general
context, the subject played the role of a personnel
manager and interviewed the confederate, who played the
role of job applicant. The job in question was
described as an entry-level management position
involving a wide range of activities (e.g., visits to
various plants and customer sites, preparation of

The "Design" subsection was included by the author. It is not mandatory. There is always a "Subjects" subsection, however.

Do not use abbreviations for subjects, experimenters, and so on.

Paragraph headings were included; these further divide the subsection. Only the first word in a paragraph heading begins with a capital letter. The heading ends with a period, and the paragraph starts on the same line.

written reports). During the interview the subject (i.e., the interviewer) read a series of questions to the applicant (i.e., the confederate). The questions were typed on index cards and were quite straightforward. For example, one asked, "What are the major goals you are seeking in your career?" Another was, "How do you get along with other people?" The confederate's responses to each question were prepared in advance and thoroughly memorized. Thus, they were identical for all subjects. These replies were designed to be simple and noncontroversial and were found, during pretesting, to be both reasonable and believable by participants.

Dependent measures. Following the final interview question, the subject was taken to a separate room where he or she rated the applicant on a number of different dimensions. Four of these were directly job related (personal suitability for the job, qualifications for this position, potential for future success, and an overall recommendation about hiring). Four other items related to personal characteristics of the applicant (intelligence, warmth, friendliness, and modesty). All ratings were made on 7-point scales.

Presence or absence of pleasant scent. In the scent-present condition, the confederates applied two small drops of the appropriate perfume or cologne behind their ears prior to the start of each day's sessions. In the scent-absent condition, they did not make use of these substances. In both conditions, the confederates refrained from employing any scented cosmetics of their own. The two scents used were Jontue for the female complices and Brut for the males. These products were chosen through pretesting in which 12 undergraduate judges (8 females, 4 males) rated 11 popular perfumes and colognes presented in identical plastic bottles. Judges rated the pleasantness of each scent and its attractiveness when used by a member of the opposite sex. Jontue and Brut received the highest mean ratings in this preliminary study. Further, they were rated above the neutral point on both dimensions by all participants.

Additional pretesting indicated that two small drops of these products placed behind the ear produced a noticeable but far-from-overpowering aroma. Because data were collected in sessions lasting from 2 to 3 hours, little fading of these scents occurred in most cases. On those few occasions when data collection occupied a longer interval, an additional single drop of scent was applied. The confederates dressed neatly in all cases, in a manner suitable for an informal job

interview (they wore slacks and a blouse). They did
not wear more formal clothing because it was felt that
such behavior, unusual for a college campus, might
arouse suspicion among subjects.

Results

Ratings of the Applicants on Job-Related Dimensions

A multivariate analysis of variance (ANOVA) was
performed on the data for the four job-related items.
This analysis yielded an interaction between sex of
subject and presence of scent. Subsequent univariate
analyses performed for each item separately revealed
that the interaction was significant for three of the
four dependent measures: qualification for the job in
question, $F(1, 37) = 4.23$, $p < .05$, potential for
future success, $F(1, 37) = 8.21$, $p < .025$, and overall
hiring recommendation, $F(1, 37) = 4.32$, $p < .05$.
Inspection of the appropriate means indicated that this
interaction took the same form in each case. The
interaction is illustrated in Figure 1 which presents

Insert Figure 1 about here

---

the means for the overall hiring recommendation. Males
assigned lower ratings to the applicants when they wore
scent than when they did not, while females assigned

Results section does not begin on a new page; the heading is centered and not underlined.

The author used optional subsection headings to break the results section into two parts. If you do this, the title of each heading would depend on your particular study and the variables you investigated. You may have as many subsections as necessary for your study.

higher ratings to the applicants when they used scent than when they did not. Thus, it appeared that male interviewers reacted negatively to the presence of artificial scent whereas female interviewers reacted in the opposite fashion.

Ratings of the Applicants on Personal Dimensions

A multivariate ANOVA was performed on the data for the four items relating to personal characteristics of the applicant (intelligence, warmth, friendliness, modesty). This analysis yielded a significant effect for sex of subject, $F(4, 34) = 4.29$, $p < .025$, and an interaction between sex of subject and scent that approached significance, $F(4, 34) = 2.51$, $p < .08$. Univariate analyses on each item revealed that the effect of sex of subject was significant for two of the four dependent measures: warmth and friendliness, $F(1, 37) = 6.24$, $p < .025$, and $F(1, 37) = 8.80$, $p < .01$, respectively. Inspection of the appropriate means indicated that this effect reflected the fact that males assigned higher ratings to the applicants on both dimensions than did females. Also, the interaction was significant for ratings of intelligence, $F(1, 37) = 4.50$, and friendliness, $F(1, 37) = 4.54$, $p < .05$. The means are shown in Table 1. Males rated the applicants as lower in intelligence

All nouns, pronouns, verbs, adjectives, adverbs, and other major words in a subsection heading begin with capital letters.

When presenting data showing statistical significance, the name of the statistical test is underlined and followed by the degrees of freedom in parentheses. Note the spacing. If your typewriter does not have a necessary symbol, write the symbol in black ink.

Most statistical symbols are underlined (e.g., F, t, M, p, df).

Figures and tables, when used, must be mentioned in the text.

241

Give instructions for placement of any figures and tables at the appropriate point in the text. The actual figures or tables are placed at the end of the paper.

Note the spelling of "questionnaire."

Smell of Success

11

Insert Table 1 about here

---

and friendliness when wearing perfume or cologne than when not using these substances. In contrast, females rated the applicants higher in intelligence and friendliness when wearing perfume or cologne than when not wearing such substances.

A third multivariate analysis was performed on the three items relating to the applicants' personal appearance (attractiveness, personal grooming, neatness of dress). This analysis yielded two effects that closely approached significance: a main effect for scent and a main effect for sex of subject. Follow-up univariate analyses on each measure revealed that males rated the applicants as being better groomed than did females, $F(1, 37) = 4.19$, $p < .05$, and almost significantly better dressed than did females, $F(1, 37) = 3.86$, $p < .06$. Similar analyses performed to examine the main effect of scent revealed that the applicants were viewed as being better dressed when wearing scent than when not using this substance, $F(1, 37) = 5.67$, $p < .025$.

An additional item on the questionnaire asked subjects to rate their liking for the applicants. An

ANOVA on these data yielded a significant interaction between sex of subject and scent, F(1, 37) = 4.28, p < .05. Consistent with findings reported earlier, this interaction reflected the fact that males reported liking the applicants less in the presence of a pleasant scent (M = 3.56) than in its absence (M = 5.10). In contrast, females reported liking the applicants more in the presence of such scent (M = 5.21) than in its absence (M = 4.62).

Subjects' Ratings of Their Own Performance as Interviewers

Two final items on the questionnaire dealt with subjects' perceptions of their own performance as interviewers. The first of these required them to rate their effectiveness in this role. An ANOVA on these data yielded an interaction between sex of subject and scent that approached significance, F(1, 37 = 3.52, p < .07. This interaction reflected the fact that males rated themselves as poorer interviewers when the applicants wore scent (M = 3.70) than when they did not (M = 4.78). In contrast, females rated themselves as slightly more effective in the presence of scent (M = 4.29) than in its absence (M = 3.92).

The second item asked subjects to rate the extent to which their evaluations of the applicants'

Note that the word "data" is plural; thus, "the data show" (not "shows"). Similarly, "criteria" is plural.

qualifications were affected by the grooming and personal appearance of these persons. An ANOVA on these data yielded a main effect for sex of subject that approached significance, $F(1, 37) = 3.13$, $p < .10$. This reflected the fact that males reported being affected to a greater degree by the applicants' personal appearance ($M = 4.47$) than did females ($M = 3.88$).

Discussion

A substantial body of research findings indicates that various aspects of personal appearance can exert powerful effects on hiring decisions (e.g., Cash et al., 1977; Dipboye et al., 1977). The present study extends this previous work by indicating that such effects can also be produced by one aspect of personal grooming not previously investigated: the use of perfume or cologne. Specifically, it was found that ratings assigned to job applicants were significantly affected by the use of such substances. Moreover, this was true both for job-related and personal characteristics. The pattern of such effects, however, was not consistent with preliminary theorizing.

Initially, it was proposed that pleasant artificial scents might either enhance ratings of job applicants through the induction of positive mood

Discussion section immediately follows the results section. The word "Discussion" is centered and not underlined.

244

Smell of Success

14

states (e.g., Clore & Byrne, 1974) or reduce such
ratings through unfavorable shifts in social perception
or attributions (see Harvey & Weary, 1981). Neither of
these patterns emerged. Instead, males and females
reacted in sharply contrasting ways to the presence of
perfume or cologne. Females assigned higher ratings to
the applicants when they used artificial scents than
when they did not, whereas the opposite was true for
males: they assigned lower ratings to these persons
when they wore perfume or cologne than when they did
not. Given that both males and females reacted
positively to the two scents used during pretesting, it
seems unlikely that these opposite reactions in the
main study stemmed from contrasting moods or affective
states. Instead, cognitive factors seem more likely to
have played a role in generating the obtained results.
One possible mechanism in this regard is suggested by
findings obtained with other dependent measures. As
may be recalled, males reported being influenced to a
greater extent than females by various aspects of the
applicants' appearance or grooming. Similarly, they
rated themselves as less effective in the role of
interviewer in the presence of perfume or cologne than
in its absence. In contrast, females perceived
themselves as slightly more effective in this role in

the presence of artificial scents than in their
absence. Together, these findings suggest that males
were more strongly affected by scent and other
extraneous aspects of the applicants' appearance or
grooming than females, and were quite aware of this
fact. To the extent this was true, it is not
surprising that they reacted negatively to the presence
of perfume or cologne. Briefly, males may have
realized that such scents would interfere with their
ability to serve as an effective interviewer. This, in
turn, caused them to experience annoyance or resentment
toward the applicants for making use of these
substances, and so to downrate them on several key
dependent measures. Females, in contrast, were less
likely to experience such reactions. Thus, they may
have responded more directly to the pleasant nature of
the two scents employed. In short, the obtained
interaction between presence of scent and sex of
subjects may have stemmed from differences in the
ability of males and females to "filter out" irrelevant
aspects of the applicants' grooming or appearance.
Although this interpretation is consistent with the
present findings, it is, of course, only tentative in
nature. It should be noted, though, that it agrees
with evidence suggesting that in many species, males

react more strongly to certain naturally occurring scents (e.g., pheromones) than do females (see Leshner, 1978).

At this point, it seems important to comment briefly on the overall significance of the present findings. Past research has called attention to the fact that job applicants' appearance and grooming can strongly affect the interview process (Dipboye et al., 1977). The present results extend this previous work by indicating that the direction of such effects is not uniformly positive. On the contrary, it appears that interviewers may sometimes react negatively to efforts at self-enhancement by job applicants. Further, such reactions appear to stem from complex cognitive mechanisms as well as from current affective states. Full comprehension of these mechanisms may add appreciably to our understanding of the job interview process. Thus, they seem worthy of further, detailed study. Until they are fully clarified, however, the practical implications of the present findings for applicants seem clear: Use artificial scents and other grooming aids with caution, for the impact may sometimes be negative.

Before concluding, it should be noted that several steps were taken to enhance the generalizability of the

present research. The description of the job in
question was quite realistic, and the questions asked
during the interview were similar to ones that might
well be posed to actual job candidates. The perfume or
cologne worn by confederates were popular national
brands, and the amount used was carefully adjusted to
reflect levels typically applied under ordinary life
conditions. These precautions, and the fact that
earlier studies employing simulated interviews have
often yielded valuable results (e.g., Imada & Hakel,
1977), suggest that the present findings may possess
considerable generality. However, it is fully realized
that the precise extent to which they may be
generalized can only be established through further
research conducted in a variety of different settings.

Smell of Success

18

References

Baron, R. A. (1981). The role of olfaction in human

social behavior: Effects of a pleasant scent on

attraction and social perception. <u>Personality and</u>

<u>Social Psychology Bulletin</u>, <u>7</u>, 611-617.

Berscheid, E., & Walster, E. (1978). <u>Interpersonal</u>

<u>attraction</u> (2nd ed.). Reading, MA: Addison-Wesley.

Cash, T. F., Gillen, B., & Burns, D. S. (1977).

Sexism and beautyism in personnel consultant

decision-making. <u>Journal of Applied Psychology</u>, <u>62</u>,

301-311.

Clore, G. L., & Byrne, D. A. (1974). A reinforcement

affect model of attraction. In T. L. Huston (Ed.),

<u>Foundations of interpersonal attraction</u> (pp.

143-170). New York: Academic Press.

Dipboye, R. L., Arvey, R. D., & Terpstra, D. E.

(1977). Sex and physical attractiveness of raters

and applicants as determinants of resume

evaluations. <u>Journal of Applied Psychology</u>, <u>62</u>,

288-294.

Harvey, J. H., & Weary, G. (1981). <u>Perspectives on</u>

<u>attributional processes</u>. Dubuque, IA: William C.

Brown.

Heilman, M. S., & Saruwatari, L. R. (1979). When

References begin on a new page. The first line of each reference is flush to the margin; subsequent lines are indented three spaces.

These references contain journal articles (Baron), books (Berscheid & Walster), chapters in books (Clore & Byrne), and unpublished papers (Levine & McBurney).

beauty is beastly: The effects of appearance and sex on evaluations of job applicants for managerial and nonmanagerial jobs. <u>Organizational Behavior and Human Performance</u>, <u>23</u>, 360-372.

Imada, A. S., & Hakel, M. D. (1977). Influence of nonverbal communication and rater proximity on impressions and decisions in simulated employment interviews. <u>Journal of Applied Psychology</u>, <u>62</u>, 295-300.

Leshner, A. I. (1978). <u>An introduction to behavioral endocrinology</u>. New York: Oxford University Press.

Levine, J. M., & McBurney, D. H. (1981, August). <u>The role of olfaction in social perception and behavior</u>. Paper presented at the Third Ontario Symposium on Personality and Social Psychology, Toronto.

Smell of Success

20

Author Notes

The author wishes to express his thanks to Mark
Mannella, Patti Schacht, Keith Short, and Linda
Thiemrodt for their able assistance in collection of
the data, and to Robert W. Horton for expert
statistical analyses. Thanks are also due to Howard
Weiss for insightful comments on an earlier draft of
this article.

Author notes are
optional. When
used, they are typed
on a separate page
following the
references.

Each table is typed on a new page. Use Arabic, not Roman, numerals to number your tables.

Note that only horizontal lines are used to separate sections of the table.

Smell of Success

21

Table 1

Mean Ratings of the Applicants on Personal Dimensions

Sex of subject	Scent Condition	
	No scent	Scent
Intelligence ratings		
Males	5.44	5.10
Females	4.08	5.64
Friendliness ratings		
Males	6.68	6.10
Females	5.30	5.85

Smell of Success

22

Figure Caption

<u>Figure 1</u>. Mean hiring recommendation as a function of sex of subject and presence of scent.

Begin the figure captions on a new page. All figure captions will go here.

Underline the figure number to begin each figure caption. Only the first word of the caption is capitalized.

The figure caption page may not be necessary for student reports. Instead, the caption would appear on the figure page.

Each figure must go on a separate page.

Pages on which figures are drawn are not numbered nor is there a page identification. To identify the figure, write the figure number in pencil on the back of the page.

Include all necessary labels for interpreting the figure.

Draw figures carefully and make sure everything is accurate.

Note that, as in all graphs, the independent variable is placed on the horizontal axis, and the dependent variable is placed on the vertical axis.

Always draw figures in black ink.

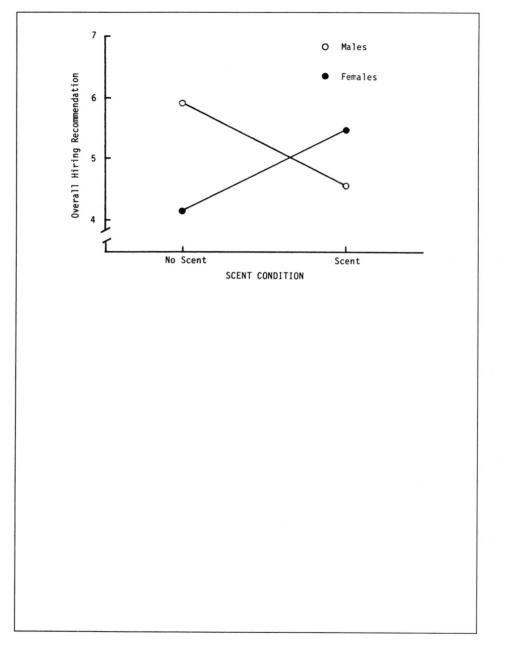

APPENDIX

B

Statistical Tests

Descriptive Statistics
Measures of Central Tendency
The Mode
The Median
The Mean
Measures of Variability
The Range
The Variance and Standard Deviation
Statistical Significance Tests
Chi-square
Example
Significance of Chi-square
Concluding Remarks
Mann–Whitney *U* Test
Example
Significance of U
Concluding remarks
Analysis of Variance (*F* Test)
Analysis of Variance: One Independent
   Variable
Sum of Squares
SS_{TOTAL}
SS_A
SS_{ERROR}
Mean Squares
Obtaining the F *Value*
Significance of F

Concluding Remarks
Analysis of Variance: Two Independent
   Variables
SS_{TOTAL}
SS_A
SS_B
$SS_{A \times B}$
SS_{ERROR}
Mean Square
Obtaining the F *Value*
Significance of F
Analysis of Variance: Repeated Measures and
   Matched Subjects
Analysis of Variance: Conclusion
Measures of Strength of Association
Contingency Coefficient
Spearman Rank-Order Correlation Coefficient
Example
Significance of rho
Pearson Product-Moment Correlation
   Coefficient
Example
Significance of r
Statistical Analysis with Computers
Statistical Programs
General Procedures

The purpose of this appendix is to provide the formulas and calculational procedures for analysis of data. All possible statistical tests are not included, but a variety of tests that should be appropriate for many of the research designs you might use are given.

We will examine both descriptive and inferential statistics. Before you study the statistics, however, you should review the properties of measurement scales described in Chapter 9. Remember that there are four types of measurement scales: nominal scales, ordinal scales, interval scales, and ratio scales. Nominal scales have no numeric properties, ordinal scales provide rank-order information only, and interval and ratio scales have equal intervals between the points on the scale. In addition, ratio scales have a true zero point. You will also recall from Chapter 9 that the appropriate statistical analysis is determined by the type of design and by the measurement scale that was used in the study. As we proceed, the discussion of the various statistical tests will draw to your attention the relevant measurement scale restrictions that apply.

The examples below use small and simple data sets so the calculations can be easily done by hand using a calculator. However, you will find that the calculations become tedious and you are more likely to make errors when working with large data sets and when you have to perform many statistical analyses in your study. Computer programs to perform statistical analyses have been developed to make the process easier and reduce calculation errors. Such programs will be described at the end of this appendix.

DESCRIPTIVE STATISTICS

With a knowledge of the types of measurement scales, we can turn to a consideration of statistical techniques. We can start with two ways of describing a set of scores: central tendency and variability.

Measures of central tendency

A measure of central tendency gives a single number that describes how an entire group scores as a whole, or on the average. Three different central tendency measures are available—the mode, the median, and the mean.

The mode The mode is the most frequently occurring score. Table B-1 shows a set of scores and the descriptive statistics that are discussed in this section. The most frequently occurring score in these data is 5: No calculations are necessary to find the mode. The mode can be used with any of the four types of measurement scales. However, it is the only measure of central tendency that can be used with nominal scale data. If you are measuring gender and find there are 100 females and 50 males, the mode is "female" because this is the most frequently occurring category on the nominal scale.

Score	Descriptive statistic
1	Mode $= 5$
2	
4	Median $= 5$
4	
5	$\overline{X} = \dfrac{\Sigma X}{N} = 4.5$
5	
5	
6	Range $= 6$
6	
7	$s^2 = \dfrac{\Sigma(X - \overline{X})^2}{N - 1} = \dfrac{\Sigma X^2 - N\overline{X}^2}{N - 1} = \dfrac{233 - 202.5}{9} = 3.388$
$\Sigma X = \overline{45}$	$s = \sqrt{s^2} = 1.84$
$\Sigma X^2 = 233$	
$N = 10$	

Table B-1
Descriptive statistics for a set of scores

The median The median is the score that divides the group in half: 50% of the scores are below the median and 50% are above the median. When the scores have been ordered from lowest to highest (as in Table B-1), the median is easily found. If there is an odd number of scores, you simply find the middle score. (For example, if there are 11 scores, the sixth score is the median, since there are five lower and five higher scores.) If there is an even number of scores, the median is the midpoint between the two middle scores. In the data in Table B-1, there are 10 scores, so the fifth and sixth scores are the two middle scores. To find the median, we add the two middle scores and divide by 2. Thus, in Table B-1 the median is

$$\frac{5 + 5}{2} = 5$$

The median can be used with ordinal, interval, or ratio scale data. It is most likely to be used with ordinal data, however. This is because calculation of the median considers only the rank ordering of scores and not the actual size of the scores.

The mean The mean does take into account the actual size of the scores. Thus, the mean is based on more information about the scores than either the mode or the median. However, it is appropriate only for interval or ratio scale data.

The mean is the sum of the scores in a group divided by the number of scores. The calculational formula for the mean can be expressed as

$$\overline{X} = \frac{\Sigma X}{N}$$

where $\overline{X}$ is the symbol for the mean. In this formula, X represents a score obtained by an individual, and the Σ symbol indicates that scores are to be summed or added. The symbol ΣX can be read as "sum of the Xs" and simply is an indication that the scores are to be added. Thus, ΣX in the data from Table B-1 is

$$1 + 2 + 4 + 4 + 5 + 5 + 5 + 6 + 6 + 7 = 45$$

The N in the formula symbolizes the number of scores in the group. In our example, $N = 10$. Thus, we can now calculate the mean:

$$\overline{X} = \frac{\Sigma X}{N} = \frac{45}{10} = 4.5$$

Measures of variability

In addition to describing the central tendency of the set of scores, we want to describe how much the scores vary among themselves. How much spread is there in the set of scores?

The range   The range is the highest score minus the lowest score. In our example, the range is 6. The range is not a very useful statistic, however, because it is based on only two scores in the distribution. It doesn't take into account all of the information that is available in the entire set of scores.

The variance and standard deviation   The variance, and a related statistic called the standard deviation, uses all the scores to yield a measure of variability. The variance indicates the degree to which scores vary about the group mean. The formula for the variance (symbolized as s^2) is

$$s^2 = \frac{\Sigma(X - \overline{X})^2}{N - 1}$$

where $(X - \overline{X})^2$ is an individual score, X, minus the mean, $\overline{X}$, and then squared. Thus, $(X - \overline{X})^2$ is the squared deviation of each score from the mean. The Σ sign indicates that these squared deviation scores are to be summed. Finally, dividing by $N - 1$ gives the mean of the squared deviations. The variance, then, is the mean of the squared deviations from the group mean. (Squared deviations are used because simple deviations would add up to zero. $N - 1$ is used in most cases for statistical purposes because the scores represent a sample and not an entire population. As the sample size becomes larger, it makes little difference whether N or $N - 1$ is used.)

The data in Table B-1 can be used to illustrate calculation of the variance. $\Sigma(X - \overline{X})^2$ is equal to

$$(1 - 4.5)^2 + (2 - 4.5)^2 + (4 - 4.5)^2 + (4 - 4.5)^2 + (5 - 4.5)^2$$
$$+ (5 - 4.5)^2 + (5 - 4.5)^2 + (6 - 4.5)^2 + (6 - 4.5)^2 + (7 - 4.5)^2$$
$$= 30.50$$

The next step is to divide $\Sigma(X - \overline{X})^2$ by $N - 1$. The calculation for the variance, then, is

$$s^2 = \frac{\Sigma(X - \overline{X})^2}{N - 1} = \frac{30.50}{9} = 3.388$$

A simpler calculational formula for the variance is

$$s^2 = \frac{\Sigma X^2 - N\overline{X}^2}{N - 1}$$

where ΣX^2 is the sum of the squared individual scores, and $\overline{X}^2$ is the mean squared. You can confirm that the two formulas are identical by computing the variance using this simpler formula (remember that ΣX^2 tells you to square each score and then sum the squared scores). This simpler formula is much easier to work with when there are many scores, because each deviation doesn't have to be calculated.

The standard deviation is the square root of the variance. Because the variance uses squared scores, the variance doesn't describe the amount of variability in the same units of measurement as the original scale. The standard deviation (s) corrects this problem. Thus, the standard deviation is the average deviation of scores from the mean.

STATISTICAL SIGNIFICANCE TESTS

This section describes several statistical significance tests. All of these tests are used to determine the probability that the outcome of the research was due to the operation of random error. All use the logic of the null hypothesis discussed in Chapter 9. We will consider three significance tests in this section: The Chi-square test, the Mann–Whitney U test, and the analysis of variance or F test.

Chi-square (χ^2)

The Chi-square (Greek letter chi, squared) test is used when dealing with nominal scale data. It is used when the data consist of frequencies—the number of subjects who fall into each of several categories.

Chi-square can be used with either the experimental or correlational method. It is used in conjunction with the experimental method when the dependent variable is measured on a nominal scale. It is used with the correlational method when both variables are measured on nominal scales.

Example Suppose you want to know whether there is a relationship between gender and hand dominance. To do this, you sample 50 males and 50 females and ask whether they are right-handed, left-handed, or ambidextrous (use both hands with equal skill). Your data collection involves classifying each person as male or female and as right-handed, left-handed, or ambidextrous.

Table B-2
Data for
hypothetical study
on hand
dominance: Chi-
square test

Sex of subject	Right	Hand dominance Left	Ambidextrous	Row totals
Male	$O_1 = 15$ $E_1 = 25$	$O_2 = 30$ $E_2 = 20$	$O_3 = 5$ $E_3 = 5$	50
Female	$O_4 = 35$ $E_4 = 25$	$O_5 = 10$ $E_5 = 20$	$O_6 = 5$ $E_6 = 5$	50
Column totals	50	40	10	$N = 100$

Computations:	Cell number	$\dfrac{(O - E)^2}{E}$	
	1	4.00	
	2	5.00	
	3	0.00	$\chi^2 = \Sigma\dfrac{(O - E)^2}{E}$
	4	4.00	$= 18.00$
	5	5.00	
	6	0.00	
		$\Sigma = 18.00$	

Fictitious data for such a study are presented in Table B-2. The frequencies labeled as "O" in each of the six cells in the table refer to the number of male and female subjects who fall into each of the three hand-dominance categories. The frequencies labeled "E" refer to frequencies that are expected if the null hypothesis is correct. It is important that each subject falls into only one of the cells when using Chi-square (that is, no subject can be counted as both male and female or both right- and left-handed).

The Chi-square test examines the extent to which the frequencies that are actually observed in the study differ from the frequencies that are expected if the null hypothesis is correct. The null hypothesis states that there is no relationship between sex and hand dominance: Males and females do not differ on this characteristic.

The formula for computing Chi-square is

$$\chi^2 = \Sigma\frac{(O - E)^2}{E}$$

where O is the *observed* frequency in each cell, E is the *expected* frequency in each cell, and the symbol Σ refers to summing over all cells. The steps in calculating the value of χ^2 are:

Step 1. Arrange the observed frequencies in a table such as Table B-2.

Note that in addition to the observed frequencies in each cell, the table presents row totals, column totals, and the total number of observations (N).

Step 2. Calculate the expected frequencies for each of the cells in the table. The expected frequency formula is

$$E = \frac{\text{Row total} \times \text{Column total}}{N}$$

where the row total refers to the row total for the cell, and the column total refers to the column total for the cell. Thus, the expected frequency for cell 1 (male right-handedness) is

$$E_1 = \frac{50 \times 50}{100} = 25$$

The expected frequencies for each of the cells are shown in Table B-2 below the observed frequencies.

Step 3. Calculate the quantity $(O - E)^2/E$ for each cell. For cell 1, this quantity is

$$\frac{(15 - 25)^2}{25} = \frac{100}{25} = 4.00$$

Step 4. Find the value of χ^2 by summing the $(O - E)^2/E$ values found in step 3. The calculations for obtaining χ^2 for the example data are shown in Table B-2.

Significance of Chi-square   The significance of the obtained χ^2 value can be evaluated by consulting a table of critical values of χ^2. A table of critical χ^2 values is presented as Table C-2 in Appendix C. The critical χ^2 values indicate the value that the *obtained* χ^2 must equal or exceed to be significant at the .10 level, the .05 level, and the .01 level.

To be able to use the table of critical values of χ^2 as well as most other statistical tables, you must understand the concept of *degrees of freedom (df)*. The critical value of χ^2 for any given study depends on the degrees of freedom. Degrees of freedom refers to the number of scores that are free to vary. In the table of categories for a Chi-square test, the number of degrees of freedom is the number of cells in which the frequencies are free to vary once we know the row totals and column totals. The degrees of freedom for Chi-square is easily calculated:

$$df = (R - 1)(C - 1)$$

where R is the number of rows in the table and C is the number of columns. In our example in Table B-1, there are two rows and three columns, so there are 2 degrees of freedom. In a study with three rows and three columns, there are 4 degrees of freedom, and so on.

In order to use Table C-2, find the correct degrees of freedom and then determine the critical value of χ^2 necessary to reject the null hypothesis at the chosen significance level. With 2 degrees of freedom, the obtained χ^2 value must be *equal to* or *greater than* the critical value of 5.991 in order to be significant at the .05 level. There is only a .05 probability that a χ^2 of 5.991 would occur if only random error is operating. Because the obtained χ^2 from our example is 18.00, we can reject the null hypothesis that there is no relationship between sex and hand dominance. (The Chi-square was based on fictitious data, but it would be relatively easy for you to determine for yourself whether there is in fact a relationship.)

Concluding remarks   The Chi-square test is extremely useful and is used frequently in all of the behavioral sciences. The calculational formula described is generalizable to expanded studies in which there are more categories on either of the variables. One note of caution, however: When both variables have only two categories, so that there are only two rows and two columns, the formula for calculating Chi-square changes slightly. In such cases, the formula is

$$\chi^2 = \sum \frac{(|O - E|) - .5)^2}{E}$$

where $|O - E|$ is the absolute value of $O - E$, and .5 is a constant that is subtracted for each cell.

Mann–Whitney U test

The Mann–Whitney U test is used to test whether there is a significant difference between two groups when the subjects were measured on an ordinal scale. The two groups may have been formed using either the experimental or the correlational method. However, the Mann–Whitney U test can only be used with an independent groups design, in which the two groups are made up of different subjects.

Example   Suppose you want to test the hypothesis that only children are less aggressive than children who have at least one brother or sister. To collect data, you go to an elementary school class and determine which pupils are only children and which have siblings. You also ask the teacher to rate each child's aggressiveness on a scale of 1 to 25 (least aggressive to most aggressive). Before collecting your data, you determine that your aggression measure is really an ordinal scale, so you decide to use the Mann–Whitney U test to evaluate your results.

Table B-3 shows fictitious results for such a study. The table shows the score the teacher gave to each child, the rank ordering of these scores, and the basic calculations for the Mann–Whitney U test. It is important to keep in mind that it is the *rank order* of scores that is crucial in the U test, not the size of the actual scores on the measurement scale.

Finding the value of U involves making two calculations:

$$(1)\ N_1 N_2 + \frac{N_1(N_1 + 1)}{2} - R_1$$

$$(2)\ N_1 N_2 + \frac{N_2(N_2 + 1)}{2} - R_2$$

Table B-3
Data for
hypothetical
experiment on
only children and
aggression:
Mann–Whitney U
test

Only children		Children with siblings	
Score	Rank	Score	Rank
1	1	5	6.5
2	2.5	5	6.5
2	2.5	9	11
3	4	10	12
4	5	11	13
6	8	13	15
7	9	14	16
8	10	16	18
12	14	19	19
15	17	23	20
	$R_1 = 73$		$R_2 = 137$

$$(1)\ N_1N_2 + \frac{N_1(N_1 + 1)}{2} - R_1 \qquad (2)\ N_1N_2 + \frac{N_2(N_2 + 1)}{2} - R_2$$

$$= (10)(10) + \frac{(10)(11)}{2} - 73 \qquad = (10)(10) + \frac{(10)(11)}{2} - 137$$

$$= 82 \qquad\qquad\qquad\qquad = 18$$

Since (2) is the smaller calculation, $U = 18$

where R_1 is the sum of the ranks in the first group, R_2 is the sum of the ranks in the second group, and N_1 and N_2 refer to the number of subjects in groups one and two, respectively. The value of U is the *smaller* of these two quantities. To calculate U, follow these steps:

Step 1. Arrange the scores in each group from lowest to highest, as was done with the scores in Table B-3. Assign a rank to each of the scores. The smallest score receives a rank of 1, the next highest score receives a rank of 2, and so on. Ranks are assigned on the basis of lowest to highest, regardless of which group the subject is in. When there are tied scores, each subject receives the mean of the rank he or she occupies. For example, in Table B-2, two subjects received a score of 2. Since these subjects occupy the 2nd and 3rd ranks, each receives the same mean rank of 2.5.

Step 2. Calculate the sum of ranks for each of the groups.

Step 3. Calculate the two quantities described above. The value of U is the *smaller* of these two quantities.

Significance of U Critical values for determining the significance of U are shown in Table C-3. To use this table, first determine your significance level. Table C-3 is made up of three smaller tables (A, B, and C) for significance levels of .10, .05, and .01.

If you choose a .05 level of significance use the table marked (B). Find the critical value of U for N_1 and N_2 in your study. In our example, $N_1 = 10$ and $N_2 = 10$. The critical value of U at the .05 level, then, is 23. To be significant, the obtained value of U must be *equal to* or *smaller than* the

263

critical value. Since the obtained value of U (18) is smaller than the critical value (23), we conclude that the results are significant at the .05 level.

A note of caution: The significance of U is determined by whether the obtained U is *smaller* than the critical value. This procedure is directly opposite to the procedures used with most other significance tests (such as the Chi-square test). With most tests, the obtained value must *exceed* the critical value to be significant.

Concluding remarks   The Mann–Whitney U test is very useful when the data are of an ordinal scale type and an independent groups design has been used. Other tests must be used, however, when the study used a repeated measures design. Such tests may be found in statistics texts.

Analysis of variance (*F* test)

The analysis of variance, or F test, is used to determine whether there is a significant difference between groups that have been measured on either interval or ratio scales. The groups may have been formed using either the experimental or the correlational method; the important thing is that at least an interval scale measure was used. The analysis of variance may be used with either independent groups or repeated measures designs. Procedures for calculating F for both types of designs are presented.

Analysis of variance: One independent variable

To illustrate the use of the analysis of variance, let's consider a hypothetical experiment on physical distance and self-disclosure. You think that people will reveal more about themselves to an interviewer when they are sitting close to the interviewer than they will when sitting farther away. To test this idea, you conduct an experiment on interviewing. Subjects are told that interviewing techniques are being studied. Each subject is seated in a room; the interviewer comes into the room and sits at one of three distances from the subject: close (2 feet, or .61 meters), medium (4 feet, or 1.22 meters), or far (6 feet, or 1.83 meters). The distance chosen by the interviewer is the independent variable manipulation. Subjects are randomly assigned to the three distance conditions, and the interviewer's behavior is constant in all conditions. The interview consists of a number of questions, and the dependent variable is the number of personal, revealing statements made by the subject during the interview.

Fictitious data for such an experiment are shown in Table B-4. Note that this is an independent groups design with five subjects in each group. The calculations of the systematic variance and error variance involve computing the *sum of squares* for the different types of variance.

Sum of squares   Sum of squares stands for the *sum of squared deviations from the mean*. Computing an analysis of variance for the data in Table B-4 involves three sums of squares: (1) SS_{TOTAL}, the sum of squared deviations of each individual score from the grand mean; (2) SS_A, the sum of squared deviations of each of the group means from the grand mean; and (3) SS_{ERROR},

	Distance (A)	
Close (A1)	Medium (A2)	Far (A3)

Table B-4
Data for
hypothetical
experiment on
distance and self-
disclosure:
Analysis of
variance

Close (A1)	Medium (A2)	Far (A3)
33	21	20
24	25	13
31	19	15
29	27	10
34	26	14
$T_{A1} = 151$	$T_{A2} = 118$	$T_{A3} = 72$
$n_{A1} = 5$	$n_{A2} = 5$	$n_{A3} = 5$
$\overline{X}_{A1} = 30.20$	$\overline{X}_{A2} = 23.60$	$\overline{X}_{A3} = 14.40$
$\Sigma X_{A1}^2 = 4623$	$\Sigma X_{A2}^2 = 2832$	$\Sigma X_{A3}^2 = 1090$
$T_{A1}^2 = 22801$	$T_{A2}^2 = 13924$	$T_{A3}^2 = 5184$

$$SS_{TOTAL} = \Sigma X^2 - \frac{G^2}{N} = (4623 + 2832 + 1090) - \frac{(151 + 118 + 72)^2}{15}$$

$$= 8545 - 7752.07$$

$$= 792.93$$

$$SS_A = \Sigma \frac{T_a^2}{n_a} - \frac{G^2}{N} = \left[\frac{(151)^2}{5} + \frac{(118)^2}{5} + \frac{(72)^2}{5}\right] - 7752.07$$

$$= 8381.80 - 7752.07$$

$$= 629.73$$

$$SS_{ERROR} = \Sigma X^2 - \Sigma \frac{T_a^2}{n_a} = 8545 - 8381.80$$

$$= 163.20$$

the sum of squared deviations of the individual scores from their respective group means. The "A" in SS_A is used to indicate that we are dealing with the systematic variance associated with independent variable A.

The three sums of squares are deviations from a mean (recall that we calculated such deviations earlier when discussing the variance in a set of scores). We could calculate the deviations directly with the data in Table B-4, but such calculations are hard to work with, so we will use simplified formulas for computational purposes. The computational formulas are

$$SS_{TOTAL} = \Sigma X^2 - \frac{G^2}{N}$$

$$SS_A = \Sigma \frac{T_a^2}{n_a} - \frac{G^2}{N}$$

$$SS_{ERROR} = \Sigma X^2 - \Sigma \frac{T_a^2}{n_a}$$

You might note here that $SS_{TOTAL} = SS_A + SS_{ERROR}$. The actual computations are shown in Table B-4.

SS_{TOTAL}   The formula for SS_{TOTAL} is

$$\Sigma X^2 - \frac{G^2}{N}$$

ΣX^2 is the sum of the squared scores of all subjects in the experiment. Each of the scores is squared first and then added. Thus, for the data in Table B-4, ΣX^2 is $33^2 + 24^2 + 31^2$ and so on until all of the scores have been squared and added. If you are doing the calculations by hand or with a pocket calculator, it may be convenient to find the ΣX^2 for the scores in each group and then add these up for your final computation. This is what I did for the data in the table. The G in the formula stands for the grand total of all of the scores. This involves adding up the scores for all subjects. The grand total is then squared and divided by N, the total number of subjects in the experiment. When computing the sum of squares, you should always keep the calculations clearly labeled, because you can simplify later calculations by referring to these earlier ones. Once you have computed SS_{TOTAL}, SS_A can be calculated.

SS_A   The formula for SS_A is

$$\Sigma \frac{T_a^2}{n_a} - \frac{G^2}{N}$$

The T_a in this formula refers to the total of the scores in group a of independent variable A. [T_a is a shorthand notation for ΣX in each group (recall the computation of ΣX from our discussion of the mean). The T_a symbol is used to avoid having to deal with too many Σ signs in our calculational procedures.] The a is used to symbolize the particular group number; thus, T_a is a general symbol for T_1, T_2, and T_3. Looking at our data in Table B-4, $T_1 = 151$, $T_2 = 118$, and $T_3 = 72$. These are the sums of the scores in each of the groups. After T_a has been calculated, T_a^2 is found by squaring T_a. Now, T_a^2 is divided by n_a, the number of subjects in group a. Once the quantity T_a^2/n_a has been computed for each group, the quantities are summed as indicated by the Σ symbol.

Notice that the second part of the formula, G^2/N, was calculated when SS_{TOTAL} was obtained. Since we already have this quantity, it needn't be calculated again when computing SS_A. After obtaining SS_A, we can now compute SS_{ERROR}.

SS_{ERROR}   The formula for SS_{ERROR} is

$$\Sigma X^2 - \Sigma \frac{T_a^2}{n_a}$$

Both of these quantities were calculated above in obtaining SS_{TOTAL} and SS_A. To obtain SS_{ERROR}, we merely have to find these quantities and perform the proper subtraction.

Source of variance	Sum of squares	df	Mean square	F
A	SS_A	$a - 1$	SS_A/df_A	MS_A/MS_{ERROR}
Error	SS_{ERROR}	$N - a$	SS_{ERROR}/df_{ERROR}	
Total	SS_{TOTAL}	$N - 1$		
A	629.73	2	314.87	23.15
Error	162.20	12	13.60	
Total	792.93	14		

As a check on the calculations, we can make sure that $SS_{TOTAL} = SS_A + SS_{ERROR}$.

The next step in the computation of the analysis of variance is to find the *mean square* for each of the sums of squares. We can then find the value of F. The necessary computations are shown in an analysis of variance summary table in Table B-5. Constructing a summary table is the easiest way to complete the computations.

Mean squares After obtaining the sum of squares, it is necessary to compute the mean squares. Mean square stands for the *mean of the sum of the squared deviations from the mean* or, more simply, the mean of the sum of squares. The mean square (MS) is the sum of squares divided by the degrees of freedom. The degrees of freedom are determined by the number of scores in the sum of squares that are free to vary. The mean squares are the variances that are used in computing the value of F.

From Table B-5, you can see that the mean squares that concern us are the mean square for A (systematic variance) and the mean square for error (error variance). The formulas are

$$MS_A = SS_A/df_A$$

$$MS_{ERROR} = SS_{ERROR}/df_{ERROR}$$

where $df_A = a - 1$ (the number of groups minus one) and $df_{ERROR} = N - a$ (the total number of subjects minus the number of groups).

Obtaining the F value The obtained F for the data in Table B-4 is found by dividing MS_A by MS_{ERROR}. If only random error is operating, the expected value of F is 1.0. The greater the F value, the lower the probability that the results of the experiment were due to chance error.

Significance of F To determine the significance of the obtained F value, it is necessary to compare the obtained F to a critical value of F. Table C-5 in Appendix C shows critical values of F for significance levels of .10, .05, and .01. To find the critical value of F, locate on the table the degrees of freedom for the numerator of the ratio (the systematic variance) and the degrees of freedom for the denominator of the F ratio (the error variance). The intersection of these two degrees of freedom on the table is the critical F value.

The appropriate degrees of freedom for our sample data are 2 and 12 (see Table B-5). The critical F value from Table C-5 is 3.89 for a .05 level of significance. For the results to be significant, the obtained F value must be equal to or greater than the critical value. Since the obtained value of F in Table B-5 (23.15) is greater than the critical value, we conclude that the results are significant and reject the null hypothesis that the means of the groups are equal in the population.

Concluding remarks   The analysis of variance for one independent variable with an independent groups design can be used when there are two or more groups in the experiment. The general formulas described are appropriate for all such designs. Also, the calculations are the same whether the experimental or the correlational method is used to form the groups. The formulas are also applicable to cases in which the number of subjects in each group is not equal (although you should have approximately equal numbers of subjects in the groups).

When the design of the experiment includes more than two levels of the independent variable (as in our example experiment, which had three groups), the obtained F value doesn't tell us whether any two specific groups are significantly different from one another. One way to examine the difference between two groups in such a study is to use the formula for SS_A to compute the sum of squares and the mean square for the two groups (the df in this case is $2 - 1$). When doing this, the previously calculated MS_{ERROR} should be used as the error variance term for computing F. More complicated procedures for evaluating the difference between two groups in such designs are available, but these are beyond the scope of this book.

Analysis of variance: Two independent variables

In this section, we will describe the computations for analysis of variance with a factorial design containing two independent variables. The formulas apply to an $A \times B$ factorial design with any number of levels of the independent variables. The formulas apply only to a completely independent groups design with different subjects in each group, and the number of subjects in each group must be equal. Once you understand this analysis, however, you should have little trouble understanding the analysis for more complicated designs with repeated measures or unequal numbers of subjects. With these limitations in mind, let's consider example data from a hypothetical experiment.

The experiment uses a 2×2 IV $\times$ SV factorial design. Variable A is the type of instruction used in a course, and variable B is the intelligence level of the students. The students are classified as either of "low" or "high" intelligence on the basis of intelligence test scores and are randomly assigned to one of two types of classes. One class uses the traditional lecture method; the other class uses an individualized learning approach with frequent testing over small amounts of material, proctors to help individual students, and a stipulation that students master each section of material before going on to

	Intelligence (B)		
	Low (B1)	High (B2)	
Traditional lecture (A1)	75 70 69 72 68	90 95 89 85 91	
	$T_{A1B1} = 354$ $\Sigma X^2_{A1B1} = 25094$ $n_{A1B1} = 5$ $\overline{X}_{A1B1} = 70.80$	$T_{A1B2} = 450$ $\Sigma X^2_{A1B2} = 40552$ $n_{A1B2} = 5$ $\overline{X}_{A1B2} = 90.00$	$T_{A1} = 804$ $n_{A1} = 10$ $\overline{X}_{A1} = 80.40$
Individualized method (A2)	85 87 83 90 89	87 94 93 89 92	
	$T_{A2B1} = 434$ $\Sigma X^2_{A2B1} = 37704$ $n_{A2B1} = 5$ $\overline{X}_{A2B1} = 86.80$	$T_{A2B2} = 455$ $\Sigma X^2_{A2B2} = 41439$ $n_{A2B2} = 5$ $\overline{X}_{A2B2} = 91.00$	$T_{A2} = 889$ $n_{A2} = 10$ $\overline{X}_{A2} = 88.90$
	$T_{B1} = 788$ $n_{B1} = 10$ $\overline{X}_{B1} = 78.80$	$T_{B2} = 905$ $n_{B2} = 10$ $\overline{X}_{B2} = 90.50$	

Table B-6
Data for hypothetical experiment on the effect of type of instruction and intelligence level on exam score: Analysis of variance

the next section. The information presented to students in the two classes is identical. At the end of the course, all students take the same test, which covers all of the material presented in the course. The score on this examination is the dependent variable.

Table B-6 shows fictitious data for such an experiment, with five subjects in each condition. This design allows us to evaluate three effects—the main effect of A, the main effect of B, and the A × B interaction. The main effect of A is whether one type of instruction is superior to the other; the main effect of B is whether high-intelligence students score differently on the test than do low-intelligence students; the A × B interaction examines whether the effect of one independent variable is different depending on the particular level of the other variable.

The computation of the analysis of variance starts with calculation of the sum of squares for the following sources of variance in the data: SS_{TOTAL}, SS_A, SS_B, $SS_{A \times B}$, and SS_{ERROR}. The procedures for calculation are similar to the calculations performed for the analysis of variance with one independent

269

Table B-7
Computations for
analysis of
variance with two
independent
variables

$$SS_{TOTAL} = \Sigma X^2 - \frac{G^2}{N}$$

$= (25094 + 40552 + 37704 + 41439)$

$- \dfrac{(354 + 450 + 434 + 455)^2}{20}$

$= 144789 - 143312.45$

$= 1476.55$

$$SS_A = \frac{\Sigma T_a^2}{n_a} - \frac{G^2}{N}$$

$= \dfrac{(804)^2 + (889)^2}{10} - 143312.45$

$= 143673.70 - 143312.45$

$= 361.25$

$$SS_B = \frac{\Sigma T_b^2}{n_b} - \frac{G^2}{N}$$

$= \dfrac{(788)^2 + (905)^2}{10} - 143312.45$

$= 143996.90 - 143312.45$

$= 684.45$

$$SS_{A \times B} = \frac{\Sigma T_{ab}^2}{n_{ab}} - \frac{G^2}{N} - SS_A - SS_B = \frac{(354)^2 + (450)^2 + (434)^2 + (455)^2}{5}$$

$- 143312.45 - 361.25 - 684.45$

$= 144639.40 - 143312.45 - 361.25 - 684.45$

$= 281.25$

$$SS_{ERROR} = \Sigma X^2 - \frac{\Sigma T_{ab}^2}{n_{ab}}$$

$= 144789 - 144639.40$

$= 149.60$

variable. The numerical calculations for the example data are shown in Table B-7. We can now consider each of these calculations.

SS_{TOTAL} The SS_{TOTAL} is computed in the same way as the previous analysis. The formula is

$$SS_{TOTAL} = \Sigma X^2 - \frac{G^2}{N}$$

where ΣX^2 is the sum of the squared scores of all subjects in the experiment, G is the grand total of all of the scores, and N is the total number of subjects. It is usually easiest to calculate ΣX^2 and G in smaller steps by calculating subtotals separately for each group in the design. The subtotals are then added. This is the procedure followed in Tables B-6 and B-7.

SS_A The formula for SS_A is

$$SS_A = \frac{\Sigma T_a^2}{n_a} - \frac{G^2}{N}$$

where ΣT_a^2 is the sum of the squared totals of the scores in each of the groups of independent variable A, and n_a is the number of subjects in each level of independent variable A. When calculating SS_A, we only consider the groups of independent variable A without considering the particular level of B. In other words, the totals for each group of the A variable are obtained by considering all subjects in that level of A, irrespective of which condition of B the subject may be in. The quantity of G^2/N was previously calculated for SS_{TOTAL}.

SS_B   The formula for SS_B is

$$SS_B = \frac{\Sigma T_b^2}{n_b} - \frac{G^2}{N}$$

SS_B is calculated in the same way as SS_A. The only difference is that we are calculating totals of the groups of independent variable B.

$SS_{A \times B}$ The formula for $SS_{A \times B}$ is

$$SS_{A \times B} = \frac{\Sigma T_{ab}^2}{n_{ab}} - \frac{G^2}{N} - SS_A - SS_B$$

The sum of squares for the $A \times B$ interaction is computed by first calculating the quantity ΣT_{ab}^2. This involves squaring the total of the scores in each of the ab conditions in the experiment. In our example experiment in Table B-6, there are four conditions; the interaction calculation considers *all* of the groups. Each of the group totals is squared, and then the sum of the squared totals is obtained. This sum is divided by n_{ab}, the number of subjects in each group. The other quantities in the formula for $SS_{A \times B}$ have already been calculated, so the computation of $SS_{A \times B}$ is relatively straightforward.

SS_{ERROR}   The quantities involved in the SS_{ERROR} formula have already been calculated. The formula is

$$SS_{ERROR} = \Sigma X^2 - \frac{\Sigma T_{ab}^2}{n_{ab}}$$

These quantities were calculated previously, so we merely have to perform the proper subtraction to complete the computation of SS_{ERROR}.

At this point, you may want to practice calculating the sums of squares using the data in Table B-6. As a check on the calculations, make sure that $SS_{TOTAL} = SS_A + SS_B + SS_{A \times B} + SS_{ERROR}$.

After obtaining the sums of squares, the next step is to find the mean square for each of the sources of variance. The easiest way to do this is to use an analysis of variance summary table like Table B-8.

Mean square   The mean square for each of the sources of variance is the sum of squares divided by the degrees of freedom. The formulas for the degrees of freedom and the mean square are shown in the top portion of Table B-8, and the computed values are shown in the bottom portion of the table.

Obtaining the F value   The F value for each of the three sources of systematic variance (main effects for A and B, and the interaction) is obtained by

271

**Table B-8
Analysis of
variance summary
table: Two
independent
variables**

Source of variance	Sum of squares	df	Mean square	F
A	SS_A	$a - 1$	SS_A/df_A	MS_A/MS_{ERROR}
B	SS_B	$B - 1$	SS_B/df_B	MS_B/MS_{ERROR}
$A \times B$	$SS_{A \times B}$	$(a - 1)(b - 1)$	$SS_{A \times B}/df_{A \times B}$	$MS_{A \times B}/MS_{ERROR}$
Error	SS_{ERROR}	$N - ab$	SS_{ERROR}/df_{ERROR}	
Total	SS_{TOTAL}			
A	361.25	1	361.25	38.64
B	684.45	1	684.45	73.20
$A \times B$	281.25	1	281.25	30.08
Error	149.60	16	9.35	
Total	1476.55	19		

dividing the appropriate mean square by the MS_{ERROR}. We now have three obtained F values and can evaluate the significance of the main effects and the interaction.

Significance of F   To determine whether an obtained F is significant, we need to find the critical value of F from Table C-5 in Appendix C. For all of the Fs in the analysis of variance summary table, the degrees of freedom are 1 and 16. Let's assume that a .01 significance level for rejecting the null hypothesis was chosen. The critical F at .01 for 1 and 16 degrees of freedom is 8.53. If the obtained F is larger than 8.53, we can say that the results are significant at the .01 level. By referring to the obtained Fs in Table B-8, you can see that the main effects and the interaction are all significant. I'll leave it to you to interpret the main effect means and to graph the interaction. If you don't recall how to do this, you should review the material in Chapter 7.

Analysis of variance: Repeated measures and matched subjects

The analysis of variance computations considered thus far have been limited to independent groups designs. This section considers the computations for analysis of variance of a repeated measures or a matched random assignment design with one independent variable.

Fictitious data for a hypothetical experiment using a repeated measures design are presented in Table B-9. The experiment examines the effect of a job candidate's physical attractiveness on judgments of the candidate's competence. The independent variable is the candidate's physical attractiveness; the dependent variable is judged competence on a 10-point scale. Subjects in the experiment view two videotapes of different females performing a mechanical aptitude task that involved piecing together a number of parts. Both females do equally well, but one is physically attractive while the other is unattractive. The order of presentation of the two tapes is counterbalanced to control for order effects.

Subjects (or subject pairs)	Condition (A)		T_S	T_S^2
	Unattractive candidate (A1)	Attractive candidate (A2)		
S#1	6	8	14	196
S#2	5	6	11	121
S#3	5	9	14	196
S#4	7	6	13	169
S#5	4	6	10	100
S#6	3	5	8	64
S#7	5	5	10	100
S#8	4	7	11	121

$$T_{A1} = 39 \qquad T_{A2} = 52 \qquad\qquad \Sigma T_S^2 = 1067$$
$$\Sigma X_{A1}^2 = 201 \qquad \Sigma X_{A2}^2 = 352$$
$$n_{A1} = 8 \qquad n_{A2} = 8$$
$$\overline{X}_{A1} = 4.88 \qquad \overline{X}_{A2} = 6.50$$

Table B-9 Data for hypothetical experiment on attractiveness and judged competence: Repeated measures analysis of variance

$$SS_{TOTAL} = \Sigma X^2 - \frac{G^2}{N} = (201 + 352) - \frac{(39 + 52)^2}{16}$$

$$= 553 - 517.56$$

$$= 35.44$$

$$SS_A = \frac{\Sigma T_a^2}{n_a} - \frac{G^2}{N} = \frac{(39)^2 + (52)^2}{8} - 517.56$$

$$= 528.13 - 517.56$$

$$= 10.57$$

$$SS_{SUBJECTS} = \frac{\Sigma T_S^2}{n_S} - \frac{G^2}{N} = \frac{1067}{2} - 517.56$$

$$= 533.50 - 517.56$$

$$= 15.94$$

$$SS_{ERROR} = SS_{TOTAL} - SS_A - SS_{SUBJECTS} = 35.44 - 10.57 - 15.94$$

$$= 8.93$$

The main difference between the repeated measures analysis of variance and the independent groups analysis described earlier is that the effect of subject differences becomes a source of variance. There are four sources of variance in the repeated measures analysis of variance, and so four sums of squares are calculated:

$$SS_{TOTAL} = \Sigma X^2 - \frac{G^2}{N}$$

$$SS_A = \frac{\Sigma T_a^2}{n_a} - \frac{G^2}{N}$$

273

**Table B-10
Analysis of
variance summary
table: Repeated
measures design**

Source of variance	Sum of squares	df	Mean square	F
A	SS_A	$a - 1$	SS_A/df_A	MS_A/MS_{ERROR}
Subjects	$SS_{SUBJECTS}$	$s - 1$	—	
Error	SS_{ERROR}	$(a - 1)(s - 1)$	SS_{ERROR}/df_{ERROR}	
Total	SS_{TOTAL}	$N - 1$		
A	10.57	1	10.57	8.26
Subjects	15.94	7	—	
Error	8.93	7	1.28	
Total	35.44	15		

$$SS_{SUBJECTS} = \frac{\Sigma T_s^2}{n_s} - \frac{G^2}{N}$$

$$SS_{ERROR} = SS_{TOTAL} - SS_A - SS_{SUBJECTS}$$

The calculations for these sums of squares are shown in the lower portion of Table B-9. The quantities in the formulas should be familiar to you by now. The only new quantity involves the calculation of $SS_{SUBJECTS}$. The term T_s^2 refers to the squared total score of each subject—that is, the squared total of the scores that each subject gives when measured in the different groups in the experiment. The quantity ΣT_s^2 refers to the sum of these squared totals for all subjects. The calculation of $SS_{SUBJECTS}$ is completed by dividing ΣT_s^2 by n_s and then subtracting by G^2/N. The term n_s refers to the number of scores that each subject gives. Since our hypothetical experiment has two groups, $n_s = 2$. The total for each subject is based on two scores.

An analysis of variance summary table is shown in Table B-10. The procedures for computing the mean squares and obtaining F are similar to our previous calculations. Note that the mean square and F for the subjects' source of variance are not computed. There is usually no reason to know or care whether subjects differ significantly from each other. The ability to calculate this source of variance does have the advantage of reducing the amount of error variance—in an independent groups design, subject differences are part of the error variance. Because there is only one score per subject in the independent groups design, it is impossible to estimate the influence of subject differences.

You can use the summary table and the table of critical F values to determine whether the difference between the two groups is significant. The procedures are identical to those discussed previously.

Analysis of variance: Conclusion

The analysis of variance is a very useful test that can be extended to any type of factorial design, including those that use both independent groups and repeated measures in the same design. The method of computing analysis of variance is much the same regardless of the complexity of the design. A section on analysis of variance as brief as this cannot hope to cover all of the many aspects of such a general statistical technique. You should now, however, have the background to compute an analysis of variance and to understand the more detailed discussions of analysis of variance in advanced statistics texts.

MEASURES OF STRENGTH OF ASSOCIATION

Finally, we will discuss several measures of the strength of association between two variables. These measures are called *correlation coefficients*. Three correlation coefficients are considered here: the contingency coefficient, the Spearman rank-order correlation coefficient, and the Pearson product-moment correlation coefficient.

Contingency coefficient

The contingency coefficient (C) is a measure of strength of association for nominal data. It is computed after obtaining the value of Chi-square. The formula is

$$C = \sqrt{\frac{\chi^2}{N + \chi^2}}$$

Thus, the value of C for the sex and hand dominance study analyzed above (Table B-2) is

$$C = \sqrt{\frac{18}{100 + 18}} = \sqrt{.153} = .39$$

Because the significance of the obtained Chi-square value has already been determined from Table C-2 in Appendix C, no further significance testing of C is necessary.

Spearman rank-order correlation coefficient

The Spearman rank-order correlation coefficient (rho) is used to measure the strength of association between pairs of variables measured on an ordinal scale. In order to use *rho*, pairs of observations must be made on each subject. These observations must be in terms of ranks; if scores rather than ranks are obtained from each subject, the scores must be converted to ranks.

    Example Suppose you are interested in the dominance rankings of a group of boys in an institutional care setting. You wish to know whether the dominance ranks during the day shift are related to the dominance ranks during the night shift, when different staff members are present. To obtain

**Table B-11
Data for
hypothetical study
on the relationship
between
dominance rank
during the day
and night shifts:
Spearman *rho***

Subject (initials)	Rank during day shift	Rank during night shift	d	d^2
B.W.	2	1	1	1
G.N.	4	3	1	1
S.P.	1	2	−1	1
R.A.	6	5	1	1
D.G.	7	7	0	0
C.M.	5	6	−1	1
J.J.	3	4	−1	1
				$\Sigma d^2 = 6$

Computation: $rho = 1 - \dfrac{6\Sigma d^2}{N^3 - N} = 1 - \dfrac{(6)(6)}{343 - 7}$

$$= 1 - \frac{36}{336}$$

$$= 1 - .107$$

$$= .893$$

pairs of observations, you determine the dominance rank of each boy during the day shift and again during the night shift.

Fictitious data for such a study, along with calculations for Spearman's *rho*, are presented in Table B-11. The seven subjects in the study were assigned ranks ranging from 1 (highest in dominance) to 7 (lowest in dominance). The calculational formula for *rho* is

$$rho = 1 - \frac{6\Sigma d^2}{N^3 - N}$$

where d is the difference between each subject's rank on the first observation and the rank on the second observation. The quantity d^2 is obtained by squaring each subject's rank difference. The quantity Σd^2 is simply the total of all subject's squared rank differences. N refers to the number of paired ranks, and N^3 is N cubed, or $N \times N \times N$. Once the value of *rho* has been obtained, the significance of *rho* can be determined.

Significance of *rho* To test the null hypothesis that the correlation in the population is 0.00, we can consult a table of critical values of *rho*. Table C-6 in Appendix C shows critical values for .10, .05, and .01 significance levels. To use the table, find the critical value of *rho* for N, the number of paired observations. The obtained value of *rho* must be greater than the critical value to be significant. The critical value at the .05 level for our example data ($N = 7$) is .79 (plus or minus). Because the obtained value of *rho* is larger than the critical value, we conclude that the dominance rankings are significantly correlated.

Subject identification number	Travel score (X)	Knowledge score (Y)	XY
01	4	10	40
02	6	15	90
03	7	8	56
04	8	9	72
05	8	7	56
06	12	10	120
07	14	15	210
08	15	13	195
09	15	15	225
10	17	14	238
	$\Sigma X = 106$	$\Sigma Y = 116$	$\Sigma XY = 1302$
	$\Sigma X^2 = 1308$	$\Sigma Y^2 = 1434$	
	$(\Sigma X)^2 = 11236$	$(\Sigma Y)^2 = 13456$	

Table B-12
Data for hypothetical study on travel and knowledge of geography: Pearson r

Computation:

$$r = \frac{N\Sigma XY - \Sigma X\Sigma Y}{\sqrt{N\Sigma X^2 - (\Sigma X)^2}\ \sqrt{N\Sigma Y^2 - (\Sigma Y)^2}}$$

$$= \frac{10(1302) - (106)(116)}{\sqrt{10(1308) - 11236}\ \sqrt{10(1434) - 13456}}$$

$$= \frac{13020 - 12296}{\sqrt{13080 - 11236}\ \sqrt{14340 - 13456}}$$

$$= \frac{724}{\sqrt{1844}\ \sqrt{884}}$$

$$= \frac{724}{1276.61}$$

$$= .567$$

Pearson product-moment correlation coefficient

The Pearson product-moment correlation coefficient (r) is used to find the strength of the relationship between two variables that have been measured on interval scales.

Example Suppose you want to know whether travel experiences are related to knowledge of geography. In your study, you give a 15-item quiz on North American geography, and you also ask how many states and Canadian provinces subjects had visited. After obtaining the pairs of observations from each subject, a Pearson r can be computed to measure the strength of relationship between travel experience and knowledge of geography.

Table B-12 presents fictitious data from such a study along with the calculations for r. The calculational formula for r is

$$r = \frac{N\Sigma XY - \Sigma X\Sigma Y}{\sqrt{N\Sigma X^2 - (\Sigma X)^2}\ \sqrt{N\Sigma Y^2 - (\Sigma Y)^2}}$$

277

where X refers to a subject's score on variable X, and Y is a subject's score on variable Y. In Table B-12, the travel experience score is variable X, and the geography knowledge score is variable Y. In the formula, N is the number of paired observations (that is, the number of subjects measured on both variables).

The calculation of r requires a number of arithmetic operations on the X and Y scores. ΣX is simply the sum of the scores on variable X. ΣX^2 is the sum of the squared scores on X (each score is first squared and then the sum of the squared scores is obtained). The quantity $(\Sigma X)^2$ is the square of the sum of the scores: The total of the X scores (ΣX) is first calculated and then this total is squared. It is important not to confuse the two quantities, ΣX^2 and $(\Sigma X)^2$. The same calculations are made, using the Y scores, to obtain ΣY, ΣY^2, and $(\Sigma Y)^2$. To find ΣXY, each subject's X score is multiplied by the score on Y; these values are then summed for all subjects. When these calculations have been made, r is computed by using the formula for r given above.

At this point, you may wish to examine carefully the calculations shown in Table B-12 to familiarize yourself with the procedures for computing r. You might then try calculating r from another set of data, such as the seating pattern and exam score study shown in Table 10-1 in Chapter 10.

Significance of r   To test the null hypothesis that the population correlation coefficient is in fact 0.00, we consult a table of critical values of r. Table C-7 in Appendix C shows critical values of r for .10, .05, and .01 levels of significance. To find the critical value, you first need to determine the degrees of freedom. The df for the significance test for r is $N - 2$. In our example study on travel and knowledge, the number of paired observations is 10, so the $df = 8$. For 8 degrees of freedom, the critical value of r at the .05 level of significance is .632 (plus or minus). The obtained r must be greater than the critical r to be significant. Since our obtained r (from Table B-12) of .567 is less than the critical value, we do not reject the null hypothesis.

Notice that we do not reject the null hypothesis in this case, even though the magnitude of r is fairly large. Recall the discussion of nonsignificant results from Chapter 9. It is possible that a significant correlation would be obtained if you used a larger sample size, or more sensitive and reliable measures of the variables.

STATISTICAL ANALYSIS WITH COMPUTERS

Computers are excellent "number crunchers." This makes them an ideal tool for performing the statistical analyses that we have been discussing. Analyses that might take several hours with a calculator can be performed almost instantaneously with a computer program. Further, the computer programs will usually be able to tell you about statistical significance so you don't have to refer to one of the tables in Appendix C. Some programs even allow you to construct tables and figures that can be used in your final report.

Some type of computer statistical program is available on most college campuses. You will have to learn the specific details of the procedures needed to use the program. The standard method is to access the program on a large mainframe computer that serves many students and faculty. Alternatively, you may use a program on a microcomputer (such as an IBM PC or an Apple Macintosh). Statistical programs for microcomputers have had problems of speed and accuracy; however, these problems have been largely overcome so that now you can conduct most analyses with ease on a microcomputer, and the cost of student versions of such programs is about the same as a textbook.

Statistical programs

Several major statistical programs have been adopted by colleges and businesses. These include SPSS (Statistical Package for the Social Sciences), BMDP (Biomedical Computer Programs), SAS (Statistical Analysis System), Minitab, and Systat. The program (or programs) used at your campus may be available on either the campus mainframe or on microcomputers. You cannot say that one program is "better" than another; they differ in the way that you input data and provide instructions for the analysis, and in the appearance of the printed reports. If you learn one program, it is generally easy to transfer your knowledge to another program if you need to do so.

General procedures

The procedures for analyzing data on a computer are much the same in all programs. The first step is to input the data. You will need to learn the rules for data input on your computer. Some programs ask you to input the data after you specify the type of statistical test you wish to use. With Minitab, you first input columns of numbers for each variable in your study. With SPSS and SAS, you construct a data file containing all of the data from your study, which are later analyzed using the statistical program. It is simplest to think of data for computer analysis as a matrix with rows and columns. Data for each subject in the study are the rows of the matrix. The columns contain subjects' scores on various measures, and often you need codes to indicate which group the subjects were in (e.g., group 1, 2, or 3). As an example, the data matrix for analyzing the data in Table B-4 (the experiment on distance and self-disclosure) would look like this:

1	33
1	24
1	31
1	29
1	34
2	21
2	25
2	19

2	27
2	26
3	20
3	13
3	15
3	10
3	14

The first column identifies whether the subject was in the close, medium, or far distance condition; the second column is the self-disclosure score. In more complex factorial designs, additional columns would identify the other independent variable levels. If additional measures were taken, the scores would appear in other columns.

The next step is to provide instructions for the statistical analysis. Again, each program uses different instructions. Also, some programs are "interactive"; that is, when you give a command, the calculations are immediately performed and you are shown the results. Other programs require you to build a set of instructions in a separate computer file and then later tell the computer to run the program using the instructions in one file with the data in another file. In either case, you will need to learn the commands to produce descriptive statistics, correlation coefficients, an analysis of variance, and other statistics you might need. As an example, in SPSS you would write instructions to name the variables in each column and then give an instruction to perform the analysis. Suppose we named the variables in the dislosure experiment DISTANCE and DISCLOSE. The SPSS instruction to perform an analysis of variance is:

ANOVA   DISCLOSE BY DISTANCE (1,3)

This instruction requests an analysis of variance (ANOVA) with scores in the DISCLOSE column representing the dependent variable, and DISTANCE as the independent variable (with values ranging from 1 to 3 for the three groups in the design). When you run the program, you are shown the calculated sums of squares, degrees of freedom, mean squares, F value, and significance level.

Statistical programs also allow you to easily do many other things with your data. You can specify that certain values represent "missing" data when subjects did not answer certain questions. You can also transform the data. This is useful when you wish to change the direction of scoring of variables. For example, if you have an attitude measure with questions worded in both positive and negative directions, you can recode the data so that high numbers indicate positive attitudes on all questions. You could do this by hand but it is much easier with a computer. You can also perform arithmetic operations on sets of variables; for example, you could create a total attitude score by adding scores on the questions you asked. You can also select out certain subjects for the analysis. For example, if you want to examine the results only for male subjects and you have coded for gender, you can tell the computer to select the male subjects and then perform the analyses.

Computer analysis of data makes it easier to perform many complex statistical calculations. You must learn how to use the programs in order for them to provide you with useful information. When you are first learning a computer analysis program, it is a good idea to practice with some data from a statistics text to make sure that you get the same results. This will assure you that you understand the instructions required by the computer program. (Note that you would get much different results in the SPSS example above if you said DISTANCE BY DISCLOSE. This is because the program requires the dependent variable to be specified first, followed by the independent variable.) You must also understand statistical theory so that you use the appropriate test for your data.

C

Statistical Tables

This appendix provides a number of tables that are frequently used in behavioral research.

RANDOM NUMBER TABLE

The random number table can be used to select data when a arbitrary sequence of numbers is needed. To obtain a series of random numbers, enter the table at any arbitrary point and read in sequence either across or down.

To use the random number table, first order your subjects in some way. This could be by name or by assigning a number to each subject. Suppose that you have three groups and want five subjects per group, for a total of 15 subjects. Following is a list of 15 subjects ordered from first to fifteenth. Enter the random number table and assign a number to each subject (if there is a duplicate number, ignore it and use the next number in the sequence). In the example here, the table was entered in the upper left-hand corner and was read downward. Now assign the subjects to groups: The five subjects who receive the lowest random numbers are assigned to group 1, the next five subjects are assigned to group 2, and the five subjects with the highest numbers are assigned to group 3. These general procedures can be followed with any number of groups in an experiment.

Subject order	Random number	Group assignment
1	10	1
2	37	2
3	08	1
4	09	1
5	12	1
6	66	2
7	31	2
8	85	3
9	63	2
10	73	2
11	98	3
12	11	1
13	83	3
14	88	3
15	99	3

To use the random number table for random sampling, first make a list of all members of your population. Enter the random number table and assign a number to each member of the population. Determine your desired sample size (N). Your sample, then, will be composed of the first N individuals. For example, if you want to take a random sample of 15 faculty members at your school, use the random number table to give each faculty member a number. The 15 faculty with the lowest numbers would be selected for the sample.

10 09 73 25 33	76 52 01 35 86	34 67 35 48 76	80 95 90 91 17	39 29 27 49 45	
37 54 20 48 05	64 89 47 42 96	24 80 52 40 37	20 63 61 04 02	00 82 29 16 65	
08 42 26 89 53	19 64 50 93 03	23 20 90 25 60	15 95 33 47 64	35 08 03 36 06	
99 01 90 25 29	09 37 67 07 15	38 31 13 11 65	88 67 67 43 97	04 43 62 76 59	
12 80 79 99 70	80 15 73 61 47	64 03 23 66 53	98 95 11 68 77	12 17 17 68 33	
66 06 57 47 17	34 07 27 68 50	36 69 73 61 70	65 81 33 98 85	11 19 92 91 70	
31 06 01 08 05	45 57 18 24 06	35 30 34 26 14	86 79 90 74 39	23 40 30 97 32	
85 26 97 76 02	02 05 16 56 92	68 66 57 48 18	73 05 38 52 47	18 62 38 85 79	
63 57 33 21 35	05 32 54 70 48	90 55 35 75 48	28 46 82 87 09	83 49 12 56 24	
73 79 64 57 53	03 52 96 47 78	35 80 83 42 82	60 93 52 03 44	35 27 38 84 35	
98 52 01 77 67	14 90 56 86 07	22 10 94 05 58	60 97 09 34 33	50 50 07 39 98	
11 80 50 54 31	39 80 82 77 32	50 72 56 82 48	29 40 52 42 01	52 77 56 78 51	
83 45 29 96 34	06 28 89 80 83	13 74 67 00 78	18 47 54 06 10	68 71 17 78 17	
88 68 54 02 00	86 50 75 84 01	36 76 66 79 51	90 36 47 64 93	29 60 91 10 62	
99 59 46 73 48	87 51 76 49 69	91 82 60 89 28	93 78 56 13 68	23 47 83 41 13	

**Table C-1
Random number
table**

283

Table C-1
(continued)

65 48 11 76 74	17 46 85 09 50	58 04 77 69 74	73 03 95 71 86	40 21 81 65 44
80 12 43 56 35	17 72 70 80 15	45 31 82 23 74	21 11 57 82 53	14 38 55 37 63
74 35 09 98 17	77 40 27 72 14	43 23 60 02 10	45 52 16 42 37	96 28 60 26 55
69 91 62 68 03	66 25 22 91 48	36 93 68 72 03	76 62 11 39 90	94 40 05 64 18
09 89 32 05 05	14 22 56 85 14	46 42 75 67 88	96 29 77 88 22	54 38 21 45 98
91 49 91 45 23	68 47 92 76 86	46 16 28 35 54	94 75 08 99 23	37 08 92 00 48
80 33 69 45 98	26 94 03 68 58	70 29 73 41 35	53 14 03 33 40	42 05 08 23 41
44 10 48 19 49	85 15 74 79 54	32 97 92 65 75	57 60 04 08 81	22 22 20 64 13
12 55 07 37 42	11 10 00 20 40	12 86 07 46 97	96 64 48 94 39	28 70 72 58 15
63 60 64 93 29	16 50 53 44 84	40 21 95 23 63	43 65 17 70 82	07 20 73 17 90
61 19 69 04 45	26 45 74 77 74	51 92 43 37 29	65 39 45 95 93	42 58 26 05 27
15 47 44 52 66	95 27 07 99 53	59 36 78 38 48	82 39 61 01 18	33 21 15 94 66
94 55 72 83 73	67 89 75 43 87	54 62 24 44 31	91 19 04 23 92	92 92 74 59 73
42 48 11 62 13	97 34 40 87 21	16 86 84 87 67	03 07 11 20 59	25 70 14 66 70
23 52 37 83 17	73 20 88 98 37	68 93 59 14 16	26 25 22 96 63	05 52 28 25 62
04 49 35 24 94	75 24 63 38 24	43 86 25 10 25	61 96 27 93 35	65 33 71 24 72
00 54 99 76 54	64 05 18 81 39	96 11 96 38 96	54 89 28 23 91	23 28 72 95 29
35 96 31 53 07	26 89 80 93 54	33 35 13 54 62	77 97 45 00 24	90 10 33 93 33
59 80 80 83 91	45 42 72 68 42	83 60 94 97 00	13 02 12 48 92	78 56 52 01 06
46 05 88 32 36	01 39 00 22 86	77 28 14 40 77	93 91 08 36 47	70 61 74 29 41
32 17 90 05 97	87 37 92 52 41	05 56 70 70 07	86 74 31 71 57	85 39 41 18 38
69 23 46 14 06	20 11 74 52 04	15 95 66 00 00	18 74 39 24 23	97 11 89 63 38
19 56 54 14 30	01 75 87 53 79	40 41 92 15 85	66 67 43 68 06	84 96 28 52 07
45 15 51 49 38	19 47 60 72 46	43 66 79 45 43	59 04 79 00 33	20 82 66 95 41
94 86 43 19 94	36 18 81 08 51	34 88 88 15 53	01 54 03 54 56	05 01 45 11 76
09 18 82 00 97	32 82 53 95 27	04 22 08 63 04	83 38 98 73 74	64 27 85 80 44
90 04 58 54 97	51 98 15 06 54	94 93 88 19 97	91 87 07 61 50	68 47 68 46 59
73 18 95 02 07	47 67 72 62 69	62 29 06 44 64	27 12 46 70 18	41 36 18 27 60
75 76 87 64 90	20 97 18 17 49	90 42 91 22 72	95 37 50 58 71	93 82 34 31 78
54 01 64 40 56	66 28 13 10 03	00 68 22 73 98	20 71 45 32 95	07 70 61 78 13
08 35 86 99 10	78 54 24 27 85	13 66 15 88 73	04 61 89 75 53	31 22 30 84 20
28 30 60 32 64	81 33 31 05 91	40 51 00 78 93	32 60 46 04 75	94 11 90 18 40
53 84 08 62 33	81 59 41 36 28	51 21 59 02 90	28 46 66 87 93	77 76 22 07 91
91 75 75 37 41	61 61 36 22 69	50 26 39 02 12	55 78 17 65 14	83 48 34 70 55
89 41 59 26 94	00 39 75 83 91	12 60 71 76 46	48 94 27 23 06	94 54 13 74 08
77 51 30 38 20	86 83 42 99 01	68 41 48 27 74	51 90 81 39 80	72 89 35 55 07
19 50 23 71 74	69 97 92 02 88	55 21 02 97 73	74 28 77 52 51	65 34 46 74 15
21 81 85 93 13	93 27 88 17 57	05 68 67 31 56	07 08 28 50 46	31 85 33 84 52
51 47 46 64 99	68 10 72 38 21	94 04 99 13 45	42 83 60 91 91	08 00 74 54 49
99 55 96 83 31	62 53 52 41 70	69 77 71 28 30	74 81 97 81 42	43 86 07 28 34
33 71 34 80 07	93 58 47 28 69	51 92 66 47 21	58 30 32 98 22	93 17 49 39 72
85 27 48 68 93	11 30 32 92 70	28 83 43 41 37	73 51 59 04 00	71 14 84 36 43
84 13 38 96 40	44 03 55 21 66	73 85 27 00 91	61 22 26 05 61	62 32 71 84 23
56 73 21 62 34	17 39 59 61 31	10 12 39 16 22	85 49 65 75 60	81 60 41 88 80
65 13 85 66 06	87 64 88 52 61	34 31 36 58 61	45 87 52 10 69	85 64 44 72 77
38 00 10 21 78	81 71 91 17 11	71 60 29 29 37	74 21 96 40 49	65 58 44 96 98
37 40 29 63 97	01 30 47 75 86	56 27 11 00 65	47 32 46 26 05	40 03 03 74 38
97 12 54 03 48	87 08 33 14 17	21 81 53 92 50	75 23 76 20 47	15 50 12 95 78
21 82 64 11 34	47 14 33 40 72	64 63 88 59 02	49 13 90 64 41	03 85 65 45 52
73 13 54 27 42	95 71 90 90 35	85 79 47 42 96	08 78 98 81 56	64 69 11 92 02

07 63 87 79 29	03 06 11 80 72	96 20 74 41 56	23 82 19 95 38	04 71 36 69 94	
60 52 88 34 41	07 95 41 98 14	59 17 52 06 95	05 53 35 21 39	61 21 20 64 55	
83 59 63 56 55	06 95 89 29 83	05 12 80 97 19	77 43 35 37 83	92 30 15 04 98	
10 85 06 27 46	99 59 91 05 07	13 49 90 63 19	53 07 57 18 39	06 41 01 93 62	
39 82 09 89 52	43 62 26 31 47	64 42 18 08 14	43 80 00 93 51	31 02 47 31 67	

Table C-1
(continued)

Source: From tables of the Rand Corporation from *A Million Random Digits with 100,000 Normal Deviates* (New York: Free Press, 1955) by permission of the Rand Corporation.

Degrees of freedom	Probability level		
	.10	*.05*	*.01*
1	2.706	3.841	6.635
2	4.605	5.991	9.210
3	6.251	7.815	11.345
4	7.779	9.488	13.277
5	9.236	11.070	15.086
6	10.645	12.592	16.812
7	12.017	14.067	18.475
8	13.362	15.507	20.090
9	14.684	16.919	21.666
10	15.987	18.307	23.209
11	17.275	19.675	24.725
12	18.549	21.026	26.217
13	19.812	22.362	27.688
14	21.064	23.685	29.141
15	22.307	24.996	30.578
16	23.542	26.296	32.000
17	24.769	27.587	33.409
18	25.989	28.869	34.805
19	27.204	30.144	36.191
20	28.412	31.410	37.566

Table C-2
Critical values of Chi-square

Source: Table adapted from Fisher and Yates. (1974). *Statistical Tables for Biological, Agricultural, and Medical Research*, 6th ed. London: Longman. Reprinted by permission.

Table C-3
Critical values of
the Mann–
Whitney U

								(A)						
							$.10$ probability level							
N_2	N_1	7	8	9	10	11	12	13	14	15	16	17	18	19	20
3		2	3	3	4	5	5	6	7	7	8	9	9	10	11
4		4	5	6	7	8	9	10	11	12	14	15	16	17	18
5		6	8	9	11	12	13	15	16	18	19	20	22	23	25
6		8	10	12	14	16	17	19	21	23	25	26	28	30	32
7		11	13	15	17	19	21	24	26	28	30	33	35	37	39
8		13	15	18	20	23	26	28	31	33	36	39	41	44	47
9		15	18	21	24	27	30	33	36	39	42	45	48	51	54
10		17	20	24	27	31	34	37	41	44	48	51	55	58	62
11		19	23	27	31	34	38	42	46	50	54	57	61	65	69
12		21	26	30	34	38	42	47	51	55	60	64	68	72	77
13		24	28	33	37	42	47	51	56	61	65	70	75	80	84
14		26	31	36	41	46	51	56	61	66	71	77	82	87	92
15		28	33	39	44	50	55	61	66	72	77	83	88	94	100
16		30	36	42	48	54	60	65	71	77	83	89	95	101	107
17		33	39	45	51	57	64	70	77	83	89	96	102	109	115
18		35	41	48	55	61	68	75	82	88	95	102	109	116	123
19		37	44	51	58	65	72	80	87	94	101	109	116	123	130
20		39	47	54	62	69	77	84	92	100	107	115	123	130	138

Note: Values are for a two-tailed test. Also, your obtained value must be less than the critical value to be significant.

								(B)						
							$.05$ probability level							
N_2	N_1	7	8	9	10	11	12	13	14	15	16	17	18	19	20
3		1	2	2	3	3	4	4	5	5	6	6	7	7	8
4		3	4	4	5	6	7	8	9	10	11	11	12	13	13
5		5	6	7	8	9	11	12	13	14	15	17	18	19	20
6		6	8	10	11	13	14	16	17	19	21	22	24	25	27
7		8	10	12	14	16	18	20	22	24	26	28	30	32	34
8		10	13	15	17	19	22	24	26	29	31	34	36	38	41
9		12	15	17	20	23	26	28	31	34	37	39	42	45	48
10		14	17	20	23	26	29	33	36	39	42	45	48	52	55
11		16	19	23	26	30	33	37	40	44	47	51	55	58	62
12		18	22	26	29	33	37	41	45	49	53	57	61	65	69
13		20	24	28	33	37	41	45	50	54	59	63	67	72	76
14		22	26	31	36	40	45	50	55	59	64	67	74	78	83
15		24	29	34	39	44	49	54	59	64	70	75	80	85	90
16		26	31	37	42	47	53	59	64	70	75	81	86	92	98
17		28	34	39	45	51	57	63	67	75	81	87	93	99	105
18		30	36	42	48	55	61	67	74	80	86	93	99	106	112
19		32	38	45	52	58	65	72	78	85	92	99	106	113	119
20		34	41	48	55	62	69	76	83	90	98	105	112	119	127

Table C-3
(*continued*)

(C)
.01 probability level

N_2	N_1	7	8	9	10	11	12	13	14	15	16	17	18	19	20
3		—	—	0	0	0	1	1	1	2	2	2	2	3	3
4		0	1	1	2	2	3	3	4	5	5	6	6	7	8
5		1	2	3	4	5	6	7	7	8	9	10	11	12	13
6		3	4	5	6	7	9	10	11	12	13	15	16	17	18
7		4	6	7	9	10	12	13	15	16	18	19	21	22	24
8		6	7	9	11	13	15	17	18	20	22	24	26	28	30
9		7	9	11	13	16	18	20	22	24	27	29	31	33	36
10		9	11	13	16	18	21	24	26	29	31	34	37	39	42
11		10	13	16	18	21	24	27	30	33	36	39	42	45	48
12		12	15	18	21	24	27	31	34	37	41	44	47	51	54
13		13	17	20	24	27	31	34	38	42	45	49	53	56	60
14		15	18	22	26	30	34	38	42	46	50	54	58	63	67
15		16	20	24	29	33	37	42	46	51	55	60	64	69	73
16		18	22	27	31	36	41	45	50	55	60	65	70	74	79
17		19	24	29	34	39	44	49	54	60	65	70	75	81	86
18		21	26	31	37	42	47	53	58	64	70	75	81	87	92
19		22	28	33	39	45	51	56	63	69	74	81	87	93	99
20		24	30	36	42	48	54	60	67	73	79	86	92	99	105

Table C-4
Critical values of *t*

df	Significance Level*			
	.05 / .10	.025 / .05	.01 / .02	.005 / .01
1	6.314	12.706	31.821	63.657
2	2.920	4.303	6.965	9.925
3	2.353	3.182	4.541	5.841
4	2.132	2.776	3.747	4.604
5	2.015	2.571	3.365	4.032
6	1.943	2.447	3.143	3.707
7	1.895	2.365	2.998	3.499
8	1.860	2.306	2.896	3.355
9	1.833	2.262	2.821	3.250
10	1.812	2.228	2.764	3.169
11	1.796	2.201	2.718	3.106
12	1.782	2.179	2.681	3.055
13	1.771	2.160	2.650	3.012
14	1.761	2.145	2.624	2.977
15	1.753	2.131	2.602	2.947
16	1.746	2.120	2.583	2.921
17	1.740	2.110	2.567	2.898
18	1.734	2.101	2.552	2.878
19	1.729	2.093	2.539	2.861
20	1.725	2.086	2.528	2.845
21	1.721	2.080	2.518	2.831
22	1.717	2.074	2.508	2.819
23	1.714	2.069	2.500	2.807
24	1.711	2.064	2.492	2.797
25	1.708	2.060	2.485	2.787
26	1.706	2.056	2.479	2.779
27	1.703	2.052	2.473	2.771
28	1.701	2.048	2.467	2.763
29	1.699	2.045	2.462	2.756
30	1.697	2.042	2.457	2.750
40	1.684	2.021	2.423	2.704
60	1.671	2.000	2.390	2.660
120	1.658	1.980	2.358	2.617
∞	1.645	1.960	2.326	2.576

*Use the top significance level when you have predicted a specific directional difference (a one-tailed test; e.g., group 1 will be greater than group 2). Use the bottom significance level when you have only predicted that group 1 will differ from group 2 without specifying the direction of the difference (a two-tailed test).

288

Table C-5
Critical values of F

df for denominator (error)	α	\multicolumn{12}{c}{df for numerator (systematic)}											
		1	2	3	4	5	6	7	8	9	10	11	12
1	.25	5.83	7.50	8.20	8.58	8.82	8.98	9.10	9.19	9.26	9.32	9.36	9.41
	.10	39.9	49.5	53.6	55.8	57.2	58.2	58.9	59.4	59.9	60.2	60.5	60.7
	.05	161	200	216	225	230	234	237	239	241	242	243	244
2	.25	2.57	3.00	3.15	3.23	3.28	3.31	3.34	3.35	3.37	3.38	3.39	3.39
	.10	8.53	9.00	9.16	9.24	9.29	9.33	9.35	9.37	9.38	9.39	9.40	9.41
	.05	18.5	19.0	19.2	19.2	19.3	19.3	19.4	19.4	19.4	19.4	19.4	19.4
	.01	98.5	99.0	99.2	99.2	99.3	99.3	99.4	99.4	99.4	99.4	99.4	99.4
3	.25	2.02	2.28	2.36	2.39	2.41	2.42	2.43	2.44	2.44	2.44	2.45	2.45
	.10	5.54	5.46	5.39	5.34	5.31	5.28	5.27	5.25	5.24	5.23	5.22	5.22
	.05	10.1	9.55	9.28	9.12	9.01	8.94	8.89	8.85	8.81	8.79	8.76	8.74
	.01	34.1	30.8	29.5	28.7	28.2	27.9	27.7	27.5	27.3	27.2	27.1	27.1
4	.25	1.81	2.00	2.05	2.06	2.07	2.08	2.08	2.08	2.08	2.08	2.08	2.08
	.10	4.54	4.32	4.19	4.11	4.05	4.01	3.98	3.95	3.94	3.92	3.91	3.90
	.05	7.71	6.94	6.59	6.39	6.26	6.16	6.09	6.04	6.00	5.96	5.94	5.91
	.01	21.2	18.0	16.7	16.0	15.5	15.2	15.0	14.8	14.7	14.5	14.4	14.4
5	.25	1.69	1.85	1.88	1.89	1.89	1.89	1.89	1.89	1.89	1.89	1.89	1.89
	.10	4.06	3.78	3.62	3.52	3.45	3.40	3.37	3.34	3.32	3.30	3.28	3.27
	.05	6.61	5.79	5.41	5.19	5.05	4.95	4.88	4.82	4.77	4.74	4.71	4.68
	.01	16.3	13.3	12.1	11.4	11.0	10.7	10.5	10.3	10.2	10.1	9.96	9.89
6	.25	1.62	1.76	1.78	1.79	1.79	1.78	1.78	1.78	1.77	1.77	1.77	1.77
	.10	3.78	3.46	3.29	3.18	3.11	3.05	3.01	2.98	2.96	2.94	2.92	2.90
	.05	5.99	5.14	4.76	4.53	4.39	4.28	4.21	4.15	4.10	4.06	4.03	4.00
	.01	13.7	10.9	9.78	9.15	8.75	8.47	8.26	8.10	7.98	7.87	7.79	7.72
7	.25	1.57	1.70	1.72	1.72	1.71	1.71	1.70	1.70	1.69	1.69	1.69	1.68
	.10	3.59	3.26	3.07	2.96	2.88	2.83	2.78	2.75	2.72	2.70	2.68	2.67
	.05	5.59	4.74	4.35	4.12	3.97	3.87	3.79	3.73	3.68	3.64	3.60	3.57
	.01	12.2	9.55	8.45	7.85	7.46	7.19	6.99	6.84	6.72	6.62	6.54	6.47
8	.25	1.54	1.66	1.67	1.66	1.66	1.65	1.64	1.64	1.63	1.63	1.63	1.62
	.10	3.46	3.11	2.92	2.81	2.73	2.67	2.62	2.59	2.56	2.54	2.52	2.50
	.05	5.32	4.46	4.07	3.84	3.69	3.58	3.50	3.44	3.39	3.35	3.31	3.28
	.01	11.3	8.65	7.59	7.01	6.63	6.37	6.18	6.03	5.91	5.81	5.73	5.67
9	.25	1.51	1.62	1.63	1.63	1.62	1.61	1.60	1.60	1.59	1.59	1.58	1.58
	.10	3.36	3.01	2.81	2.69	2.61	2.55	2.51	2.47	2.44	2.42	2.40	2.38
	.05	5.12	4.26	3.86	3.63	3.48	3.37	3.29	3.23	3.18	3.14	3.10	3.07
	.01	10.6	8.02	6.99	6.42	6.06	5.80	5.61	5.47	5.35	5.26	5.18	5.11
10	.25	1.49	1.60	1.60	1.59	1.59	1.58	1.57	1.56	1.56	1.55	1.55	1.54
	.10	3.29	2.92	2.73	2.61	2.52	2.46	2.41	2.38	2.35	2.32	2.30	2.28
	.05	4.96	4.10	3.71	3.48	3.33	3.22	3.14	3.07	3.02	2.98	2.94	2.91
	.01	10.0	7.56	6.55	5.99	5.64	5.39	5.20	5.06	4.94	4.85	4.77	4.71

Table C-5
(continued)

df for de-nomi-nator (error)	α	df for numerator (systematic)											
		1	2	3	4	5	6	7	8	9	10	11	12
11	.25	1.47	1.58	1.58	1.57	1.56	1.55	1.54	1.53	1.53	1.52	1.52	1.51
	.10	3.23	2.86	2.66	2.54	2.45	2.39	2.34	2.30	2.27	2.25	2.23	2.21
	.05	4.84	3.98	3.59	3.36	3.20	3.09	3.01	2.95	2.90	2.85	2.82	2.79
	.01	9.65	7.21	6.22	5.67	5.32	5.07	4.89	4.74	4.63	4.54	4.46	4.40
12	.25	1.46	1.56	1.56	1.55	1.54	1.53	1.52	1.51	1.51	1.50	1.50	1.49
	.10	3.18	2.81	2.61	2.48	2.39	2.33	2.28	2.24	2.21	2.19	2.17	2.15
	.05	4.75	3.89	3.49	3.26	3.11	3.00	2.91	2.85	2.80	2.75	2.72	2.69
	.01	9.33	6.93	5.95	5.41	5.06	4.82	4.64	4.50	4.39	4.30	4.22	4.16
13	.25	1.45	1.55	1.55	1.53	1.52	1.51	1.50	1.49	1.49	1.48	1.47	1.47
	.10	3.14	2.76	2.56	2.43	2.35	2.28	2.23	2.20	2.16	2.14	2.12	2.10
	.05	4.67	3.81	3.41	3.18	3.03	2.92	2.83	2.77	2.71	2.67	2.63	2.60
	.01	9.07	6.70	5.74	5.21	4.86	4.62	4.44	4.30	4.19	4.10	4.02	3.96
14	.25	1.44	1.53	1.53	1.52	1.51	1.50	1.49	1.48	1.47	1.46	1.46	1.45
	.10	3.10	2.73	2.52	2.39	2.31	2.24	2.19	2.15	2.12	2.10	2.08	2.05
	.05	4.60	3.74	3.34	3.11	2.96	2.85	2.76	2.70	2.65	2.60	2.57	2.53
	.01	8.86	6.51	5.56	5.04	4.69	4.46	4.28	4.14	4.03	3.94	3.86	3.80
15	.25	1.43	1.52	1.52	1.51	1.49	1.48	1.47	1.46	1.46	1.45	1.44	1.44
	.10	3.07	2.70	2.49	2.36	2.27	2.21	2.16	2.12	2.09	2.06	2.04	2.02
	.05	4.54	3.68	3.29	3.06	2.90	2.79	2.71	2.64	2.59	2.54	2.51	2.48
	.01	8.68	6.36	5.42	4.89	4.56	4.32	4.14	4.00	3.89	3.80	3.73	3.67
16	.25	1.42	1.51	1.51	1.50	1.48	1.47	1.46	1.45	1.44	1.44	1.44	1.43
	.10	3.05	2.67	2.46	2.33	2.24	2.18	2.13	2.09	2.06	2.03	2.01	1.99
	.05	4.49	3.63	3.24	3.01	2.85	2.74	2.66	2.59	2.54	2.49	2.46	2.42
	.01	8.53	6.23	5.29	4.77	4.44	4.20	4.03	3.89	3.78	3.69	3.62	3.55
17	.25	1.42	1.51	1.50	1.49	1.47	1.46	1.45	1.44	1.43	1.43	1.42	1.41
	.10	3.03	2.64	2.44	2.31	2.22	2.15	2.10	2.06	2.03	2.00	1.98	1.96
	.05	4.45	3.59	3.20	2.96	2.81	2.70	2.61	2.55	2.49	2.45	2.41	2.38
	.01	8.40	6.11	5.18	4.67	4.34	4.10	3.93	3.79	3.68	3.59	3.52	3.46
18	.25	1.41	1.50	1.49	1.48	1.46	1.45	1.44	1.43	1.42	1.42	1.41	1.40
	.10	3.01	2.62	2.42	2.29	2.20	2.13	2.08	2.04	2.00	1.98	1.96	1.93
	.05	4.41	3.55	3.16	2.93	2.77	2.66	2.58	2.51	2.46	2.41	2.37	2.34
	.01	8.29	6.01	5.09	4.58	4.25	4.01	3.84	3.71	3.60	3.51	3.43	3.37
19	.25	1.41	1.49	1.49	1.47	1.46	1.44	1.43	1.42	1.41	1.41	1.40	1.40
	.10	2.99	2.61	2.40	2.27	2.18	2.11	2.06	2.02	1.98	1.96	1.94	1.91
	.05	4.38	3.52	3.13	2.90	2.74	2.63	2.54	2.48	2.42	2.38	2.34	2.31
	.01	8.18	5.93	5.01	4.50	4.17	3.94	3.77	3.63	3.52	3.43	3.36	3.30
20	.25	1.40	1.49	1.48	1.46	1.45	1.44	1.43	1.42	1.41	1.40	1.39	1.39
	.10	2.97	2.59	2.38	2.25	2.16	2.09	2.04	2.00	1.96	1.94	1.92	1.89
	.05	4.35	3.49	3.10	2.87	2.71	2.60	2.51	2.45	2.39	2.35	2.31	2.28
	.01	8.10	5.85	4.94	4.43	4.10	3.87	3.70	3.56	3.46	3.37	3.29	3.23

Table C-5
(*continued*)

df for denominator (error)	α	df for numerator (systematic)											
		1	2	3	4	5	6	7	8	9	10	11	12
22	.25	1.40	1.48	1.47	1.45	1.44	1.42	1.41	1.40	1.39	1.39	1.38	1.37
	.10	2.95	2.56	2.35	2.22	2.13	2.06	2.01	1.97	1.93	1.90	1.88	1.86
	.05	4.30	3.44	3.05	2.82	2.66	2.55	2.46	2.40	2.34	2.30	2.26	2.23
	.01	7.95	5.72	4.82	4.31	3.99	3.76	3.59	3.45	3.35	3.26	3.18	3.12
24	.25	1.39	1.47	1.46	1.44	1.43	1.41	1.40	1.39	1.38	1.38	1.37	1.36
	.10	2.93	2.54	2.33	2.19	2.10	2.04	1.98	1.94	1.91	1.88	1.85	1.83
	.05	4.26	3.40	3.01	2.78	2.62	2.51	2.42	2.36	2.30	2.25	2.21	2.18
	.01	7.82	5.61	4.72	4.22	3.90	3.67	3.50	3.36	3.26	3.17	3.09	3.03
26	.25	1.38	1.46	1.45	1.44	1.42	1.41	1.39	1.38	1.37	1.37	1.36	1.35
	.10	2.91	2.52	2.31	2.17	2.08	2.01	1.96	1.92	1.88	1.86	1.84	1.81
	.05	4.23	3.37	2.98	2.74	2.59	2.47	2.39	2.32	2.27	2.22	2.18	2.15
	.01	7.72	5.53	4.64	4.14	3.82	3.59	3.42	3.29	3.18	3.09	3.02	2.96
28	.25	1.38	1.46	1.45	1.43	1.41	1.40	1.39	1.38	1.37	1.36	1.35	1.34
	.10	2.89	2.50	2.29	2.16	2.06	2.00	1.94	1.90	1.87	1.84	1.81	1.79
	.05	4.20	3.34	2.95	2.71	2.56	2.45	2.36	2.29	2.24	2.19	2.15	2.12
	.01	7.64	5.45	4.57	4.07	3.75	3.53	3.36	3.23	3.12	3.03	2.96	2.90
30	.25	1.38	1.45	1.44	1.42	1.41	1.39	1.38	1.37	1.36	1.35	1.35	1.34
	.10	2.88	2.49	2.28	2.14	2.05	1.98	1.93	1.88	1.85	1.82	1.79	1.77
	.05	4.17	3.32	2.92	2.69	2.53	2.42	2.33	2.27	2.21	2.16	2.13	2.09
	.01	7.56	5.39	4.51	4.02	3.70	3.47	3.30	3.17	3.07	2.98	2.91	2.84
40	.25	1.36	1.44	1.42	1.40	1.39	1.37	1.36	1.35	1.34	1.33	1.32	1.31
	.10	2.84	2.44	2.23	2.09	2.00	1.93	1.87	1.83	1.79	1.76	1.73	1.71
	.05	4.08	3.23	2.84	2.61	2.45	2.34	2.25	2.18	2.12	2.08	2.04	2.00
	.01	7.31	5.18	4.31	3.83	3.51	3.29	3.12	2.99	2.89	2.80	2.73	2.66
60	.25	1.35	1.42	1.41	1.38	1.37	1.35	1.33	1.32	1.31	1.30	1.29	1.29
	.10	2.79	2.39	2.18	2.04	1.95	1.87	1.82	1.77	1.74	1.71	1.68	1.66
	.05	4.00	3.15	2.76	2.53	2.37	2.25	2.17	2.10	2.04	1.99	1.95	1.92
	.01	7.08	4.98	4.13	3.65	3.34	3.12	2.95	2.82	2.72	2.63	2.56	2.50
120	.25	1.34	1.40	1.39	1.37	1.35	1.33	1.31	1.30	1.29	1.28	1.27	1.26
	.10	2.75	2.35	2.13	1.99	1.90	1.82	1.77	1.72	1.68	1.65	1.62	1.60
	.05	3.92	3.07	2.68	2.45	2.29	2.17	2.09	2.02	1.96	1.91	1.87	1.83
	.01	6.85	4.79	3.95	3.48	3.17	2.96	2.79	2.66	2.56	2.47	2.40	2.34
200	.25	1.33	1.39	1.38	1.36	1.34	1.32	1.31	1.29	1.28	1.27	1.26	1.25
	.10	2.73	2.33	2.11	1.97	1.88	1.80	1.75	1.70	1.66	1.63	1.60	1.57
	.05	3.89	3.04	2.65	2.42	2.26	2.14	2.06	1.98	1.93	1.88	1.84	1.80
	.01	6.76	4.71	3.88	3.41	3.11	2.89	2.73	2.60	2.50	2.41	2.34	2.27
∞	.25	1.32	1.39	1.37	1.35	1.33	1.31	1.29	1.28	1.27	1.25	1.24	1.24
	.10	2.71	2.30	2.08	1.94	1.85	1.77	1.72	1.67	1.63	1.60	1.57	1.55
	.05	3.84	3.00	2.60	2.37	2.21	2.10	2.01	1.94	1.88	1.83	1.79	1.75
	.01	6.63	4.61	3.78	3.32	3.02	2.80	2.64	2.51	2.41	2.32	2.25	2.18

Table C-6
Critical values of
***rho* (Spearman**
rank-order
correlation
coefficient)

N	Level of significance for two-tailed test		
	.10	.05	.01
5	.90	1.00	
6	.83	.89	1.00
7	.71	.79	.93
8	.64	.74	.88
9	.60	.70	.83
10	.56	.65	.79
11	.54	.62	.76
12	.50	.59	.73
13	.48	.56	.70
14	.46	.54	.68
15	.45	.52	.66
16	.43	.51	.64
17	.41	.49	.62
18	.40	.48	.61
19	.39	.46	.60
20	.38	.45	.58
21	.37	.44	.56
22	.36	.43	.55
23	.35	.42	.54
24	.34	.41	.53
25	.34	.40	.52
26	.33	.39	.51
27	.32	.38	.50
28	.32	.38	.49
29	.31	.37	.48
30	.31	.36	.47

The significance level is halved for a one-tailed test.

df	Level of significance for two-tailed test		
	.10	.05	01
1	.988	.997	.9999
2	.900	.950	.990
3	.805	.878	.959
4	.729	.811	.917
5	.669	.754	.874
6	.622	.707	.834
7	.582	.666	.798
8	.549	.632	.765
9	.521	.602	.735
10	.497	.576	.708
11	.476	.553	.684
12	.458	.532	.661
13	.441	.514	.641
14	.426	.497	.623
15	.412	.482	.606
16	.400	.468	.590
17	.389	.456	.575
18	.378	.444	.561
19	.369	.433	.549
20	.360	.423	.537
25	.323	.381	.487
30	.296	.349	.449
35	.275	.325	.418
40	.257	.304	.393
45	.243	.288	.372
50	.231	.273	.354
60	.211	.250	.325
70	.195	.232	.303
80	.183	.217	.283
90	.173	.205	.267
100	.164	.195	.254

Table C-7
Critical values of r
(Pearson product-moment correlation coefficient)

The significance level is halved for a one-tailed test.

293

D

Constructing a Latin Square

A Latin Square to determine the orders of any N number of conditions will have N arrangements of orders. Thus, if there are four conditions, there will be four orders in a 4×4 Latin Square; eight conditions will produce an 8×8 Latin Square. The method for constructing a Latin Square shown below will produce orders in which (1) each condition or group appears once at each order and (2) each condition precedes and follows each other condition one time.

Use the following procedures for generating a Latin Square when there is an even number of conditions:

1. Determine the number of conditions. Use letters of the alphabet to represent your N conditions: ABCD for four conditions, ABCDEF for six conditions, and so on.

2. Determine the order for the first row, using the following ordering:

$$A, B, L, C, L-1, D, L-2, E$$

and so on. L stands for the last or final treatment. Thus, if you have four conditions (ABCD), your order will be

$$A, B, D, C$$

With six conditions (ABCDEF), the order will be

$$A, B, F, C, E, D$$

because F is the final treatment (L), and E is the next to final treatment ($L - 1$).

3. Determine the order for the second row, by increasing one letter at each position of the first row. The last letter cannot be increased, of course, so it reverts to the first letter. With six conditions, the order of the second row becomes

B, C, A, D, F, E

4. Continue this procedure for the third and subsequent rows. For the third row, increase one letter at each position of the second row:

C, D, B, E, A, F

The final 6 × 6 Latin Square will be

A B F C E D
B C A D F E
C D B E A F
D E C F B A
E F D A C B
F A E B D C

5. Randomly assign each of your conditions to one of the letters to determine which condition will be in the A position, the B position, and so on.

If you have an odd number of conditions, you must make two Latin Squares. For the first square, simply follow the procedures shown above. Now create a second square that reverses the first one; that is, in each row the first condition becomes the last, the second condition is next to last, and so on. Join the two squares together to create the final Latin Square (actually a rectangle!). Thus, if there are five conditions, you will have ten possible orders to run in your study.

Glossary

Alternate forms reliability
>A reliability coefficient determined by the correlation between scores on one form of a measure administered at one time with scores on an alternative version of the measure given at a later time.

Analysis of covariance
>A statistical technique to control for the correlation between a subject variable and a dependent variable in an experiment. This procedure removes the error variance that results from the fact that variability in scores on the dependent variable is due in part to the effect of the subject variable.

Analysis of variance
>*See* F test.

Archival research
>The use of existing sources of information for research. Sources include statistical records, survey archives, and written records.

Bar graph (histogram)
>Graphic display of the scores in a frequency distribution; vertical or horizontal bars represent the frequencies of each score.

Baseline
>In a single-subject design, the subject's behavior during a control period before introduction of the experimental manipulation.

Between-subjects design
>*See* Independent groups design.

Carry-over effect
>A problem that may occur in repeated measures designs if the effects of one treatment are still present when the next treatment is given.

Case study
>A descriptive account of the behavior, past history, and other relevant factors concerning a specific individual.

Ceiling effect
>Failure of a measure to detect a difference because it was too easy (*also see* Floor effect).

Central tendency

A single number or value that describes the typical or central score among a set of scores.

Cluster sampling

A method of sampling in which clusters of individuals are identified. Clusters are sampled, and then all individuals in each cluster are included in the sample.

Coding system

A set of rules used to categorize observations.

Cohort

A group of people born at about the same time and exposed to the same societal events; cohort effects are confounded with age in a cross-sectional study.

Conceptual replication

Replication of research using different procedures for manipulating or measuring the variables.

Confederate

A person posing as a subject in an experiment who is actually part of the experiment.

Confounding

Failure to control for the effects of a third variable in an experimental design.

Construct validity

The degree to which a measurement device accurately measures the theoretical construct it is designed to measure.

Content analysis

Systematic analysis of the content of written records.

Control series design

An extension of the interrupted time series quasi-experimental design in which there is a comparison or control group.

Correlation coefficient

An index of how strongly two variables are related to each other in a group of subjects.

Correlational method

A method of determining whether two variables are related by measurement or observation of the variables.

Counterbalancing

A method of controlling for order effects in a repeated measures design by either including all orders of treatment presentation or randomly determining the order for each subject.

Criterion validity

The degree to which a measurement device accurately predicts behavior on a criterion measure.

Criterion variable

A behavior that a researcher wishes to predict using a predictor variable.

Cross-cultural research

Research that studies the relationship between variables across different cultures.

Cross-sectional method

A developmental research method in which persons of different ages are studied at only one point in time; conceptually similar to an independent groups design.

297

Curvilinear relationship
>   A relationship in which increases in the values of the first variable are accompanied by both increases and decreases in the values of the second variable.

Debriefing
>   Explanation of the purposes of the research that is given to subjects following their participation in the research.

Degrees of freedom (*df*)
>   The number of observations that are free to vary given that there are certain restrictions placed on the set of observations.

Demand characteristics
>   Cues that inform the subject how he or she is expected to behave.

Dependent variable
>   The variable that is the subject's response to, and dependent on, the level of the manipulated independent variable.

Descriptive statistics
>   Statistical measures that describe the results of a study; descriptive statistics include measures of central tendency (e.g., mean), variability (e.g., standard deviation), and correlation (e.g., Pearson *r*).

Electroencephalograph (EEG)
>   An apparatus that measures the electrical activity of the brain.

Error variance
>   Random variability in a set of scores that is not the result of the independent variable. Statistically, the variability of each score from its group mean.

Exact replication
>   Replication of research using the same procedures for manipulating and measuring the variables that were used in the original research.

Experimental control
>   In an experiment, keeping all extraneous variables constant so that only the independent variable can affect the dependent variable.

Experimental method
>   A method of determining whether variables are related in which the researcher manipulates the independent variable and controls all other variables either by randomization or by direct experimental control.

Experimental realism
>   The extent to which the independent variable manipulation has an impact on and involves subjects in an experiment.

Experimenter bias (expectancy effects)
>   Any intentional or unintentional influence that the experimenter exerts on subjects to confirm the hypothesis under investigation.

External validity
>   The degree to which the results of an experiment may be generalized.

F test (analysis of variance)
>   A statistical significance test for determining whether two or more means are significantly different. *F* is the ratio of systematic variance to error variance.

Face validity
>   The degree to which a measurement device appears to accurately measure a variable.

Factorial design

A design in which all levels of each independent variable are combined with all levels of the other independent variables. A factorial design allows investigation of the separate main effects and interactions of two or more independent variables.

Fatigue effect

An order effect in which performance deteriorates as a result of repeated experience with a task.

Field experiment

An experiment that is conducted in a field, rather than laboratory, setting.

Field observation

Descriptions of observations made in a complex social setting (the "field"). Also called field work.

Filler items

Items included in a questionnaire measure to help disguise the true purpose of the measure.

Floor effect

Failure of a measure to detect a difference because it was too difficult (*also see* Ceiling effect).

Frequency distribution

An arrangement of a set of scores from lowest to highest that indicates the number of times each score was obtained.

Frequency polygon

A graphic display of a frequency distribution in which the frequency of each score is plotted on the vertical axis, with the plotted points connected by straight lines.

Functional design

An experiment that contains many levels of the independent variable in order to determine the exact functional relationship between the independent and dependent variables.

Galvanic Skin Response (GSR)

The electrical conductance of the skin, which changes when sweating occurs.

Haphazard sampling

Selecting subjects in a haphazard manner, usually on the basis of availability, and not with regard to having a representative sample of the population; a type of nonprobability sampling.

Histogram

See Bar graph.

History

As a threat to the internal validity of an experiment, refers to any outside event that is not part of the manipulation that could be responsible for the results.

Hypothesis

A statement that makes an assertion about what is true in a particular situation; often, a statement asserting that two or more variables are related to one another.

Independent groups design

An experiment in which different subjects are assigned to each group. Also called between-subjects design.

Independent variable

The variable that is manipulated to observe its effect on the dependent variable.

Inferential statistics

Statistics designed to determine whether results based on sample data are generalizable to a population.

Informed consent

In research ethics, the principle that subjects in an experiment be informed in advance of all aspects of the research that might influence their decision to participate.

Institutional Review Board

An ethics review committee established to review research proposals. The IRB is composed of scientists, nonscientists, and legal experts.

Instrument decay

As a threat to internal validity, the possibility that a change in the characteristics of the measurement instrument is responsible for the results.

Interaction effect

The differing effect of one independent variable on the dependent variable, depending on the particular level of another independent variable.

Internal validity

The certainty with which results of an experiment can be attributed to the manipulation of the independent variable rather than to some other, confounding variable.

Interrupted time series design

A design in which the effectiveness of a treatment is determined by examining a series of measurements made over an extended time period both before and after the treatment is introduced. The treatment is not introduced at a random point in time.

Interval scale

A scale of measurement in which the intervals between numbers on the scale are all equal in size.

Interviewer bias

Intentional or unintentional influence exerted by an interviewer in such a way that the actual or interpreted behavior of respondents is consistent with the interviewer's expectations.

Item-total reliability

A reliability coefficient based upon the average correlation between the score on each item of a measure with the total score.

IV × SV design

A factorial design that includes both an experimental independent variable (IV) and a correlational subject variable (SV).

Latin Square

A technique to control for order effects without having all possible orders.

Longitudinal method

A developmental research method in which the same persons are observed repeatedly as they grow older; conceptually similar to a repeated measures design.

Main effect

The direct effect of an independent variable on a dependent variable.

Manipulation check

A measure used to determine whether the manipulation of the independent variable has had its intended effect on a subject.

Matched random assignment

A method of assigning subjects to groups in which pairs of subjects are first matched on some characteristic and then individually assigned randomly to groups.

Maturation

As a threat to internal validity, the possibility that any naturally occurring change within the individual is responsible for the results.

Mean

A measure of central tendency, obtained by summing scores and then dividing the sum by the number of scores.

Measurement error

The degree to which a measurement deviates from the true score value.

Median

A measure of central tendency; the middle score in a distribution of scores that divides the distribution in half.

Meta-analysis

A set of statistical procedures for combining the results of a number of studies in order to provide a general assessment of the relationship between variables.

Mixed factorial design

A design that includes both independent groups (between-subjects) and repeated measures (within-subjects) variables.

Mode

A measure of central tendency; the most frequent score in a distribution of scores.

Mortality

The loss of subjects who decide to leave an experiment. Mortality is a threat to internal validity when the mortality rate is related to the nature of the experimental manipulation.

Multiple baseline design

Observing behavior before and after a manipulation under multiple circumstances (across different individuals, different behaviors, or different settings).

Multiple correlation

A correlation between one variable and a combined set of predictor variables.

Mundane realism

The extent to which the independent variable manipulation is similar to events that occur in the real world.

Negative case analysis

In field observation, an examination of observations that do not fit with the explanatory structure devised by the researcher.

Negative linear relationship

A relationship in which increases in the values of the first variable are accompanied by decreases in the values of the second variable.

Nominal scale

A scale of measurement with two or more categories that have no numeric (less than, greater than) properties.

Nonequivalent control group design

A poor experimental design in which nonequivalent groups of subjects participate in the different experimental groups, and there is no pretest.

301

Nonequivalent control group pretest-posttest design
A quasi-experimental design in which nonequivalent groups are used, but a pretest allows assessment of equivalency and pretest-posttest changes.

Nonprobability sampling
Type of sampling procedure in which one cannot specify the probability that any member of the population will be included in the sample.

Nonsignificant results
Results that are probably due to error factors and indicative of a decision to not reject the null hypothesis.

Null hypothesis
The hypothesis, used for statistical purposes, that the variables under investigation are not related in the population, that any observed effect based upon sample results is due to random error.

Odd-even reliability
A reliability coefficient determined by the correlation between scores based on the odd-numbered items of a measure with scores on the even-numbered items.

Operational definition
Definition of a concept that specifies the operation used to measure or manipulate the concept.

Order effect
In a repeated measures design, the effect that the order of introducing treatment has on the dependent variable.

Ordinal scale
A scale of measurement in which the measurement categories form a rank order along a continuum.

Panel study
In survey research, questioning the same people at two or more points in time.

Partial correlation
The correlation between two variables with the influence of a third variable statistically controlled for.

Pilot study
A small-scale study conducted prior to conducting an actual experiment; designed to test and refine procedures.

Placebo group
In drug research, a group given an inert substance to assess the psychological effect of receiving a treatment.

Population
The defined group of individuals from which a sample is drawn.

Positive linear relationship
A relationship in which increases in the values of the first variable are accompanied by increases in the values of the second variable.

Posttest-only design
A true experimental design in which the dependent variable (posttest) is measured only once, after manipulation of the independent variable.

Practice effect
An order effect in which performance improves as a result of repeated practice with a task.

Prediction

A statement that makes an assertion concerning what will occur in a particular research investigation.

Predictor variable

A measure that is used to predict behavior on another measure (a criterion variable).

Pretest-posttest design

A true experimental design in which the dependent variable is measured both before (pretest) and after (posttest) manipulation of the independent variable.

Probability

The likelihood that a given event (among a specific set of events) will occur.

Probability sampling

Type of sampling procedure in which one is able to specify the probability that any member of the population will be included in the sample.

Program evaluation

Research designed to evaluate programs (e.g., social reforms, innovations) that are designed to produce certain changes or outcomes in a target population.

Projective measure

A measure consisting of an ambiguous stimulus to which subjects respond and thus "project" elements of their personality, values, and so on.

Psychobiography

A type of case study in which the life of an individual is analyzed using psychological theory.

Quasi-experimental design

A type of design that approximates the control features of true experiments to infer that a given treatment did have its intended effect.

Quota sampling

A sampling procedure in which the sample is chosen to reflect the numerical composition of various subgroups in the population. A haphazard sampling technique is used to obtain the sample.

Random error

An unexplained and unsystematic variability from a true score.

Randomization

Controlling for the effects of extraneous variables by ensuring that the variables operate in a manner determined entirely by chance.

Randomized response technique

In survey research, a procedure to encourage people to respond honestly to sensitive questions. Subjects randomly determine whether to answer an innocuous or sensitive question, and statistical procedures are used to estimate the actual proportion of people who had engaged in the sensitive behavior.

Ratio scale

A scale of measurement in which there is an absolute zero point, indicating an absence of the variable being measured. An implication is that ratios of numbers on the scale can be formed (generally these are physical measures such as weight, or timed measures such as duration or reaction time).

Reactivity

A problem of measurement in which the measure changes the behavior being observed.

303

Regression equation
> A mathematical equation that allows prediction of one behavior when the score on another variable is known.

Reliability
> The degree to which a measure is consistent.

Repeated measures design
> An experiment in which the same subjects are assigned to each group. Also called within-subjects design.

Replication
> Repeating a research study to determine whether the results can be duplicated.

Research hypothesis
> The hypothesis that the variables under investigation are related in the population, that the observed effect based on sample data is true in the population.

Response set
> A pattern of individual response to questions on a self-report measure that is not related to the content of the questions.

Reversal design
> A single-subject design in which the treatment is introduced after a baseline period and then withdrawn during a second baseline period. It may be extended by adding a second introduction of the treatment. Sometimes called a "withdrawal" design.

Role-playing
> A procedure for studying behavior in which individuals are asked to indicate how they would respond to a given situation rather than being observed in action in the situation.

Sampling
> The process of choosing members of a population to be included in a sample.

Selection differences
> Differences in the type of subjects who make up each group in an experimental design; this situation occurs when subjects elect which group they are to be assigned to.

Sensitivity
> The ability of a measure to detect differences between groups.

Sequential design
> A combination of the cross-sectional and longitudinal design to study developmental research questions.

Significance level
> The probability of rejecting the null hypothesis when it is true.

Significant result
> An outcome of a study that has a low probability of occurrence if the null hypothesis is true; a result that leads to a decision to reject the null hypothesis.

Simple random assignment
> Assigning subjects to groups in a random manner such that assignment is determined entirely by chance.

Simple random sampling
> A sampling procedure in which each member of the population has an equal probability of being included in the sample.

Simulator group

In hypnosis research, a group that is not actually hypnotized but whose members are instructed to act as if they were hypnotized.

Single-subject experiment

An experiment in which the effect of the independent variable is assessed using data from a single subject.

Split-half reliability

A reliability coefficient determined by the correlation between scores on the first half of the items on a measure with scores on the second half of a measure.

Standard deviation

The average deviation of scores from the mean (the square root of the variance).

Statistical regression

The tendency of extreme scores on a measure to become less extreme (regress toward the mean) when the measurement is made a second time.

Statistical significance

Rejection of the null hypothesis when an outcome has a low probability of occurrence (usually .05 or less) if in fact the null hypothesis is correct.

Stratified random sampling

A sampling procedure in which the population is divided into strata followed by random sampling from each stratum.

Stratum (*pl.* strata)

Subdivision of a population based upon specified characteristics of its members.

Structural model

A model of an expected pattern of relationships among a set of variables. The proposed pattern is based upon a theory of how the variables are causally related to one another.

Systematic observation

Observations of one or more specific variables usually made in a precisely defined setting.

Systematic variance

Variability in a set of scores that is the result of the independent variable; statistically, the variability of each group mean from the grand mean of all subjects.

Testing

A threat to internal validity in which taking a pretest changes behavior without any effect on the independent variable.

Test-retest reliability

A reliability coefficient determined by the correlation between scores on a measure given at one time with scores on the same measure given at a later time.

True score

An individual's actual score on a variable being measured, as opposed to the score the individual obtained on the measure itself.

Type I error

An incorrect decision to reject the null hypothesis when it is true.

Type II error

An incorrect decision to accept the null hypothesis when it is false.

Unobtrusive measure

A measure of behavior that is made without the subject's awareness.

Validity

The degree to which a measurement instrument measures what it is intended to measure.

Variability

The amount of dispersion of scores about some central value.

Variable

A general class or category of objects, events, or situations within which specific instances are found to vary.

Variance

A measure of the variability of scores about a mean; the mean of the sum of squared deviations of scores from the group mean.

References

Aiello, J. R., Baum, A., & Gormley, F. P. (1981). Social determinants of residential crowding stress. *Personality and Social Psychology Bulletin, 4*, 643–649.

Ajzen, I., & Fishbein, M. (1980). *Understanding attitudes and predicting social behavior.* Englewood Cliffs, NJ: Prentice-Hall.

American Psychological Association. (1967). *Casebook on ethical standards of psychologists.* Washington, DC: Author.

American Psychological Association. (1973). Ethical principles in the conduct of research with human participants. *American Psychologist, 28*, 79–80.

American Psychological Association. (1981). *Ethical principles of psychologists.* Washington, DC: Author.

American Psychological Association. (1982). *Ethical principles in the conduct of research with human participants.* Washington, DC: Author.

American Psychological Association. (1983). *Publication manual of the American Psychological Association.* Washington, DC: Author.

American Psychological Association. (1986). Guidelines for ethical conduct in the care and use of animals. *Journal of the Experimental Analysis of Behavior, 45*, 127–132.

American Psychological Association. (1990). Ethical principles of psychologists [Amended June 2, 1989]. *American Psychologist, 45*, 390–395.

American Psychological Association. (1991, June). Draft of APA ethics code published. *APA Monitor*, pp. 30–35.

Anderson, C. A., & Anderson, D. C. (1984). Ambient temperature and violent crime: Test of the linear and curvilinear hypotheses. *Journal of Personality and Social Psychology, 46*, 91–97.

Anderson, D. R., Lorch, E. P., Field, D. E., Collins, P. A., & Nathan, J. G. (1986). TV viewing at home. *Child Development, 57*, 1024–1033.

Aristotle. (1954). Rhetoric. In *Aristotle, rhetoric, and poetics* (W. Rhys Roberts, Trans.). New York: Modern Library.

Aronson, E. (1984). *The social animal* (4th ed.). San Francisco: W. H. Freeman.

Aronson, E., Brewer, M., & Carlsmith, J. M. (1985). Experimentation in social psychology. In G. Lindzey & E. Aronson (Eds.), *Handbook of social psychology* (3rd ed.). New York: Random House.

Aronson, E., Stephan, C., Sikes, J., Blaney, N., & Snapp, M. (1978). *The jigsaw classroom*. Newbury Park, CA: Sage.

Astin, A. (1987). *The American freshman: Twenty year trends, 1966–1985*. Los Angeles: Higher Education Research Institute, Graduate School of Education, University of California.

Bakeman, R., & Brownlee, J. R. (1980). The strategic use of parallel play: A sequential analysis. *Child Development, 51*, 873–878.

Bakeman, R., & Gottman, J. M. (1986). *Observing interaction*. Cambridge: Cambridge University Press.

Bales, R. F. (1970). *Personality and interpersonal behavior*. New York: Holt, Rinehart & Winston.

Barlow, D. H., & Hersen, M. (1984). *Single case experimental designs*. New York: Pergamon Press.

Barton, E. M., Baltes, M. M., & Orzech, M. J. (1980). Etiology of dependence in older nursing home residents during morning care; the role of staff behavior. *Journal of Personality and Social Psychology, 38*, 423–431.

Baum, A., Gachtel, R. J., & Schaeffer, M. A. (1983). Emotional, behavioral, and psychological effects of chronic stress at Three Mile Island. *Journal of Consulting and Clinical Psychology, 51*, 565–572.

Beach, F. A. (1950). The snark was a boojum. *American Psychologist, 5*, 115–124.

Beaman, A. (1991). An empirical comparison of meta-analytic and traditional reviews. *Personality and Social Psychology Bulletin, 17*, 252–257.

Becker, H. S. (1963). *Outsiders: Studies in the sociology of deviance*. New York: Free Press.

Bem, D. J. (1981). Writing the research report. In L. H. Kidder (Ed.), *Research methods in social relations*. New York: Holt, Rinehart & Winston.

Berry, T. D., & Geller, E. S. (1991). A single-subject approach to evaluative vehicle safety belt reminders: Back to basics. *Journal of Applied Behavior Analysis, 24*, 13–22.

Berscheid, E., Baron, R. S., Dermer, M., & Libman, M. (1973). Anticipating informed consent: An empirical approach. *American Psychologist, 28*, 913–925.

Bouchard, T. J., Jr., & McGue, M. (1981). Familial studies of intelligence: A review. *Science, 212*, 1055–1059.

Bramel, D. (1962). A dissonance theory approach to defensive projection. *Journal of Abnormal and Social Psychology, 64*, 121–129.

Brogden, W. J. (1962). The experimenter as a factor in animal conditioning. *Psychological Reports, 11*, 239–242.

Brooks, C. I., & Rebata, J. L. (1991). College classroom ecology: The relation of sex of student to classroom performance and seating preference. *Environment and Behavior, 23*, 305–313.

Byrne, D. (1971). *The attraction paradigm*. New York: Academic Press.

Byrne, D., Ervin, C. R., & Lamberth, J. (1970). Continuity between the experimental study of attraction and real-life computer dating. *Journal of Personality and Social Psychology, 16*, 157–165.

Cacioppo, J. T., & Petty, R. E. (Eds.). (1983). *Social psychophysiology: A sourcebook*. New York: Guilford Press.

Cacioppo, J. T., & Tassinary, L. G. (1990). Inferring psychological significance from physiological signals. *American Psychologist, 45,* 16–28.

Campbell, D. T. (1968). Quasi-experimental design. In D. L. Gillis (Ed.), *International encyclopedia of the social sciences* (Vol. 5). New York: Macmillan and Free Press.

Campbell, D. T. (1969). Reforms as experiments. *American Psychologist, 24,* 409–429.

Campbell, D. T., & Stanley, J. C. (1966). *Experimental and quasi-experimental designs for research.* Chicago: Rand McNally.

Cavan, S. (1966). *Liquor license: An ethnography of bar behavior.* Chicago: Aldine.

Chaiken, S., & Pliner, P. (1987). Women, but not men, are what they eat: The effect of meal size and gender on perceived femininity and masculinity. *Personality and Social Psychology Bulletin, 13,* 166–176.

Cialdini, R. B. (1988). *Influence: Science and practice* (2nd ed.). Glenview, IL: Scott, Foresman.

Cialdini, R. B., Borden, R., Walker, M. R., Freeman, S., Shuma, P., Braver, S. L., Ralls, M., Floyd, L., Reynolds, L., Crandall, R., & Jellison, J. M. (1974). Wearing the warm glow of success: A (football) field study. *Proceedings of the Division of Personality and Social Psychology, 1,* 13–15.

Clark, K. B., & Clark, M. P. (1947). Racial identification and preference in Negro children. In T. M. Newcomb & E. L. Hartley (Eds.), *Readings in social psychology.* New York: Holt, Rinehart & Winston.

Clubb, J. M., Austin, E. W., Geda, C. L., & Traugott, M. W. (1985). Sharing research data in the social sciences. In S. E. Fienber, M. E. Martin, & M. L. Straff (Eds.), *Sharing research data.* Washington, D.C.: National Academy Press.

Coile, D. C., & Miller, N. E. (1984). How radical animal activists try to mislead humane people. *American Psychologist, 39,* 700–701.

Conoley, J. C., & Kramer, J. J. (1989). *Tenth mental measurements yearbook.* Lincoln: Buros Institute of Mental Measurements, University of Nebraska-Lincoln.

Converse, J. M., & Presser, S. (1986). *Survey questions: Handcrafting the standardized questionnaire.* Newbury Park, CA: Sage.

Cook, T. D., & Campbell, D. T. (1979). *Quasi-experimentation: Design and analysis issues for field settings.* Chicago: Rand McNally.

Cooper, H. M., & Rosenthal, R. (1980). Statistical versus traditional procedures for summarizing research findings. *Psychological Bulletin, 87,* 442–449.

Coovert, M. D., Penner, L. A., & MacCallum, R. (1990). Covariance structure modeling in personality and social psychological research: An introduction. In C. Hendrick & M. S. Clark (Eds.), *Review of personality and social psychology* (Vol. 11). Newbury Park, CA: Sage.

Costa, P. T., Jr., & McCrae, R. R. (1985). *The NEO personality inventory manual.* Odessa, FL: Psychological Assessment Resources.

Curtiss, S. R. (1977). *Genie: A psycholinguistic study of a modern-day "wild child."* New York: Academic Press.

Darley, J. M., & Latané, B. (1968). Bystander intervention in emergencies: Diffusion of responsibility. *Journal of Personality and Social Psychology, 8,* 377–383.

Denmark, F., Russo, N. P., Frieze, I. H., & Sechzer, J. A. (1988). Guidelines for avoiding sexism in psychological research: A report of the Ad Hoc Committee on Nonsexist Research. *American Psychologist, 43,* 582–585.

Department of Health and Human Services. (1981, January 26). Final regulations amending basic HHS policy for the protection of human research subjects. *Federal Register, 46*(16), 8366–8392.

Dill, C. A., Gilden, E. R., Hill, P. C., & Hanslka, L. L. (1982). Federal human subjects regulations: A methodological artifact? *Personality and Social Psychology Bulletin, 8*, 417–425.

Douglas, J. D. (1976). *Investigative social research: Individual and team field research.* Newbury Park, CA: Sage.

Duncan, S., Rosenberg, M. J., & Finklestein, J. (1969). The paralanguage of experimenter bias. *Sociometry, 32*, 207–219.

Eagly, A. H., Ashmore, R. D., Makhijani, M. G., & Longo, L. C. (1991). What is beautiful is good, but . . . : A meta-analytic review of research on the physical attractiveness stereotype. *Psychological Bulletin, 110*, 109–128.

Ellsworth, P. C., Carlsmith, J. M., & Henson, A. (1972). The stare as a stimulus to flight in human beings: A series of field experiments. *Journal of Personality and Social Psychology, 21*, 302–311.

Elms, A. (1976). *Personality in politics.* New York: Harcourt Brace Jovanovich.

Epstein, Y. M., Suedfeld, P., & Silverstein, S. J. (1973). The experimental contract: Subjects' expectations of and reactions to some behaviors of experimenters. *American Psychologist, 28*, 212–221.

Everett, P. B., Hayward, S. C., & Meyers, A. W. (1974). The effects of a token reinforcement procedure on bus ridership. *Journal of Applied Behavior Analysis, 7*, 1–10.

Fazio, R. H., Cooper, M., Dayson, K., & Johnson, M. (1981). Control and the coronary-prone behavior pattern: Responses to multiple situational demands. *Personality and Social Psychology Bulletin, 7*, 97–102.

Fidler, D. S., & Kleinknecht, R. E. (1977). Randomized response versus direct questioning: Two data-collection methods for sensitive information. *Psychological Bulletin, 84*, 1045–1049.

Fischer, K., Schoeneman, T. J., & Rubanowitz, D. E. (1987). Attributions in the advice columns: II. The dimensionality of actors' and observers' explanations of interpersonal problems. *Personality and Social Psychology Bulletin, 13*, 458–466.

Fishbein, M., & Ajzen, I. (1975). *Belief, attitude, intention, and behavior: An introduction to theory and research.* Reading, MA: Addison-Wesley.

Fiske, S. T., Bersoff, D. N., Borgida, E., Deaux, K., & Heilman, M. E. (1991). Social science research on trial: Use of sex stereotyping in Price Waterhouse v. Hopkins. *American Psychologist, 46*, 1049–1060.

Fiske, S. T., & Taylor, S. E. (1984). *Social cognition.* New York: Random House.

Flavell, J. H. (1985). *Cognitive development.* Englewood Cliffs, NJ: Prentice-Hall.

Freedman, J. L. (1969). Role-playing: Psychology by consensus. *Journal of Personality and Social Psychology, 13*, 107–114.

Freedman, J. L., Klevansky, S., & Ehrlich, P. R. (1971). The effect of crowding on human task performance. *Journal of Applied Social Psychology, 1*, 7–25.

Freedman, J. L., Levy, A. S., Buchanan, R. W., & Price, J. (1972). Crowding and human aggressiveness. *Journal of Experimental Social Psychology, 8*, 528–548.

Gallup, G. G., & Suarez, S. D. (1985). Alternatives to the use of animals in psychological research. *American Psychologist, 40*, 1104–1111.

Gans, H. (1962). *Urban villagers*. New York: Free Press.

Gardner, G. T. (1978). Effects of federal human subjects regulations on data obtained in environmental stressor research. *Journal of Personality and Social Psychology, 34*, 774–781.

Gardner, L. E. (1988). A relatively painless method of introduction to the psychological literature search. In M. E. Ware & C. L. Brewer (Eds.), *Handbook for teaching statistics and research methods*. Hillsdale, NJ: Erlbaum.

Gelfand, H., & Walker, C. J. (1990). *Mastering APA style*. Washington, DC: American Psychological Association.

Geller, E. S., Russ, N. W., & Altomari, M. G. (1986). Naturalistic observations of beer drinking among college students. *Journal of Applied Behavior Analysis, 19*, 391–396.

Gergen, K. J. (1973). The codification of research ethics: Views of a Doubting Thomas. *American Psychology, 28*, 907–912.

Green, J., & Wallaf, C. (1981). *Ethnography and language in educational settings*. New York: Ablex.

Greenwald, A. G. (1976). Within-subjects designs: To use or not to use? *Psychological Bulletin, 83*, 314–320.

Gross, A. E., & Fleming, I. (1982). Twenty years of deception in social psychology. *Personality and Social Psychology Bulletin, 8*, 402–408.

Gwaltney-Gibbs, P. A. (1986). The institutionalization of premarital cohabitation: Estimates from marriage license applications, 1970 and 1980. *Journal of Marriage and the Family, 48*, 423–434.

Hawking, S. W. (1988). *A brief history of time: From the big bang to black holes*. New York: Bantam Books.

Health and Human Services, Department of. (1981, January 26). Final regulations amending basic HHS policy for the protection of human research subjects. *Federal Register, 46*(16), 8366–8392.

Hearnshaw, L. S. (1979). *Cyril Burt, psychologist*. Ithaca, NY: Cornell University Press.

Henle, M., & Hubbell, M. B. (1938). "Egocentricity" in adult conversation. *Journal of Social Psychology, 9*, 227–234.

Hill, C. T., Rubin, Z., & Peplau, L. A. (1976). Breakups before marriage: The end of 103 affairs. *Journal of Social Issues, 32*, 147–168.

Hill, L. (1990). Effort and reward in college: A replication of some puzzling findings. In J. W. Neuliep (Ed.), *Handbook of replication in the behavioral and social sciences*. [Special issue] *Journal of Social Behavior and Personality, 5*(4), 151–161.

Holden, C. (1987). Animal regulations: So far, so good. *Science, 238*, 880–882.

Holsti, O. R. (1969). *Content analysis for the social sciences and humanities*. Reading, MA: Addison-Wesley.

Hood, T. C., & Back, K. W. (1971). Self-disclosure and the volunteer: A source of bias in laboratory experiments. *Journal of Personality and Social Psychology, 17*, 130–136.

Hostetler, A. J. (1987, May). Fraud inquiry revives doubt: Can science police itself? *APA Monitor*, pp. 1, 12.

Hovland, C., & Weiss, W. (1951). The influence of source credibility on communication effectiveness. *Public Opinion Quarterly, 15*, 635–650.

311

Humphreys, L. (1970). *Tearoom trade*. Chicago: Aldine.

James, L. R., Mulaik, S. A., & Brett, J. M. (1982). *Causal analysis: Assumptions, models, and data*. Newbury Park, CA: Sage.

Jones, R., & Cooper, J. (1971). Mediation of experimenter effects. *Journal of Personality and Social Psychology, 20*, 70–74.

Jourard, S. M. (1969). The effects of experimenters' self-disclosure on subjects' behavior. In C. Spielberger (Ed.), *Current topics in community and clinical psychology*. New York: Academic Press.

Joy, L. A., Kimball, M. M., & Zabrack, M. L. (1986). Television and children's aggressive behavior. In T. M. Williams (Ed.), *The impact of television: A natural experiment in three communities*. Orlando, FL: Academic Press.

Joynson, R. B. (1989). *The Burt affair*. London: Routledge.

Judd, C. M., Smith, E. R., & Kidder, L. H. (1991). *Research methods in social relations* (6th ed.). Ft. Worth: Holt, Rinehart & Winston.

Kamin, L. G. (1974). *The science and politics of IQ*. New York: Wiley.

Kelman, H. C. (1967). Human use of human subjects: The problem of deception in social psychological experiments. *Psychological Bulletin, 67*, 1–11.

Kenny, D. A. (1979). *Correlation and causality*. New York: Wiley.

Keyser, D. J., & Sweetland, R. C. (Eds.). (1991). *Test critiques*. Kansas City, MO: Test Corporation of America.

Kidder, L. H., & Judd, C. M. (1986). *Research methods in social relations* (5th ed.). New York: Holt, Rinehart & Winston.

King, J. C. (1985, August). *The impact of "The Day After" on anti-nuclear war behavior*. Paper presented at the annual meeting of the American Psychological Association, Los Angeles.

Kintz, N. L., Delprato, D. J., Mettee, D. R., Persons, C. E., & Schappe, R. H. (1965). The experimenter effect. *Psychological Bulletin, 63*, 223–232.

Koocher, G. P. (1977). Bathroom behavior and human dignity. *Journal of Personality and Social Psychology, 35*, 120–121.

Koop, C. E. (1987). Report of the Surgeon General's workshop on pornography and public health. *American Psychologist, 42*, 944–945.

Lana, R. E. (1969). Pretest sensitization. In R. Rosenthal & R. Rosnow (Eds.), *Artifact in behavioral research*. New York: Academic Press.

Langer, E. J., & Abelson, R. P. (1974). A patient by any other name . . . : Clinical group difference in labeling bias. *Journal of Consulting and Clinical Psychology, 42*, 4–9.

Langer, E. J., & Rodin, J. (1976). The effects of choice and enhanced personal responsibility for the aged: A field experiment in an institutional setting. *Journal of Personality and Social Psychology, 34*, 191–198.

Latané, B., & Darley, J. M. (1970). *The unresponsive bystander: Why doesn't he help?* New York: Appleton-Century-Crofts.

Leventhal, H. (1970). Findings and theory in the study of fear communications. In L. Berkowitz (Ed.), *Advances in experimental social psychology* (Vol. 5). New York: Academic Press.

Levin, J. R. (1983). Pictorial strategies for school learning: Practical illustrations. In

M. Pressley & J. R. Levin (Eds.), *Cognitive strategy research: Educational applications* (pp. 213–238). New York: Springer-Verlag.

Levine, R. V. (1990). The pace of life. *American Scientist, 78,* 450–459.

Linz, D., Donnerstein, E., & Penrod, S. (1987). The findings and recommendations of the Attorney General's Commission on Pornography: Do the psychological "facts" fit the political fury? *American Psychologist, 42,* 946–953.

Lofland, J. (1971). *Analyzing social settings.* Belmont, CA: Wadsworth.

Lofland, J. (1976). *Doing social life: The qualitative study of human interaction in natural settings.* New York: Wiley.

Loftus, E. (1979). *Eyewitness testimony.* Cambridge, MA: Harvard University Press.

Luria, A. R. (1968). *The mind of a mnemonist.* New York: Basic Books.

McGuigan, F. J. (1963). The experimenter: A neglected stimulus. *Psychological Bulletin, 60,* 421–428.

Marlatt, G. A. (1983). The controlled-drinking controversy: A commentary. *American Psychologist, 38,* 1097–1110.

Marlatt, G. A., & Rohsenow, D. R. (1980). Cognitive processes in alcohol use: Expectancy and the balanced placebo design. In N. K. Mello (Ed.), *Advances in substance abuse* (Vol. 1). Greenwich, CT: JAI Press.

Matteson, M. T., & Ivancevich, J. M. (1983). Note on tension discharge rate as an employee health status predictor. *Academy of Management Journal, 26,* 540–545.

Middlemist, R. D., Knowles, E. S., & Matter, C. F. (1976). Personal space invasion in the lavatory: Suggestive evidence for arousal. *Journal of Personality and Social Psychology, 33,* 541–546.

Middlemist, R. D., Knowles, E. S., & Matter, C. F. (1977). What to do and what to report: A reply to Koocher. *Journal of Personality and Social Psychology, 35,* 122–124.

Migdal, S., Abeles, R. P., & Sherrod, L. R. (1985). *An inventory of longitudinal studies of middle and old age.* New York: Social Science Research Council.

Milgram, S. (1963). Behavioral study of obedience. *Journal of Abnormal and Social Psychology, 67,* 371–378.

Milgram, S. (1964). Group pressure and action against a person. *Journal of Abnormal and Social Psychology, 69,* 137–143.

Milgram, S. (1965). Some conditions of obedience and disobedience to authority. *Human Relations, 18,* 57–76.

Milgram, S. (1970, June). The lost letter technique. *Psychology Today,* p. 30.

Miller, A. G. (1972). Role-playing: An alternative to deception? *American Psychologist, 27,* 623–636.

Miller, A. G. (1986). *The obedience experiments: A case study of controversy in social science.* New York: Praeger.

Miller, G. A. (1969). Psychology as a means of promoting human welfare. *American Psychologist, 24,* 1063–1075.

Miller, N. E. (1985). The value of behavioral research on animals. *American Psychologist, 40,* 423–440.

Nisbett, R. E., & Ross, L. (1980). *Human inference: Strategies and shortcomings of social judgment.* Englewood Cliffs, NJ: Prentice-Hall.

Nisbett, R. E., & Wilson, T. D. (1977). Telling more than we can know: Verbal reports on mental processes. *Psychological Review*, *84*, 231–259.

Orne, M. T. (1962). On the social psychology of the psychological experiment: With particular reference to demand characteristics and their implications. *American Psychologist*, *17*, 776–783.

Osgood, C. E., Suci, G. J., & Tannenbaum, P. H. (1957). *The measurement of meaning.* Urbana, IL: University of Illinois Press.

Oskamp, S., King, J. C., Burn, S. M., Konrad, A. M., Pollard, J. A., & White, M. A. (1985). The media and nuclear war: Fallout from TV's "The Day After." In S. Oskamp (Ed.), *Applied social psychology annual* (Vol. 6). Newbury Park, CA: Sage.

Patterson, G. R., & Moore, D. (1979). Interactive patterns as units of behavior. In M. E. Lamb, S. J. Sumoi, & G. R. Stephenson (Eds.), *Social interaction analysis: Methodological issues* (pp. 77–96). Madison, WI: University of Wisconsin Press.

Paulus, P. B., Annis, A. B., Seta, J. J., Schkade, J. K., & Matthews, R. W. (1976). Crowding does affect task performance. *Journal of Personality and Social Psychology*, *34*, 248–253.

Pendery, M. L., Maltzman, I. M., & West, L. J. (1982). Controlled drinking by alcoholics? New findings and a reevaluation of a major affirmative study. *Science*, *217*, 169–174.

Peterson, J. L., & Zill, N. (1986). Marital disruption, parent-child relationships, and behavior problems in children. *Journal of Marriage and the Family*, *48*, 295–307.

Petty, R. E., & Cacioppo, J. T. (1986). *Communication and persuasion: Central and peripheral routes to attitude change.* New York: Springer-Verlag.

Petty, R. E., Cacioppo, J. T., & Goldman, R. (1981). Personal involvement as a determinant of argument-based persuasion. *Journal of Personality and Social Psychology*, *41*, 847–855.

Pfungst, O. (1911). *Clever Hans (the horse of Mr. von Osten): A contribution to experimental, animal, and human psychology* (C. L. Rahn, Trans.). New York: Holt, Rinehart & Winston. (Republished 1965.)

Piaget, J. (1952). *The origins of intelligence in children.* New York: International Universities Press.

Piliavin, I. M., Rodin, J., & Piliavin, J. A. (1969). Good samaritanism: An underground phenomenon? *Journal of Personality and Social Psychology*, *4*, 289–299.

Posavac, E. J., & Carey, R. G. (1989). *Program evaluation: Methods and case studies* (3rd ed). Englewood Cliffs, NJ: Prentice-Hall.

Prinsky, L. E., & Rosenbaum, J. L. (1987). "Leer-ics" or lyrics: Teenage impressions of rock 'n' roll. *Youth and Society*, *18*, 384–397.

Punnett, B. J. (1986). Goal setting: An extension of the research. *Journal of Applied Psychology*, *71*, 171–172.

Reed, J. G., & Baxter, P. M. (Eds.). (1991). *Library use: A handbook for psychology* (2nd ed.). Washington, DC: American Psychological Association.

Richardson, B., Sorenson, J., & Soderstrom, E. J. (1987). Explaining the social and psychological impact of a nuclear power plant accident. *Journal of Applied Social Psychology*, *17*, 507–518.

Ring, K. (1967). Experimental social psychology: Some sober questions about frivolous values. *Journal of Experimental Social Psychology*, *3*, 113–123.

314

Ring, K., Wallston, K., & Corey, M. (1970). Mode of debriefing as a factor affecting subjective reaction to a Milgram-type obedience experiment: An ethical inquiry. *Representative Research in Social Psychology*, *1*, 67–68.

Riordan, C. A., & Marlin, N. A. (1987). Some good news about some bad practices. *American Psychologist*, *42*, 104–106.

Roberson, M. T., & Sundstrom, E. (1990). Questionnaire design, return rates, and response favorableness in an employee attitude questionnaire. *Journal of Applied Psychology*, *75*, 354–357.

Robinson, J. P., Athanasiou, R., & Head, K. B. (1969). *Measures of occupational attitudes and occupational characteristics*. Ann Arbor, MI: Institute for Social Research.

Robinson, J. P., Rusk, J. G., & Head, K. B. (1968). *Measures of political attitudes*. Ann Arbor, MI: Institute for Social Research.

Robinson, J. P., Shaver, P. R., & Wrightsman, L. S. (1991). *Measures of personality and social psychological attitudes* (Vol. 1). San Diego, CA: Academic Press.

Rodin, J., & Langer, E. J. (1977). Long-term effects of a control-relevant intervention with the institutionalized aged. *Journal of Personality and Social Psychology*, *35*, 897–902.

Rosenblatt, P. C., & Cozby, P. C. (1972). Courtship patterns associated with freedom of choice of spouse. *Journal of Marriage and the Family*, *34*, 689–695.

Rosenblatt, P. C., de Mik, L., Anderson, R. M., & Johnson, P. A. (1985). *The family in business*. San Francisco: Jossey-Bass.

Rosenhan, D. (1973). On being sane in insane places. *Science*, *179*, 250–258.

Rosenthal, R. (1965). The volunteer subject. *Human Relations*, *18*, 389–406.

Rosenthal, R. (1966). *Experimenter effects in behavior research*. New York: Appleton-Century-Crofts.

Rosenthal, R. (1967). Covert communication in the psychological experiment. *Psychological Bulletin*, *67*, 356–367.

Rosenthal, R. (1969). Interpersonal expectations: Effects of the experimenter's hypothesis. In R. Rosenthal & R. L. Rosnow (Eds.), *Artifacts in behavioral research*. New York: Academic Press.

Rosenthal, R. (1984). *Meta-analytic procedures for social research*. Newbury Park, CA: Sage.

Rosenthal, R., & Jacobson, L. (1968). *Pygmalion in the classroom: Teacher expectation and pupils' intellectual development*. New York: Holt, Rinehart & Winston.

Rosenthal, R., & Rosnow, R. L. (1975). *The volunteer subject*. New York: Wiley.

Rosnow R. L., & Rosnow, M. (1992). *Writing papers in psychology* (2nd ed.). Belmont, CA: Wadsworth.

Rossi, P. H., & Freeman, H. E. (1989). *Evaluation: A systematic approach* (4th ed.). Newbury Park, CA: Sage.

Rubin, Z. (1970, December). Jokers wild in the lab. *Psychology Today*, pp. 18, 20, 22–24.

Rubin, Z. (1973). Designing honest experiments. *American Psychologist*, *28*, 445–448.

Rubin, Z. (1975). Disclosing oneself to a stranger: Reciprocity and its limits. *Journal of Experimental Social Psychology*, *11*, 233–260.

Rubin, Z. (1985). Deceiving ourselves about deception: Comment on Smith and

Richardson's "Amelioration of deception and harm in psychological research." *Journal of Personality and Social Psychology, 48*, 252–253.

Rubin, Z., & Peplau, L. A. (1973). Belief in a just world and reactions to another's lot: A study of participants in the national draft lottery. *Journal of Social Issues, 29*, 73–93.

Runyan, W. K. (1981). Why did Van Gogh cut off his ear? The problem of alternative explanations in psychobiography. *Journal of Personality and Social Psychology, 40*, 1070–1077.

Russell, C. H., & Megaard, I. (1988). *The general social survey, 1972–1986: The state of the American people.* New York: Springer-Verlag.

Schachter, S. (1959). *The psychology of affiliation.* Stanford, CA: Stanford University Press.

Schaie, K. W. (1986). Beyond calendar definitions of age, time, and cohort: The general developmental model revisited. *Developmental Review, 6*, 252–277.

Schoeneman, T. J., & Rubanowitz, D. E. (1985). Attributions in the advice columns: Actors and observers, causes and reasons. *Personality and Social Psychology Bulletin, 11*, 315–325.

Schreiber, F. R. (1973). *Sybil.* Chicago: Regnery.

Schwartz, S. (1986). *Classic studies in psychology.* Mountain View, CA: Mayfield.

Sears, D. O. (1986). College sophomores in the laboratory: Influences of a narrow data base on social psychology's view of human nature. *Journal of Personality and Social Psychology, 51*, 515–530.

Seaver, W. B. (1973). Effects of naturally induced teacher expectancy effects. *Journal of Personality and Social Psychology, 28*, 333–342.

Sebald, H. (1986). Adolescents' shifting orientation toward parents and peers: A curvilinear trend over recent decades. *Journal of Marriage and the Family, 48*, 5–13.

Shaw, M. E., & Wright, J. M. (1967). *Scales for the measurement of attitudes.* New York: McGraw-Hill.

Shepard, R. N., & Metzler, J. (1971). Mental rotation of three-dimensional objects. *Science, 171*, 701–703.

Sidman, M. (1960). *Tactics of scientific research.* New York: Basic Books.

Siegel, S., & Castellan, N. J. (1988). *Nonparametric statistics for the behavioral sciences.* New York: McGraw-Hill.

Silverman, I. (1975). Nonreactive methods and the law. *American Psychologist, 30*, 764–769.

Skinner, B. F. (1953). *Science and human behavior.* New York: Macmillan.

Smart, R. (1966). Subject selection bias in psychological research. *Canadian Psychologist, 7*, 115–121.

Smith, C. P. (1983). Ethical issues: Research on deception, informed consent, and debriefing. In L. Wheeler & P. Shaver (Eds.), *Review of personality and social psychology* (Vol. 4). Newbury Park, CA: Sage.

Smith, M. L., & Glass, G. V. (1977). Meta-analysis of psychotherapy outcome studies. *American Psychologist, 32*, 752–760.

Smith, R. J., Lingle, J. H., & Brock, T. C. (1978). Reactions to death as a function of perceived similarity to the deceased. *Omega, 9*, 125–138.

Smith, S. S., & Richardson, D. (1983). Amelioration of harm in psychological research:

The important role of debriefing. *Journal of Personality and Social Psychology*, *44*, 1075–1082.

Smith, S. S., & Richardson, D. (1985). On deceiving ourselves about deception: A reply to Rubin. *Journal of Personality and Social Psychology*, *48*, 254–255.

Smith, V. L., & Ellsworth, P. C. (1987). The social psychology of eyewitness accuracy: Misleading questions and communicator expertise. *Journal of Applied Psychology*, *72*, 294–300.

Sobell, M. B., & Sobell, L. C. (1973). Individualized behavior therapy for alcoholics. *Behavior Therapy*, *4*, 49–72.

Soeken, K. L., & Macready, G. B. (1982). Respondents' perceived protection when using randomized response. *Psychological Bulletin*, *92*, 487–489.

Solomon, R. L. (1949). An extension of control group design. *Psychological Bulletin*, *46*, 137–150.

Steinberg, L., & Dornbusch, S. M. (1991). Negative correlates of part-time employment during adolescence: Replication and elaboration. *Developmental Psychology*, *27*, 303–313.

Stephan, W. G. (1983). Intergroup relations. In D. Perlman & P. C. Cozby (Eds.), *Social psychology*. New York: Holt, Rinehart & Winston.

Sternberg, R. J. (1988). *The psychologist's companion: A guide to scientific writing for students and researchers*. Cambridge: Cambridge University Press.

Stevenson, H. W., & Allen, S. (1964). Adult performance as a function of sex of experimenter and sex of subject. *Journal of Abnormal and Social Psychology*, *68*, 214–216.

Sullivan, D. S., & Deiker, T. E. (1973). Subject-experimenter perceptions of ethical issues in human research. *American Psychologist*, *28*, 587–591.

Swim, J., & Borgida, E. (1987). Public opinion on the psychological and legal aspects of television rape trials. *Journal of Applied Social Psychology*, *17*, 507–518.

Tanaka, J. S., Panter, A. T., Winborne, W. C., & Huba, G. J. (1990). Theory testing in personality and social psychology with structural equation models: A primer in 20 questions. In C. Hendrick & M. S. Clark (Eds.), *Review of personality and social psychology* (Vol. 11). Newbury Park, CA: Sage.

Tufte, E. R. (1983). *The visual display of quantitative information*. Cheshire, CT: Graphics Press.

Tversky, A., & Kahneman, D. (1983). Extensional vs. intuitive reasoning: The conjunction fallacy in probability judgment. *Psychological Review*, *90*, 293–315.

Verdonik, F., & Sherrod, L. R. (1984). *An inventory of longitudinal research on childhood and adolescence*. New York: Social Science Research Council.

Viney, L. L. (1983). The assessment of psychological states through content analysis of verbal communications. *Psychological Bulletin*, *94*, 542–563.

Vitz, P. C. (1966). Preference for different amounts of visual complexity. *Behavioral Science*, *11*, 105–114.

Webb, E. J., Campbell, D. T., Schwartz, R. D., Sechrest, R., & Grove, J. B. (1981). *Nonreactive measures in the social sciences* (2nd ed.). Boston: Houghton Mifflin.

Wilson, D. W., & Donnerstein, E. (1976). Legal and ethical aspects of nonreactive social psychological research. *American Psychologist*, *31*, 765–773.

Winograd, E., & Soloway, R. M. (1986). On forgetting the location of things stored in special places. *Journal of Experimental Psychology: General*, *115*, 366–372.

Yin, R. K. (1984). *Case study research: Design and methods*. Newbury Park, CA: Sage.

Zajonc, R. B. (1976). Family configuration and intelligence. *Science, 192,* 227–236.

Zimbardo, P. G. (1973). The psychological power and pathology of imprisonment. In E. Aronson & R. Helmreich (Eds.), *Social psychology*. New York: Van Nostrand.

Zuckerman, M. (1979). *Sensation seeking: Beyond the optimal level of arousal*. Hillsdale, NJ: Erlbaum.

Index